PROBLEMS OF AMERICAN SOCIETY
Bernard Rosenberg, General Editor

| *Functionaries* |

Functionaries

F. WILLIAM HOWTON

Quadrangle Books | *Chicago*

Library of Congress Catalog Card Number: 69–20156

TO *Erica, Joey, and Louise*

Acknowledgments

I want to thank Bernard Rosenberg for suggesting the book, for giving it a name, and for being a good colleague, adviser, and friend throughout the period it was written. Joseph Bensman, another colleague whom I count as friend and mentor, did a brilliant job of close reading and editing of the first part of the book; I am responsible for the final version, of course, but if I have managed to achieve some measure of lucidity it is because Bensman knows how to take an argument apart and explain its structure. Ivan Dee, my editor at Quadrangle, made valuable suggestions on organization and style, and offered informed encouragement when it was most needed.

Donal E. J. MacNamara and Edward Sagarin read parts of the chapter on "Power Struggle in the Prison" and gave me the benefit of their advice. The Ford Foundation assisted in the field research phase of that study by providing funds through its administrative internship program. I want to acknowledge the generous help, the good will, and the intelligent interest and courtesy shown by people at all levels of the Northeastern City Department of Corrections, and at Faulkner's Point. Drawn as

I was by ties of professional kinship and point of view to the rehabilitationists at the prison, I am delighted to say that I found a common ground of interest with several custodians, and I learned a good deal from them.

Finally, I should like to acknowledge my debt to my teachers at the University of California, Berkeley: Robert A. Brady and Lloyd H. Fisher, now deceased; and Reinhard Bendix, Philip Selznick, Tamotsu Shibutani, Seymour Martin Lipset, and Wolfram Eberhard.

I have dedicated this book to my wife and children, who were not only kind and forbearing but gave me a good deal of encouragement during the difficult time of writing it.

F. W. H.

New York, 1968

Contents

| *Functionaries* |

Introduction

In the 1920's the Czech playwright Karel Capek wrote a play with the cryptic, sinister title *R.U.R.*—Rossem's Universal Robots.[1] It was an expressionist fantasy about a future world in which the manufacture of humanoid machines—robots—had reached such an advanced state that the thing created was technically superior to its creator, man. Nearly forty years later an American psychologist, B. F. Skinner, offered his own version of the idea, now long since become an obsession, in *Walden II,*[2] a novel that is not so much fantasy as cool speculation about how technology may, quite soon, be able to bring men near to machine-like perfection through the use of applied psychology.

Between Capek and Skinner, just after World War II, a number of works appeared that considered what might be called the sociological version of the theme: man is becoming machine-like because society is a machine, and the individual is a cog in it. One thinks of Sloan Wilson's *The Man in the Gray Flannel Suit,* Herman Wouk's *The Caine Mutiny,* Alan Harrington's *Life in the Crystal Palace* (nonfiction), and George Orwell's masterpiece, *1984.*[3] These writers differed in the attitude they took toward their subject. Harrington found it maddeningly funny; Wouk apparently thought it revealed God's design; and Wilson did not know what to make of it. Orwell alone decoded the logic of the ultimate totalitarian horror he saw us drifting into, and laid it out so graphically no one could misunderstand.

Regardless of their differences, these novelists, and the essayist Harrington, all show man dehumanized by society.

Dehumanization as such is not new as a human and at times as a social problem, but the explicit association with technology and social organization is. Novelists and playwrights and poets and artists of all sorts were the first to see it, or to see it dramatically, as chunks of experience people actually have. Philosophers and social scientists are not necessarily less sensitive to what is happening to people and society. It just takes them longer to come up from factual chronicling and down from abstract theorizing to find the point at which their insights connect with inchoate experience to show that the troubles of individuals are problems for society.

The kind of dehumanization that the playwright Capek foresaw with horror—and the psychologist Skinner with an attitude close to eager anticipation—was taken up by sociologists and sociological journalists in the early 1950's, most notably in C. Wright Mills's *White Collar* and William H. Whyte's *The Organization Man*.[4] Mills, a sociologist, sought to describe a new exploited class, the white-collar worker. Whyte, an editor of *Fortune* magazine, was not so much interested in the plight of the little man in big organizations as in the problems of conscience and meaning that afflict the middle manager. The big organization, as he saw it, had made the old "Puritan Ethic" obsolete. The new breed of business executives and managers had found the "Social Ethic" to be much more useful and sound as a guide to conduct.

Exploited or self-exploited, it seemed clear to Whyte that the conditions of work and the kind of interpersonal relations in the giant organization dehumanized the men in them. This conclusion was disturbing, but while feeling indignant one could make jokes about how to cheat on personality tests, and about the man who got passed over for the Big Job because his wife did poorly in *her* interview.

The jokes, bitter but funny, a sort of Organization Man's gallows humor, are still told. But soon after Whyte's book the discussion moved into a new and nightmarish dimension, beyond wit, with the accumulating evidence that the Nazis who had organized and carried out the genocidal destruction of virtually the entire Jewish population of Europe—more than five million people—were not demons, monsters, or demented sadists, but quite ordinary types such as one might find living next door or working at the office.

Raul Hilberg's *The Destruction of the European Jews* [5] appeared in 1961. Its subject is how the apparatus of the Nazi state was able to carry out the "final solution to the Jewish question," in bureaucratic euphemism. (The fact itself, that the Nazis did accomplish the worst single atrocity in the memory of man, was established by the Nuremberg Trials of 1948.) Hilberg's book was followed soon after by the revelations in Jerusalem of the Eichmann trial (Eichmann was the SS official responsible for organizing the transportation of Jews to Auschwitz and other killing centers), and Hannah Arendt's controversial account of it. [6]

Eichmann appears to have been the type of man who was impersonal about the content of his work but took its method to heart; he was conscientious, skillful, ingenious in devising new and better procedures—in short, he was the very model of the dutiful functionary whom we shall meet throughout this book. His defense at court was that he was not responsible for policy, he merely carried it out.

The big organization dehumanizes the individual by turning him into a functionary. In doing so it makes everything possible by creating a new kind of man, one who is morally unbounded *in his role* as functionary. The only limits he knows come from rationality applied to the choice and use of means in relation to a given end—in other words, functional rationality. His ethic is the ethic of the good soldier: take the order, do the job, *do it the best way you know how,* because that is your honor, your virtue, your pride-in-work.

Whyte was wrong. The successor to the Puritan Ethic is not the Social Ethic,[7] it is the Functional Ethic. The Social Ethic makes the individual responsible for the collective act in which his work has meaning. The logic of the functionary's work situation forbids him to take account of ends, because to do so would introduce an irrational element into his choice of means.

Whyte's basic error was to see the Organization Man as touched only lightly by the kind of work he did, but very much by his place and prospects in the organization. (Throughout the book Whyte's view is too narrowly psychological. For example, he takes it as obvious that the individual is free to think out ways to resist the organization and preserve his integrity. This is true in marginal instances, such as learning how to cheat on personality tests. But if it were true generally it would mean that most people in organizations are either hypocrites or else so severely alienated from their work that they border on the schizoid. This is hardly plausible.) In fact it is more nearly the reverse: the work an individual does determines with whom and how he relates to others, and in this way it strongly affects the position he has in the organization.

The only useful insight the "organization man" concept offers as a point of departure is that organization men are different from other people in ways that are odd and frightening and have something to do with organizational bigness.

There is a considerable literature about "the bureaucrat" as a social type, but it does not help much in understanding the functionary either, mainly because it puts the bureaucrat in an organizational work situation now rapidly becoming archaic, and because the description tends to be exclusively psychological: it fails to relate his psychological characteristics to the structure of the work environment. The bureaucrat is usually portrayed as a sort of a 1910 customs inspector: self-important but essentially idiotic, smugly self-righteous but at the same time cowardly and irresponsible. The term "government functionary" still has this connotation in the minds of editorial writers on provincial newspapers. Even social scientists show their parochial bias by choosing to study "red tape," the evils of overcentralization, and the "decision-making process" when they study the work situation of the bureaucrat.

The traditional concept of the bureaucrat is that of a man who exercises authority delegated to the office of which he is the incumbent. As an official he does not *do* anything, he merely *decides* things. This emphasis makes it difficult to study meaningfully the content of the work he does, or its spirit and structure as they reflect the logic of his work situation.

The trouble is, scholarly and popular accounts of the bureaucrat and of bureaucracy have been limited until very recently to what Anthony Downs calls "non-market bureaucracies," of which the apparatus of government is the best example.[8]

Max Weber's work is virtually the lone exception. His complex ideal-type concept of bureaucracy is sufficiently general to be as applicable to bureaucracy in industry (Downs's "market bureaucracies") as it is to government. And the same is true of the axioms, propositions, and corollaries about the process of bureaucratization that follow from it. But Weber was handicapped by lack of data about bureaucratization in industry, in part because the process had not yet advanced very far in that sector by the time of his death in 1919.

Weber isolated the essential characteristics of the specifically modern, rational-legal form of bureaucracy and associated them in such a way that they articulated logically—they formed a new constitution. Moreover, this new constitution comprised the basis or plan of an institutional form never before known in history. There were other bureaucracies, of course—perhaps he should have called them quasi-bureaucracies—to be found near the beginnings of urban civilization, as in ancient Egypt. But they were either traditional or charismatic rather than rational-legal in character.

Weber's theory of bureaucracy and bureaucratization (as amplified by Reinhard Bendix,[9] for example) has been misread by a good many sociologists as a set of hypotheses about how bureaucratic organizations *work* instead of a set of abstract descriptions of what bureaucracy *is*. Weber wanted to identify bureaucracy. His interest was in providing terms for distinguishing between bureaucratic and pre-bureaucratic elements in a concrete organization, because he saw bureaucratization as one aspect of a larger process he called "world disenchantment," or secularization and rationalization.

Bureaucratization in the narrow sense refers to the process by which more and more authority is taken away from men and delegated to officials, rank upon rank in descending order. Rationalization applies to the way offices are defined and officers found to fill them. A rational-legal bureaucracy is a hierarchical body of officials, wielders of authority which is not their own but is attached to the office they hold. In principle, each official knows and follows the abstract rules governing the amount, the kind, and the functional jurisdiction of the authority of his office.

Weber began his scholarly career with an interest in the history of economic and legal institutions. It is not hard to see that he was rather more interested in the rights and duties men have as officials in large organizations than in the kind of work they do. Bureaucratization in the broad sense includes functionalization, the thoroughgoing application of rationality to the division of labor, both as a concept implicit in Weber's theory and as a reasonable inference from the facts we see around us: rationalization of the division of labor both fosters and is fostered by rationalization of the structure of authority, and both processes occur when there are rapid advances in the technology of production and communications.

Functionalization is the process by which the division of labor within an organization becomes progressively rationalized. Looked at one way, narrowly, it is analogous to bureaucratization and complementary to it. Looked at another way, broadly, it is a hitherto undeveloped branch of bureaucratization theory.

Now, to return to the functionary as an organization person with problems, and to the plan of this book.

We must follow the lead of the concept of functionalization and look closely at the work that organization people do instead of the position they occupy—I should say, *as well as* the position they occupy. Position is important, but it has been "done," and, besides, it is related to work in ways that have not been explored: holding a position is a warrant to do certain kinds of work, but it is also true that, typically, assignment or promotion to a position is the result of a certain kind of work done a certain way— "successfully"—in the past. It is no longer very useful to look at a person's place and prospects only. The "official" or the "organization man" is too broad a category. The work he does is the thing; it is character-defining both generically and specifically.

Part I which follows is concerned with the functionary and the organization. Its purpose is to characterize the functionary as a social type, in a preliminary, problem-posing way, and then to review some of the literature about images and perspectives on organization and the leading strands of organization theory in formal social science works.

Part II develops a theory of functionalization, in somewhat loose-jointed fashion, by considering the military man, the government man, the businessman, and the functionary in voluntary associations. The first is treated historically, in order to provide a time dimension; the second, the government man, is quasi-historical in that it deals with types that overlap in time as government operations expand. In the third, industry, commerce, and the services are treated as different spheres of business activity. Finally, the consideration of the functionary in voluntary associations sets forth a fairly elaborate theory of functionalization and applies it to religious, fraternal, and political associations.

Part III presents two special studies. The first is a case of conflict between custodial and rehabilitation staffs in a penal institution, in which each group claims the right to define the mission and run the apparatus. The second section is an essay which analyzes the interrelation between extreme situations and total institutions and the role of the functionary in them.

Part One

1

The functionary

The history of modern society, Max Weber wrote, is buried in its languages.

Consider the changing appropriateness of the term "mere" as a characterizer of social identities. One no longer says "a mere woman" without sounding quaint, or "a mere surgeon" or "a mere writer" without seeming plain idiotic. Women are still handicapped in life chances and social honor, but not much. Writers influence heads of state and surgeons earn $100,000 a year now, when only a few generations ago barbers did surgery and writers were "scribblers"—and functionaries were "mere" functionaries.

An angered European head of government recently referred to the United States Secretary of State as "a functionary." It was meant to be an expression of contempt which would wound, and it did. If it was a successful insult, the second ranking statesman of the most powerful nation on earth may very well have something of the character of the functionary, and if he does, the social type we have been calling by that name has certainly come up in the world. The remark would have sounded churlish and nonsensical even two decades ago, so his rise must have been recent. And it had to be a sudden climb because public discussion in our time shows little more than a glimmering of awareness that the functionary has arrived.

The rise of the functionary creates problems for people, for public policy, and for intellectual self-clarification.

THE PROBLEM FOR PEOPLE

As human beings we have our preferences and our dilemmas. The individual lives in a community, bears its distinctive outlook and traditions, and embodies it in a positive self-image that justifies his existence. He objectifies this self-image in a social type. He has an identity. He yearns for immortality in the sense that he wants his social type to go on, and he seeks to provide for it by standing up for certain values and opposing others. He seeks to preserve his type's identity by passing it on to his offspring, trying as best he can to rear them in his image. But he tempers his egoism. He accommodates his immediately felt wishes to the wishes of both his own peer group and the peer group of his child, and he makes still another accommodation by encouraging his child to be flexible and open and always to stand ready to chase down the main chance as the world changes.

The problem for people is how to be themselves and at the same time be what a changing society demands.

Middle-class people must find ways to adjust to the meanings and disciplines of work in modern, large bureaucratic organizations, meanings and disciplines exemplified in the functionary's social and occupational type. The self must accept remolding as the conditions of work change; but if the process goes too far and too fast, one reaches a point where too much of his identity is lost. The individual may suffer mental or emotional disorder; younger and older generations may find themselves alienated from one another. (The young activist spokesmen for the Free Speech Movement in Berkeley at the University of California in

1964 said, "We don't trust anybody over thirty.") People know that in their own selves they embody the values and style of a certain kind of human nature, or social character. By a sociological law of conservation of energy, the character they have can change, but not at an unlimited pace or in an unlimited range.

The individual may or may not actually become a functionary, but he must learn to cope with such people, to relate to them, to empathize with them enough to be able to live and work in a society whose style of interpersonal relations and institutional structure reflects the logic of the functionary's work situation.

THE PROBLEM FOR PUBLIC POLICY

Bureaucratization and the rapidly evolving division of labor pose grave public problems. The welfare of the polity always is threatened during a period of change, because the leading institutional sectors tend to pull away from the trailing ones. For example, dramatic exploits in aerospace technology make the decrepit state of our public services even more glaring than they would be otherwise. If scientists can put a man on the moon, why are educators unable to teach a child to read? If supersonic jet transports will soon get us from New York to London in two hours, why does it still take us an hour to get from the city to the airport? If our per capita national income is half again as high as that of the second richest country in the world, why do we have forty million people living in poverty? The looting and burning and rioting by Negroes which affected 110 cities after the assassination of Martin Luther King in 1968; the insurrectionary militance of black-power advocates; the repudiation of the President in time of war by half the country—these events and the conditions behind them indicate that in 1968 many Americans thought the nation's fundamental social arrangements were unjust and unsound.

Some loss of faith in social institutions is necessary for reconstruction, but if the process of "world disenchantment" goes too far too fast there may soon be nothing left to build with. The statesman reflects that men need the bread of myth: they must believe to some extent that existing institutions are right, or the walls will come tumbling down all at once.

Rapid social change since the French Revolution has eroded many favorite myths and the traditional form of legitimacy. But the statesman is always opposed to theorists who would press desacralization all the way and order society in accordance with the dictates of reason instead of the appeals of sentiment. His problem is in the short or intermediate range. The statesman is a man of action, and his interest and responsibility are not only to pick a suitable goal for public policy but to guide the ship of state and look to its safety in the course of the voyage.

Social problems for the statesman are analogous to self problems for the individual.

The person acting for himself alone is a sort of self-appointed statesman for his social type. He wants his "constituency" to gain the whole world but not to lose its soul in doing it. Self problems grow out of the individual's effort to maintain his integrity while remaining sufficiently flexible to be able to choose and use means that will be effective in reaching a given end. Social problems are the result of society's simultaneous pursuit of the good-for-you and the good-in-itself; the one sensitizes those who claim to speak in the name of all to the existence of an undesirable and theoretically correctable condition, and the other sets limits on what actually can be done to correct it by forbidding the use of certain means.

Both the private person and the civic polity choose who they are and what they are by deciding what is to be done and how it is to be done, because the choice of ends and the use of means is character-defining.

The rise of the functionary thus forces society to make an anguished choice. The greater the prestige and power of the functionary, the more capable society is of solving its problems —but the weaker the will of the polity is to do it. The strength of the collective will to act depends directly upon the viability of the collective myth—the American Dream, or what have you. But what the functionary does, even more his style of doing it, projects values which erode the credibility of all mythic thought. Beliefs about what is right and ought to be done, which have nourished generation after generation, are swept away in the tide of conviction that efficiency and discipline must have their way. Society needs its myths, but it needs the functionary more; and so it learns to live with the restless giant as he knocks the old gods and heroes off their pedestals and puts up instead a single new god-hero: himself.

The statesman is afraid that if he replaces all the varied symbols of collective identity with this one featureless monolith, however, he may so soften and weaken the social bond that there will be no future. Lacking an idealistic vision, civilization may fall victim to its own success and sink back into barbarism.

THE PROBLEM FOR INTELLECTUAL SELF-CLARIFICATION

So far we have considered the rise of the functionary from the viewpoints of the private person and the statesman. One speaks for himself, the other for the civic polity. The private person's need is to accommodate himself to the world of the functionary, in some sense to become a functionary, without making too great a sacrifice of personal integrity. The statesman's need is to incorporate the functionary into society without undermining its moral foundation in the process.

There is a third viewpoint, too, that of the socially unattached intellectual.

The intellectual's interest lies in the clarity, completeness, and usefulness of men's explanations of the world. In other words, the amount and quality of the knowledge we have about the world, how far it ranges, how well it is organized, and its relevance and accessibility—what we know should be relevant to the needs of and available to the man-who-must-act. This means it should be in the right form, and the user should have the right equipment, character, and skill to use it.

One must bear in mind that the "private person," the "states-man," and the "intellectual" are abstractions, and yet most in-dividuals actually experience what it means to take the viewpoint of each of the three at some juncture of life. An individual tends to become primarily a private person or a statesman or an intel-lectual as time goes on, depending on the course of his life and the central life interests he develops. The dialectic of continuing socialization, shuttling back and forth between material and ideal interests, ideally produces a firmer and firmer identity. And the firmer one's identity, the more circumscribed are his ideological options: both the intellectual and the statesman develop a "trained incapacity" to empathize with each other. One conse-quence is that the perspective of those who specialize in cultivat-ing knowledge *about* society tends in the long run to diverge from the perspective of those whose work not only calls for but gen-erates knowledge *of* society.

For the private person (who acts for himself) and the states-man (who imagines that he acts for society), the intellectual is a source of information and an object to be manipulated, as well as a human subject with whom to identify and perhaps sympathize.

The intellectual seeks self-clarification, but the "self" he wants to be clear about is not his own private individual self but the self of all of us, "human nature" at our world-historical moment. (If he is a sociologist he defines the problem more narrowly as "the social character of his stratum and generation in relation to social structure and its changes.") He wants information about what people do and what they think and what their doing and thinking mean to them. He gets it by observing, questioning, interacting (relating socially to others, role-playing), reading, reflecting, ana-lyzing—posing questions and trying to get answers about how and why people are what they are and do what they do.

The intellectual's will-o'-the-wisp is insight. But isn't it everybody's? Of course, but the intellectual is a specialist. He has a certain expertise in knowing what we do not know and yet ought to know. He is a professional in knowing what things need to be explained, either because there is no explanation or because what passes for explanation is defective, and in the art of explaining itself.

The rise of the functionary as a social type intrigues the intellectual in two respects.

In the first place, throughout history there has been mutual fascination and ambivalence between the man-who-would-act and the man-who-would-know. The statesman claims to act in the name of all, and the intellectual theorizes about the good of all. The intellectual needs the statesman because the experience and conduct of the statesman, inadvertently or directly, test the intellectual's explanations. Through close observation, or even vicarious participation, the intellectual learns whether or not the old theories stand up and what new explanations are needed. The statesman needs the intellectual, too, for technical advice: what the facts are, what alternatives of action are open, how the decision should be cast ideologically in order to win compliance from those affected by it. For the intellectual this is a source of both help and hindrance. He often must function as the court wizard, and this is bound to compromise his detachment—in the extreme, he becomes a prostitute. (But he may be able to redeem his honor later on: more than one sometime lackey and apologist of power has been able to use his access to the secrets of the inner circle to write a valuable scholarly treatise.)

The functionary intrigues the intellectual, in the second place, because he feels closer to him than to most statesmen. There is much less social distance between the two than there is between a royal prince and his wise men. Both intellectual and functionary are likely for the most part to be self-made men, valued more for their demonstrated competence than for nonrational attributes such as personal charisma or family eminence. Indeed, the functionary-statesman not infrequently was himself an intellectual at an earlier stage of his career, and he may even continue to be one in some avocational capacity.

We may take it as self-evident, however, that neither a functionary *as* functionary nor a statesman *as* statesman can be an intellectual in the course of his work. The logics are too different to be commensurable.

It is precisely this qualified affinity that leads the intellectual to distrust the functionary and to fear his rise as a social type. The intellectual looks at the functionary and sees a mindless technician, neutral, nonresponsible, a man of intelligence and skill who rents his ingenuity and his competence to the highest bidder. Or else he sees something far worse: a committed and responsible "Dr. Strangelove" who so deifies technique that his credo becomes "what can be done must be done."

It goes without saying that these two images of the functionary, devil worshiper or whore, are the projections of the intellectual. He sees himself, or possibilities of himself, mirrored in the functionary. But projection and bias can also be a source of insight.

To sum up, the problem for intellectual self-clarification presented by the functionary is that the conditions of work in a bureaucracy make him into a quasi-intellectual or an ex-intellectual. He cannot be an intellectual in the course of doing his work, because his method of operating is inherently different; but he can and sometimes does adopt the taste and culture and life-style of the true intellectual, and so creates a problem. The intellectual, identifying with the role of the hypothetical enlightened functionary, may allow himself to believe that "just putting in some good men" will make all the difference in solving the problems of big bureaucratic organizations and of a bureaucratically organized society. When this does not work, or does not work as well as it should, he is inclined to blame it on individuals who are either underinvolved (mindless technicians) or overinvolved (Dr. Strangelove characters) with technique and its uses.

Up to now we have been concerned with how we know the functionary in our common experience, and how the rise of his social type has created problems for the private person, the statesman, and the intellectual. Now we shall try to clarify what the functionary is by developing the implications of four abstract, characterizing statements: he is an organization man; he is ubiquitous; he is prototypic; and he is a new elitist.

THE FUNCTIONARY IS AN ORGANIZATION MAN

By now this is obvious. The point of defining the functionary as an organization man is to spell out what he is not. Specifically, he is *not:*

—a proprietor, free professional, or otherwise self employed; or
—a manual worker.

And he is only marginally:

—a white-collar worker of the comparatively immobile lower ranks; or
—an administrator on the policy-making level.

High administrators are formally above the organization, but still they are "of" it in part; they are creatures of it, to some degree, because either they came up through the ranks or they learned on the job that to be effective one must know first where the bodies are, and then how to relate to them.

Seymour Martin Lipset shows vividly in his book *Agrarian Socialism* [1] that an established bureaucratic organization is far from helpless against a new administrator. The CCF (Cooperative Commonwealth Federation), a moderate socialist party, won an electoral victory in the province of Saskatchewan in the late 1930's. The new ministers found that the entrenched, Tory-oriented bureaucracy at first was able to sabotage almost every effort to initiate a new program of reform. Eventually the new ministers learned to meet the professionals halfway and, somewhat later, to win authority in fact as well as in form. The administrator must accommodate himself, his method of operation, his personal style, even his values and his interpretation of his mandate, to the organization. In that sense he becomes "of" it although not exactly "in" it; the logic of his situation requires him to keep a certain distance from the regular apparatus.

Another category of organization people who are of it but not quite in it includes the clerks, typists, and lower white-collar workers generally. They are at the opposite end of the hierarchy of power and status from the administrator, but they share with him the need to be stamped with the organization's mark. They are its creatures, too, just as he is, and for basically the same reason if not to the same degree: they cannot do their work effectively unless they have some understanding of how the thing works and can empathize with those who work it, the true functionaries.

Administrative function is the key. The lower white-collar worker is a tool of the organization, not a part of it in the sociological sense—"it" being the apparatus of functionaries. And so he is of it but not in it. The proof lies in those subtle but unmistakable boundary markers on the social landscape, artifacts of the shared understanding of functionaries and subfunctionaries to maintain distance and not confuse roles.

One of the benign consequences of the subfunctionary's exclusion is his freedom to identify with the organization or to disidentify, as long as he is not too noisy about it. The functionary has no choice; he must identify.

Self-employed persons are by definition neither of nor in the organization. Manual workers are also outside the organization, although unlike the self-employed they are subject to it. The logic of the manual worker's situation makes any investment of self in the work he does or the functionally meaningful relationships he forms altogether fortuitous. There is no need for it, and so whether he identifies or disidentifies with the organization is a matter of indifference to it. He can make all the noise he wants.

The functionary is an organization man in every sense. He is the organization's creature and at the same time part of its apparatus; he *works* the apparatus and yet he *is* the apparatus. He is in it and of it and for it.

The functionary is essentially the middle and upper manager. He acts in the name of the organization, and he has the power to do so as long as he operates within guidelines. Moreover, in the ideal case what *he* does *he* chooses to do. His act is rational and meaningful from his own standpoint for that reason; it is rational from the standpoint of the organization—ideally, I repeat—because he is at one with it. He must invest the core of his self in his work if he is deeply and fully to understand it, which he must if he is to do it well. He cannot follow the logic and conform to the ethic of functional rationality—the application of technique to the choice of the best available means toward the end of making the organization work—without being personally attuned to the organization's needs and wants.

The functionary is an organization man in the sense, finally, that he is the organization's man: he is a constituent part of its conscience as well as its brain.

THE FUNCTIONARY IS UBIQUITOUS

Most of the work in modern society is done by formal organizations, not as it once was by communal collectivities or individuals working alone. "Who says organization says functionaries," to borrow the rhetorical form and some of the substance of Robert Michels' "Iron Law of Oligarchy." (In Michels' classic of social science literature, *Political Parties,*[2] he studies the Marxist-oriented trade union movement in Europe shortly after the turn of the century and concludes that: "Who says organization says oligarchy.") Organizations act *because of* and *by means of* non-functionaries—respectively, high administrators and manual workers—but they necessarily act *through* functionaries. The functionary is the commissioned agent of the organization; moreover, the functionary never acts except in combination with the whole body of functionaries who make up the organization's apparatus.

There are still individuals whose work act is altogether their own, uncomplicated by a need to work through others or with others and therefore uncontaminated by the spirit of functional rationality, yet who produce things recognized to be of social value. The artist is the best single example, but all self-employed persons have something of the artist's freedom to be himself and nothing but himself while at work.

The proportionate volume of such work is small, however, and steadily shrinking. This is the bureaucratic revolution's effect on the small producer.

There is also a certain amount of work still done communally. In such instances the individual works for love, not money; he gets his satisfaction out of working with and being with others. The product is not "mine" or "its" but "ours." "We" made it. The typical example is work done by a civic association or a team of volunteers (hospital visitors like the Gray Ladies, or canvassers during a political campaign), or by a large family unit engaged in business or farming, or by a voluntaristic community such as a religious or political movement. But a good part of even this sort of work is "coordinated," that is, administered, by functionaries.

In both these deviant types of work situations, efficiency, the optimal adjustment of means to ends among a large number of workers or employees, is not a prime value. The self-employed man does not have to "meet a payroll" or anything like it, except that he must maintain himself and his family. Within this imperative he is free to organize his work activities any way he pleases. He is not compelled by the logic of his situation to systematically minimize waste, maximize output, and in general to govern his relations with people and things under the press of rational necessity. He is free to be irrational or nonrational as long as he makes enough to live on.

The same is true of the family, the civic association, and the voluntaristic community as production units. The logic imposed by the technological division of labor is not very compelling. Individuals act in concert with others in doing their work, but there is nothing inherently illogical—given the fact that the object of their joint endeavor is to gain personal and social satisfactions as well as to generate an output—in their not following a rationally conceived plan for cooperation. They may prefer to follow a "sloppy" scheme of coordination because it is "more fun" or "more natural." They may pay a price in achieving less than maximum efficiency, but they may think it's worth it.

The functionary is ubiquitous in modern society because the organization of work, any kind of work, including the work of visiting hospitals or running a political campaign, usually accepts large-scale efficiency as an overriding value. Given the techniques available—and such techniques include modes of relating to people as well as to things—a high level of efficiency demands a large primary production unit whose work tasks and duties are differentiated according to the logic of functional rationality. This calls for a bureaucratic apparatus of officials and technicians to design, arrange, and oversee the operation of the production system of people and facilities.

The deviant types of work organization, individualistic and communalistic, only make it clear that the "normal" form of work organization in our society is bureaucratic: it is not only efficient but uniform, predictable, continuous in its operation, and stable. Because of this, more and more the only "normal" and "rational" way to get work done, as these standards are socially defined, is to make sure that the functionary operates the organization. Holdouts such as the family farm continue to shrink as a major source of employment and production.

THE FUNCTIONARY IS PROTOTYPIC

The functionary is ubiquitous and the functionary is prototypic: both statements are corollaries of Weber's master proposition that the bureaucratization of institutions in modern society continues to broaden and deepen, and this defines its main drift.

There is a difference, however.

To say the functionary is ubiquitous is to say that he is "all over," that he is to be found throughout society; and the explanation for this lies in the necessities of the organization of work. There is the technological factor, the availability of means, the related cultural factor, the commitment to efficiency as a prime value, and the underlying economic factor—the advantages of bureaucracy in cutting costs through increasing the scale of production. Thus the functionary and his style invade more and more areas of work formerly held by individualists and communalists.

To say the functionary is prototypic is something else: it means that his occupational type has become a pattern and mold for all other occupations—a master symbol of the culture of modern society.

There are other prototypic occupations, some of which continue from the past. The free entrepreneur is one; the free professional is a variant and so is the free or proprietary farmer. Much of our national mythology still reflects the individualizing bent of the entrepreneur, with its characteristic bias toward money-making as the only worthwhile object for a man of energy and talent. The free professional ("the old family doctor," "the family lawyer") is still held up as an example of wisdom and courage and self-reliance mixed with altruism, and the farmer has long stood for the peculiar kind of purity that follows from choosing work that is intrinsically honest and satisfying and directly productive. But doctors and lawyers and farmers have been expected to behave like businessmen, because the archetypal businessman, the free entrepreneur determined to get rich all on his own, has been America's hero without parallel. With the exception of clergymen and scholars, honored in form but with a patronizing air—as often as not secretly despised—it has been taken for granted by most people that all occupational types, even or perhaps especially the manual worker, would pattern themselves after this mythic, fast disappearing type of businessman.

The great depression of the 1930's diminished the prestige of the businessman, however. The New Deal securely established a bureaucracy of welfare and planning technicians to fill the vacuum left by the collapse of old-style business leadership. At the same time, federal hearings and inquiries such as those of the Temporary National Economic Committee (TNEC), and studies by scholars in law and the social sciences, showed that the free entrepreneur had become not much more than a myth.[3] Instead, unassuming men who styled themselves "industrial lieutenants," "managers," and "white-collar men" took charge of American business and industry. The hot war of the forties and the Cold War of the fifties accelerated the trend. The bureaucratic expert, whether in management or technology or some meld of the two, has now almost eclipsed the old-fashioned free entrepreneur as a mover and shaker. Whether in industry, in the military, or in government, the new man of the new age is the functionary. In an earlier era, men in all occupational walks of life took the free entrepreneur as their model; now we look to the functionary.

Doctors, lawyers, farmers, workers, politicians, professors— almost everyone unconsciously shapes his occupational character to resemble the functionary's. The way he walks and talks, organizes his private life, thinks and feels about the world, *the way he solves problems in the course of doing his work* sets the standard. This comes out in superficial ways—in the quasi–Ivy League "Brooks Brothers look" in style of dress; the beyond-the-suburbs "exurbanite" [4] style of private life; the cool, smooth, "uptown hipster" or "Madison Avenue" style of conversation and self-presentation.[5] In ways that count more deeply, it affects career patterns, attitudes toward work, and interpretations of success. More and more of us see a high rate of spatial and social mobility as normal, for example, as more and more people find it possible to treat their acquired organizational expertise as a kind of portable capital: they get ahead by skipping back and forth from company to company, industry to industry, and even between industry and government, government and academia, the military and some scholarly institute, or from any pair of these to another pair in an ever more elaborate series.

The great majority of people do not, really, and cannot, realistically, look forward to the glamorous jet-age career that a comparative few highly publicized individuals achieve. Such people form an elite of functionaries which is itself an elite. And yet these men, or our images of them, have careers we emulate in our own work lives. The significance of the rise of the functionary as a prototypic occupation is that it provides a reference point for assessing the reality and the value of our own work experience. We decide what is right or wrong, good or bad, true or false, correct or incorrect, on the basis of our own direct experience; but our experience is conditioned by our understanding of the logic of the functionary's work situation and of his intellectual and moral style in coping with it, and by our fascination with the whole package. Regardless of how appropriate it is to do so, we approach our own work problems in the spirit of the functionary. And thus we learn to become functionaries, or quasi-functionaries, whether or not we ought to, have to, or even consciously want to.

THE FUNCTIONARY IS A NEW ELITIST

Etymologically, to be "elite" is to be "the best."

It was French commercial practice in the nineteenth century to classify the very best grade of commercial goods "elite" and to sell them at a premium. (Perhaps the nearest equivalent term in English, applied to commercial practice, is "select.") In the twentieth century the term became applied to people and groups of people—in itself evidence of the process of dehumanization described succinctly in Paul Goodman's phrase, "from people to personnel." We now speak of an "elite corps" of military men (the Nazi SS, for example, or the American Special Forces), or a "power elite," or even an "elite" of fashion designers. In each case, we refer to a relatively small group of persons who stand out from others because of some special quality of excellence attributed to them.

Functionaries have become an elite; to say this is not to judge their value but to assess their place in society. It is a matter of objective social fact. Some individuals excel in a given line of activity, and some lines of activity are more prestigious than others. Those who occupy high places in a prestigious occupation constitute an elite, by definition.

In big institutions and organizations, for example, the growth in power and influence of a leadership stratum confers elitehood on its individual leaders in the society at large as well, *outside* the organization, especially as the elite actively claims deference because of the newly arisen influence and power of the institution they direct.

Most large elitists are affluent, some are rich and influential, some are genuinely powerful—if only because they are not too indifferent or too maladroit to seize opportunities for the material gain that so often comes with social honor, or too diffident to take a hand in the game of power. But some are. There are always a few individual elitists, a deviant minority within a minority, who squander fruitlessly the social capital they initially won, or else let it lie. They remind us that great wealth and real power are not the automatically conferred emoluments of elitehood, but must be sought with a convincing show of competence and responsibility.

There is an elite-within-the-elite, moreover, because the closer one approaches the apex of wealth and power in society, the more restrictive become the rules of the game. The ability to perform and achieve, and the qualities of moral fitness necessary for the move up, become more and more "Establishmentarian." This fact discourages some, quashes others, and puts off still others. Some minor functionaries never become major functionaries for this reason. On the other hand, some major functionaries take a broad view of their elite role and think of themselves as quasi-statesmen, while others take a narrow view and do not seek to project themselves into the national power elite, the elite of elites at the apex of all others.

But before a man moves up as a functionary, he must enter an occupation—if it is an occupation, properly speaking. One does not take up an apprenticeship or enroll in a trade or professional school to become a functionary, or take an examination or secure a license or credential or degree. One does not simply take a beginning job at the base of a tall hierarchy—as in the civil service or the military—in the hope of working up to a certain higher job with the title "functionary." Still, any one of these preparatory steps can be the first move in a career pattern that carries an individual into the realm of the true functionary.

The functionary as an occupational type transcends specialism in his work and responsibilities. Typically, he is a man who begins as a specialist, however, and he uses his technical expertise to win his first laurels by demonstrating superior achievement in a line of work for which he is objectively, impersonally qualified. His show of proficiency in applying a narrow range of skills then puts him in line for advancement to a position in which the content of his proven competence is no more than marginally useful —and may even be a handicap. Unless he can transcend the success he has had, leave it behind, he finds himself unhappy in his new work, or at any rate less than fully effective. He was a specialist; now he must learn to become a proficient generalist.

There is a lesson in the fact that the price of success as a doctor or lawyer, for example, is that one must accept becoming a luminary of the profession, an elitist, and take on duties of teaching or consulting or administering that limit the time one can devote to the substance of professional practice. The same is true of an engineer or scientist, or even of a production specialist or a sales specialist in industry who advances within his organization. The irony is that a man who does superbly well in his line of work is rewarded by being compelled to leave it, to move up into a higher occupation; but this is precisely how functionaries are recruited.

The functionary claims that the content of his work involves expertise based not only on craftsmanlike skill but also on administrative judgment. He has "know-who" as well as "know-what" and "know-how," as he sees it. He "gets things done," which means he makes the social arrangements men need to do their work, the same work which is socially necessary within the frame of the organization. There is no question but that the functionary must have administrative judgment (although he often makes a mystique of it). But skills—craftsmanlike, technical—are another matter.

Skills in general are open, public, "objective," teachable, and transferable, as opposed to talent or "genius," which is personal, private, unique, not transferable. Skills can be monopolized by organized groups who restrict access to avenues leading to their acquisition and application; but individuals cannot do likewise. Functionaries are not an organized group, they have no guild or craft union, and so they are not able to monopolize skills by that means. And they do not take a course of study to become what they are.

The fact that individuals very often become functionaries without going through any sort of formalized training supposed to guarantee competence, such as getting a Ph.D. in order to qualify for a professorship, must be contrasted to the generally accepted idea that a functionary's competence in any field may be effectively transferred to almost any other field. Executives transfer with apparent ease from one industry to another (and between industry and government and industry and the military), and this interchangeability is strong evidence that a common body of skills applies to all bureaucratic situations. But it is difficult to say what these are.

Civil service examinations, academic degrees, licenses and certificates of all sorts attest that the recipient is qualified for a particular line of work, but not—or not directly—the work of the functionary. There are professional schools of business and public administration, of course, but not even the most enthusiastic booster will claim that an M.B.A. certifies its holder to be a qualified functionary.

Functionary technique may be inherently somewhat nebulous

because, as in any elite occupation, over and above skill there is an existential element: a man must *be* (become) what he *is* in order to *do* what he does effectively; he must be able to make his *self* pliable and place it in the service of his intellect as an instrument. One may know a lot more than one can do: it is not necessary to be Caesar in order to understand Caesar, as Weber remarked, but it is necessary to be Caesar to do what Caesar did. (Needless to say, there are hundreds of thousands of competent functionaries, and almost all are men without extraordinary personal qualities. The chance of finding a potential world conquerer on the management staff of the local tool-and-die works is remote.) The point is, the role makes the man; and the man must be capable of being made—more accurately, made over—by the role regardless of his skills in using teachable and learnable techniques.

The functionary's role as a new elitist is also disguised by his lack of responsibility for policy—he merely carries it out. He takes his orders from a type above him we have called the "statesman," who is the politically appointed minister in charge of a civil service bureaucracy, for example, or the civilian chief of a military bureaucracy, or the chairman of the governing board in industry or in a nonprofit corporation. The functionary has authority *within* the organization, but the statesman has authority *over* it.

The difference between the functionary and the statesman is often more formal than real, however, depending on circumstances. The statesman is himself something of a functionary, for one thing. Either he came up through the ranks or was "broken in" by the organizational apparatus in order to be effective in discharging his responsibilities. And the functionary, especially the higher functionary, is himself something of a statesman. He cannot do his work well unless he understands thoroughly the organization's mission and the general policy line laid down by the statesman; he must think like a statesman while being a functionary. He takes on statesmanlike qualities in order to communicate with the statesman and to influence him to see things as they appear from the functionary's point of view.

Means, the province of the functionary, inevitably become more important than ends in the large organization. The apparatus and its mode of operation become institutionalized; it becomes an establishment with its own momentum, vested interests, habits, and routines, and it thereby acquires the capability to tailor ends to suit the means available for their realization. It is always hard to know what these means really are and what their capability is, but the functionary is in a better position than the statesman to make an informed assessment. The functionary comes to have a virtual monopoly of knowledge of how the apparatus works. The statesman must rely for the most part on the advice of experts, who in the nature of the case are functionaries with a vested interest in seeing goals and policy phrased in the way that expresses their habits of mind, interests, perspectives, and preferred procedures. Over time, the statesman becomes socialized to the functionaries' point of view; he is coopted or beguiled into accepting it as his own.

Social ends, in broad historical perspective, increasingly get defined in terms of the socially established means available for their realization. (We climb the mountain "because it is there." We go ahead with plans to build a supersonic jet transport aircraft "because we can," not because we demonstrably need it. We decide to "contain communism" in Southeast Asia because our "counterinsurgency capability" is "irresistible," without paying much attention to whether or not we are prepared to meet the cost of using it.) Because the functionaries now mostly "own" the means, it follows that they are a new elite in society. Their mind and spirit, reflecting the logic of their work situation, become the mind and spirit of all of us. Citizens and statesmen—anyone who takes thought and cares—find it increasingly hard to think and feel clearly and relevantly without using functionary logic.

In discussing the "who" and the "what" of the functionary in modern society, his identity and place, we have found that he is an organization man, he is ubiquitous, he is prototypic, and he is a new elitist.

Now we can attempt to understand him abstractly as a social type, to discover his image of the world, his basic attitudes, his public and private ethics and morality. We can attempt to discover the sense in which his world-views are the product of his organizational perspective and the nature of his work, and how this influences his self-definition and self-consciousness as a member of an elite group. If he does define himself as an elitist, we are interested not only in the claims he makes on others because of his status, but in the special and unique qualities he upholds to justify these claims.

These characteristics can be stated in propositional form: the functionary is both detached from his work and engrossed in it; the logic of his work situation places functional ahead of substantive rationality; and, finally, the functionary's occupational ethic evaluates the public good in terms of a bureaucratic "private" interest.

THE FUNCTIONARY IS BOTH DETACHED FROM HIS WORK AND ENGROSSED IN IT

This is a paradoxical statement, but the functionary's work is paradoxical.

He is supposed to pour himself into his work, to accept being "owned by the job," and yet to maintain an attitude of reasonableness and unruffled calm when things go wrong. He is expected to be loyal both to colleagues in his department and to the company—but his "loyalty" is portable: he may be pirated away by another company and expected to be loyal to it, even though his new employer had to entice him into an act of disloyalty to get him. His private life is company business (his wife and home may be informally inspected and rated if he is up for hiring or promotion), and yet the way he conducts the company's business is his own responsibility if it involves violation of antitrust and similar laws. If he is a scientist or technologist or any sort of professional man, his professional business is company business, but at the same time he is expected to "keep up" by publishing, corresponding, attending conventions, and all the things a normally situated professional man does. The functionary must walk a tightrope between being too engrossed in his company's work and not engrossed enough.

Some individuals become so wrapped up in their immediate work that they cut themselves off from other people, even though the substance of their work in large part lies precisely in dealing with people. This detachment is possible through involvement in paperwork: memoranda, letters, reports, schedules, manuals—the list is endless. It works for a time; a man can even make a good mark for efficiency this way, but only in the short run. Systems of interpersonal relations, clique formations, informal channels of communication (the "grapevine") grow and change and adapt, and thus the world of paper is never the real operating world. The pencil pusher works harder and harder but to less and less avail, because his paper world is a fiction.[6]

At the other extreme is the type of functionary who spends all his time and energy "keeping in touch." He knows dozens of counterparts in other departments by first name and is on the telephone or at lunch with them as often as possible. He knows the personal life of each member of his staff and of his boss's staff. It is hard to tell whether his activities within the organization are work or play. They can be called work and sometimes they are. But very often the functionary who engages in them is not really wrapped up in work but is playing at work. A variation in the pattern is the type of higher official who spends four afternoons a week at long lunches or golfing or "touring," which may include a nap at home. Playing at work in this case is barely distinguishable from "goofing off."

The problem of striking a balance between being overengrossed and underengrossed in work is different on the departmental and the company levels.

The overengrossed departmentalist is one who suffers from parochialism, localism, mental and emotional hardening of the arteries. He is so attached to his office and to his formally defined function that he *is* that office and function. He is conservative, intransigent, ritualistic. He resists all innovations automatically as "setting a dangerous precedent." He cannot see the forest for the trees, and he makes himself a bore at departmental or interdepartmental meetings by insisting that trees are the only thing. He may or may not work hard and conscientiously, but if he does the thrust is likely to be not so much to realize the mission as to forestall changes that will, he is convinced, thwart the ritualistic pseudo-production in which he has a large vested interest.

The opposite of the "localite" just described is the "cosmopolitan." He thinks and tries to operate on the company rather than the departmental level. He may or may not be truly engrossed in his *work,* realizing the mission, but he is certain not to be engrossed in his *job,* which is the inherited procedure he is supposed to follow in pursuing the mission. He takes a longer and larger view. The trouble is, he has a hard time seeing the trees for the forest. He often has grandiose plans for reorienting goals and reorganizing apparatus. He is the idea man, the sparkplug, the promoter, the entrepreneur in a bureaucratic setting. His greatest interest is in things that affect the company from outside rather than inside. His enthusiasm takes the form of devotion to ends— the mission—more than means—the welfare of the apparatus. He thinks of himself as a general rather than as a sergeant or lieutenant. If his dreams fail he becomes an "operator," full of plans and schemes against "the System." If these operations come to nothing too, he withdraws from work as well as job and starts looking around for a better place.

THE LOGIC OF THE FUNCTIONARY'S WORK SITUATION TENDS TO PUT FUNCTIONAL AHEAD OF SUBSTANTIVE RATIONALITY

Max Weber and Karl Mannheim, grand masters of the study of large-scale organization, detected the Achilles heel of bureaucracy:

rationality of means is not a simple derivative of rationality of ends, and in fact tends to pervert it.

Rationality in substance is rationality applied to ends. Means are not unlimited, and somehow a choice has to be made between guns and butter; between better highways to and through the city and better public rapid-transit facilities within the city; between spending $30 billion to put one man on the moon or about the same amount (assuming it costs $30,000 per man in new investment) to place a million unemployed Negroes in jobs.

There is no rational solution to such problems because they concern ultimate ends and values, and everyone knows a value judgment cannot be proved or disproved. (I think life is better than death; but if you deny it, what facts can I cite, what fallacy of logic can I expose that will compel you to concede error?)

The choice of ultimate ends is neither rational nor irrational, but nonrational. The clash of material and ideal interests which constitutes political conflict grows out of irreconcilable differences about what is "good" and "right" and "fair." Barring an unbreakable stalemate, one or the other party is defeated, eventually, or else a compromise is reached which settles nothing except that nothing fundamental can be settled. There follows a period of "cold war" or "peaceful coexistence," depending on the swing of the pendulum and one's point of view. Looked at objectively, victory or compromise is not the result of rational choice but the outcome of a power struggle.

And yet we do try to be rational in choosing ends, which implies that we think we can be. Either we are deluded in this endeavor, and there is no such thing as a rationality of ends, or else we are not deluded, in which case we must decide how there can be any real difference between a rationality of ends and a rationality of means.

The problem must be approached sociologically rather than logically. A strictly logical analysis leads up a blind alley.

The point of departure is to realize that there is no firm distinction to be made *objectively* between means and ends. In actual human experience, one shades off into the other. The defining quality of things called "means" and other things called "ends" must be found in the situation of the actor, not in the object of the human act.

Take the case of the proposed crosstown expressway for lower Manhattan in New York City. Whether it is seen as a means or an end depends on the standpoint of the viewer, his interests and commitments, his situation, and his role in that situation. Those who want the expressway for the most part see it primarily as a means. For them it is a necessary link in the greater New York City expressway net, so it is a means to the end of improved facilities for automobile and truck transportation. But at the same time it is an end in itself, at least for some: those who are so involved in it that it acquires the meaning of a mission or a project with its own intrinsic value.

Those who are against the expressway also see it both as a means and an end. They oppose it as a means either because they see it as a rational means to an irrational end, an irrational means to a rational end, or an irrational means to an irrational end; but some may also oppose it as a bad thing in itself, as an end. They may try to block it in order to block the realization of the larger end ("something for cars instead of people"), not caring too much one way or another about that particular project; or it may be that the expressway itself is ultimately obnoxious and not so much the end it is intended to implement. (This would be the point of view of local residents and businessmen who object to being uprooted by construction.)

From the standpoint of policy, when there is a conflict over ends the groups involved go further back in their valuation schema in order to find some more ultimate set of ends they can agree upon. If they succeed they go on to determine the degree of proximity and the relative importance of immediate ends to ultimate ends. Then they attempt (in theory) to discover which immediate ends, if acted upon, would result in the sacrifice of certain other immediate ends, and what those ends would be. This provides the basis for weighing certain immediate ends against ultimate ends held in common. All of this rests upon *agreement* on ultimate ends. Without that, only force and power make any difference. It is prior agreement rather than the objective validity of ends that is socially operative.

Tolstoy, with admirable economy, observed that the fundamental and inescapable concern of a human being is "what to do" and "how to live." These are questions of ultimate ends, not means. One must conclude, he said, that since these are the only important questions, and since science cannot answer them, it follows that science is useless. In effect, he spurned any "rationality of means" and devoted his whole attention to questions of a "rationality of ultimate ends." We have seen that it is part of our common experience to sit continuously in judgment on what-to-do and how-to-live decisions, mulling over, deliberating, finally deciding (or perhaps finally not deciding) that this or that accomplishment or contemplated action is "good" or "bad," "right" or "wrong" as an individual act. This is the process we have termed rationality in substance, because, in the style of Tolstoy, it is concerned with ultimate ends. Now we turn to functional rationality, the rationality and the ethic of the functionary.

The functionary differs from the ordinary person in that he acts on behalf of a formally constituted organization. Most of us do not, or if we do it takes up only a small part of our total social existence. The functionary is more likely to be "on the job" all the time, as we have seen, and so to a comparatively greater extent than the rest of us the logic of his work relationships carries over into his private life. Moreover, he is a culture-bearer, a style-setter, a power-wielder in modern society. His logic tends to become the logic we all follow, not only at work but also in civic affairs, at leisure, and even in the most intimate moments of our private lives.

The functionary is like the ordinary person in that he is a human being first (although we must gravely emend this statement later), and so he is caught up with problems of substantive rationality as much as the rest of us. At least we can say this as a first approximation. He knows all the nonfunctionary knows about what Stephen Potter calls "lifemanship," [7] and something more, something very potent and character defining: in addition to being human he must know how to be a machine.

A man cannot be a machine in the literal sense—although some try—but he can organize his relations with others according to machine logic, and he can build that logic into his very conscience.

Because he acts publicly not on behalf of individuals but of the company and the organization, the functionary learns to base his decisions on "the impersonal laws of cause and effect," a habit of mind that Veblen [8] admired but Weber regarded as a dehumanized canon of conduct in work.[9] The functionary sees personalization as a distortion equivalent to anthropomorphism; it is to treat a thing as if it had human qualities, and in this new logic *people are really things*. Their humanity is incidental and irrelevant to the functionary's set of mind. The fact that people are unique individuals is an irritant to the system, sand in the gears: one must take time out to relate to them as persons, that is, on non-rational grounds, grounds of sentiment, and this interferes with getting the work done with maximum organizational efficiency. Even one's own uniqueness is annoying because it introduces an infirm parameter into the system, one that may vary at any time and in incalculable ways. The ideal production system has no individuals at all in it.

The practice of substantive rationality on the job and in the course of doing one's work is a clear violation of bureaucratic procedure, a matter of taking the rules into one's own hands. The organization is not a civic polity, and any widespread concern with the equivalent of "our national purpose"—ultimate goals—testifies to a breakdown of the division of functions between policy-makers and executors. The functionary's feeling in such situations is, "I don't know where I stand, so how can I act?"

If the functionary does not know ends, the organizational mission, it is because the ultimate makers of policy, the "statesmen," have failed to define them as they apply to him in his place in the organizational scheme of things. The world he prefers is a world in which ends are given and only means, *his* means, are problematic. His expertise is in means-rationality, not ends-rationality. He has no special qualifications for saying *what* should be done, but he has a lot to say, and he can speak with authority, on *how* it should be done.

Not infrequently it happens that a vacuum develops on the level of top leadership, however, and the functionary is sucked up into it whether he likes it or not. Being a man of action, he responds to requests for advice in the spirit of such military maxims as "When in doubt, attack," or "Do something, do anything; the one unforgivable sin is to do nothing." He quite naturally defines ends in terms of means, because means are what he knows; he phrases problems of substantive rationality in terms of a calculus suited to problems of *functional* rationality. If his advice prevails, the effect is to adapt ends to means instead of means to ends, and the organization is set upon a course calculated to realize an objective which requires the use of means it has proved capable of using effectively in the past. Carried to an extreme, the intrinsic merit of the end is hardly examined at all—the mountain is climbed "because it is there" and "we have the means and the know-how to do it."

The only name for this perverse state of affairs is mindless, ritualistic activism.

THE FUNCTIONARY'S OCCUPATIONAL ETHIC EVALUATES THE PUBLIC GOOD IN TERMS OF A BUREAUCRATIC "PRIVATE" INTEREST

It was a United States Secretary of Defense, formerly president of the world's largest manufacturing corporation (and one whose stock ownership was dominated at the time by a single family, the duPonts), who said, "What's good for General Motors is good for the country."

There is a certain superficial resonance between the tone of Charles E. Wilson's statement and the public-be-damned sentiments often expressed by the Robber Barons of the heroic age of American capitalism, from the 1870's to just after the turn of the century. But the similarity is more apparent than real. Wilson spoke in the style of the modern functionary-become-statesman, not the old-style tycoon. He made his mark first as a functionary and only then as the chief of a vast private bureaucracy, and so he was considered fit to run a vast public bureaucracy. The significance of his remark is not so much that it betrays "capitalist arrogance" as that it exhibits a kind of parochialism of the mind which has a character similar to that of pure functionaries.

Every occupational type has its own psychosis, and the functionary's is a trained incapacity to deal with problems of work organization in substantive rather than functional terms. Much of this has been touched upon already. Now we must assess the implications for public policy of the rise of the functionary—how does his occupational interest square with the public interest?

The distinction we commonly make between "public" and "private" bureaucracies is more a matter of form than substance, considered from the standpoint of their internal arrangements. Functionaries are not very different in either; the logic of the two sets of work situations is essentially the same. Of greater importance in explaining differences are the goals of the "private" bureaucracy. During wartime, for example, extraordinary arrangements—"working partnerships"—are entered into between business and government; government puts up the capital for new plants, and industry provides the operating staff on a cost-plus basis. When the war is over and the partnership dissolved, government withdraws and private industry resumes its command of profitable fields of production—this is called the private sector —and government goes back to overseeing the socially necessary but profitless remainder, the public sector.

The mission of a private industrial organization is quite simply to grow and make money. The mission of a similar organization in the public sector is to produce goods and services economically, that is, at the lowest possible cost, but without calculating the effect production decisions have on growth and profitability. They are "nonmarket" organizations; they get their orders in the form of a mandate from a public body, such as Congress, or from a high public official. This complicates the policy-making job and gives it a distinctive character, as compared with private industry. But the "government bureaucrats" and "industrial bureaucrats" on the level below are mostly of the same species: functionary. This is shown by the very considerable amount of interchange of managerial and higher technical personnel between the public and private sectors.

"Bureaucratic interest," therefore, is not synonymous with "property interest." It is found in the public sector as well as in the private. The hybrid type of functionary-statesman represented by Secretary Wilson and, more recently, by Secretary Robert S. McNamara can be found in countries such as the Soviet Union which do not even have a private sector. One would suppose that somewhere in recent history there is a Russian counterpart of Wilson's famous gaffe—uttered, perhaps, by a former industrialist not yet seasoned to the political realities of his new job as Commissar of Industrial Procurement for the Red Army. This is a flight of fancy, but it does illustrate the point that the underlying phenomenon is neither "capitalist" nor "socialist," properly speaking. It is a case of the rhetoric of an occupational group being passed off as the rhetoric of a civic polity; more precisely, it is the universal rhetoric of the functionary, whose characteristic bent is to define ends in terms of means, and the world in terms of the needs and perspectives of a particular bureaucracy and its bureaucrats.

Ideally, the functionary is a public person with public responsibilities only in the passive sense. He is an interpreter of public policy—in order to implement it if he is a "public" official, in order to accommodate it if he is a "private" official—rather than a maker of it. But in recent years, ostensibly private organizations have taken on more and more of a public role, and people who are supposed to make policy, the "statesmen," in fact are relying more and more on the functionary's expertise and are ever more inclined to defer to his power because of his entrenched place in the organizational apparatus. The functionaries find themselves makers of policy, definers of the public interest through default. After the Bay of Pigs fiasco in 1962, President Kennedy wondered bitterly how he could have been "stupid enough to trust the experts."

1961

The functionary's characteristic version of the public interest reflects both a pious, self-effacing, "good-soldier" ethic and a monumental arrogance fit for a Florentine nobleman. The arrogance grows out of the piety; in fact, it is made possible by the piety: "I am in the service of a Cause; everything I do is for It, nothing is for Me." The nothing-for-me part of the official credo (unofficially it is not all that neat) makes it possible for the functionary, in good conscience, to interpret and act on a conception of the public interest that is actually a projection onto society at large of the "private" interests of an organization in the business of transporting coal or catching criminals or making automobiles.

It has come to be accepted that the operation of a large organization in the private sector is "affected with a public interest," and if it is in the public sector it has a legitimate sphere of "private" interest. This makes it seem reasonable for spokesmen and officials in either kind of organization to take a leading role in saying what is good for America. And the fact that the big bureaucratic organization is impersonal makes it seem objective— right as well as reasonable. After all, concludes the functionary-statesman, those who ultimately benefit when public authorities are "friendly" and "understanding" and thus permit the work to go forward are "the people, all the people." This is his rationale for consciously and deliberately interpreting the public interest, more and more, as nothing but a special version of the "private" interests of big, quasi-public bureaucracies.

2

Work and the organization

The pure functionary does his work in a modern large-scale organization. Authority is hierarchically delegated, labor is functionally divided, rules are abstract and articulated so they mesh throughout the organization, and all is ordered according to a bureaucratically rationalized scheme. People are hired, fired, and promoted according to technical qualifications and with respect for tenure, and interpersonal relations are impersonal throughout.[1]

This is the ideal situation of the functionary. In reality things are not so neat, of course. But, with due regard for the unevenness and incompleteness of an evolutionary phenomenon, the different real-life situations have enough in common to provoke social scientists (in economics, psychology, political science, and sociology) to develop what has come to be known as "the field of complex organizations," or "organization theory"[2] for short.

We have seen what the functionary is, how we encounter him in our everyday experience, how his existence is in itself a social problem and calls attention to others, and what his salient social-psychological characteristics are. Now we turn from the functionary as a social type to the nature of his milieu: the organization—in particular, to perspectives on the organization and the place of work in it, to images of the organization and to concepts and theories about the organization.

The discussion below is concerned first with what Durkheim and Weber had to say about work and organization. It turns then to organization theory as it has developed over the past several decades, primarily in the United States, and then concludes with a note on the question of organization power and research bias. The guiding theme throughout is that we can know what the organization *is* only by first giving attention to what practical men and scholars have *thought it to be;* ideology is a hindrance to a sure grasp of truth, but, no less for that, it is also a source of insight. The better we understand the organization in its abstract form, the better we can understand the functionary. A review of organization perspectives and theory is a necessary prolegomenon to a closer look at the functionary as he exists in various contexts of action.

It is a striking fact that the two undisputed founding fathers of modern sociology turned their attention early in their careers, a little before and just after the turn of the twentieth century, to the problems of what Daniel Bell has called aptly "work and its discontents." [3] The perspectives they brought were different and yet complementary. Looking back now, from a vantage point two-thirds of a century later, one marvels at how prescient they were. The issues they raised are still very much alive, and they still constitute two major aspects of the impact of the large-scale organization on work: the problem of the social bond, and the problem of meaning in work.

DURKHEIM'S PERSPECTIVE: A SATISFYING SOCIAL BOND

Emile Durkheim was a French sociologist who did most of his scientific work between 1882 and 1912. He was concerned with what he saw as a loss of a sense of community in modern society, a fragmenting, a pulling apart which was due ultimately to the progress of the division of labor (the title of his doctoral dissertation and his first book).

Durkheim foresaw quite early that modern man was going to have to learn to live by the credo: "Make yourself . . . fulfill a determinate function." [4] He meant that productive work was inexorably taking on a different shape and meaning, and that character and the social self would have to accept being remolded to suit the imperatives of modern industry. The old communal basis for free and voluntary cooperative work was gone, or going rapidly. No longer was the kind of work a man did a function of his social existence; rather, his social existence, what he was and who he was, depended on and reflected the kind of work he did.

Contrary to the rationalistic, laissez-faire economic and psychological philosophers of individualism of his time, however, Durkheim understood that a line of work is not simply something one "takes up," either as a rational expression of self-interest or as a meaningless, drifting, inconsequential adaptation to circumstance. Instead it is the crucial act by which the individual integrates into society and finds a definition of self that corresponds to his place in it. The communal order of society, the *Gemeinschaft,*[5] the society of "mechanical" or "segmental" solidarity (cohesion based on a sense of likeness), had broken down and was being replaced. Its successor was to be not a society of rational human atoms, free and capable of choosing, but of individuals existing in relation to each other in society by virtue of their instrumental role in it (cohesion based on a sense of reciprocity).

There is a degree of hopefulness in Durkheim's view because he sees satisfaction and fulfillment in work as a group rather than an individual phenomenon. (Following Ruth Benedict's use of the terms, he leaned toward the "Apollonian" and away from the "Dionysian" in the fundamentals of his world-view.[6]) If only men can learn to recognize in their work relationships that they are functionally akin to others similarly situated—not as a class in the Marxian sense but as a corporate body engaged in one given line of production—they can develop a sense of communal self-consciousness capable of providing the locus within which new bonds of cohesion appropriate to the modern world, "organic solidarity," can develop.

Work is important, said Durkheim, but not as a thing in itself. Its real significance lies in the fact that it locates workers in relation to each other and provides the existential grounding of the social bond that (latently) unites them. Durkheim was thinking primarily of the common man, not the upper managerial elitist or the expert technologist.

Much of Durkheim's perspective is evident in the works of Mayo and Roethlisberger and Dickson, who analyzed the results of the famed Hawthorne Studies of management and the worker in the late 1920's and early 1930's, and of the social anthropologist W. Lloyd Warner, who carried out the Yankee City studies in the thirties, and of the contemporary industrial sociologist William Foote Whyte.[7] Their concern has been with the disaffected production worker, not the bored or frustrated management man. (This is true even though, ironically, as Clark Kerr and Lloyd Fisher [8] point out, the main impact of the "human relations in industry" movement has been to change the way management and technical men relate to each other. The supervisor-operative relationship has been much less affected.)

To sum up, Durkheim's thesis is that the division of labor is a progressive and irreversible feature of modern industrial-urban society, and that its logic, on the one hand, subverts bonds of communal solidarity, and, on the other, creates the basis for a new form of solidarity—corporate self-consciousness—suited to the modern world. The important thing is the social bond: work is merely an occasion for its development, it has no meaning intrinsic to itself. The functional equivalent of the old medieval *Gemeinschaft* of men working cooperatively together because they felt the tug of kinship, or quasi-kinship, must be reconstituted on a different foundation.

Max Weber was interested not so much in the division of labor and its effects on the bonds of social cohesion as in the evolution of what he took to be the master institutional form of modern society: bureaucracy.

Durkheim worried about the community. Weber's concern was for the individual. In spite of the difference in emphasis, however, the two men reached conclusions not dissimilar on one key point. In Weber's view the new society, more and more brought under the influence of bureaucratization, was a milieu of social and work relationships that made the rationalistic, self-dependent individual obsolescent at the same time the old communal organization of work was becoming little more than a dim memory. Looking only a short distance into the future, he saw men at work as spiritless cogs in huge bureaucratic machines, a "nullity . . . without heart . . . that imagines it has built the greatest civilization the world has ever known." [9] Durkheim would have agreed, given only the assumption that man will in fact not realize his fondest hope for the future: to develop corporate self-consciousness and save society as a community. But Durkheim was not willing to accept such an assumption.

Weber was not alone in his bitter pessimism. His despair about the future of meaningful work and the kind of social character he valued is echoed in the later work of the economist Joseph Schumpeter, who deplored the passing of the "daemonic entrepreneur" in industry and his replacement by a "faceless army of white-collar workers." Even the "creative destruction" Schumpeter saw as the vital heart and secret of success of the giant industrial corporation was coming more and more under the "rule of routine"—standardized, reduced to formula, denied meaning for the functionaries who carry on its operations.[10]

Weber was fascinated by bureaucracy, just as Durkheim was by the division of labor. Taking, as always, the standpoint of the ethically responsible and uniquely valuable individual, he praised bureaucracy for vastly extending man's grasp but denounced it for taking away all reason for reaching. In bureaucracy there is no meaning in work—and this is dreadful. A man is made, his character is formed at least as much from what he does and the logic of his doing it as from his membership in a community of fellow doers.

The chief difference between Durkheim and Weber is that Durkheim emphasizes the satisfying social bond growing out of man's social relations at work—community or quasi-community—while Weber's interest is in the meaning of the work itself. Not surprisingly, the main concern of Durkheim and the Durkheimians is with the nonfunctionary or the subfunctionary, the common man in industry. The blue-collar and lower white-collar types are those most likely to emphasize social satisfactions incidental to the job and to show no more than a resigned, perfunctory interest in the content of their work. Higher technicians, technologists, and their compeers on the supervisory and managerial levels are more likely to want "challenge," "opportunity," "a chance to do something interesting and worthwhile." They want the work they do to be intrinsically meaningful; they have something of Veblen's "instinct of workmanship"; and of course they are the ones to whom the Weberian emphasis mostly applies.

THE TRANSITIONALISTS

Follett

Mary Parker Follett, an American professor of public administration, is remembered as one of the first to reject the rationalism and individualism still taken for granted by most scholars and theorists in the 1920's. She insisted instead that administration should be viewed as a "creative process." Successful administrators are those who take a "dynamic view" of their situation and do not hesitate to allow a considerable role for intuition in forming judgments and carrying out policies. She saw the organization as something like an "organism," with its own "life process." The individual's natural bent is not to be hedonistically self-seeking but to act in such a way that he expresses a sense of oneness with others. The individual experiences his own act as part of a larger collective act which is continually being built up over a period of time.[11]

The consequences of looking at the individual in the organization in this way are twofold. The rank-and-filer, for one thing, is conceived to be naturally energetic and group-minded. He wants to act and he wants to do the right thing because his motivation is primarily social. He cares deeply about the opinions of others, his peers no less than his superiors.

The administrator, once he understands this, will not drive, pull, push, or passively "administer" but genuinely lead. He knows that his subordinates want to be shown the way, not just once but continuously, because the one thing they cannot do themselves is choose goals and coordinate efforts so that all become effectively one. They resent being pushed or driven, and they feel insulted by a carrot-and-stick doctrine of command. In the logic of their situation they feel a personal stake in the outcome of the large collective act in which they have a small but intensely real part. The wise administrator, knowing this, takes compliance for granted and treats the question of sanctions as marginal, reserving his best energy and thought for coping with the problem of how to fit the part-acts together into a meaningful and effective whole.

Mayo

Elton Mayo was a social anthropologist by training who spent most of his career teaching industrial management at Harvard. Like Mary Follett, he found himself out of sympathy with the rationalistic individualism of the dominant school of management and organization theory in the twenties. And, like certain of his fellow anthropologists (notably W. Lloyd Warner and Margaret Mead), he felt and responded to a sense of mission: civilized society must learn to understand itself by studying the social institutions and the culture and psychology of "simple" peoples— "primitive tribes," to use old-fashioned language—and somebody will have to midwife the insights thus to be born.

One of the most important lessons from these studies, according to Mayo, is that *collaboration cannot be left to chance* in modern society, and most especially in the industrial enterprise, "the plant community." If we look at the societies of preliterates, societies supposedly "closer to nature," we see that individuals naturally cohere into groups; collaboration can be left to chance because such societies are small and the division of labor is simple. Is it not possible that the same is true of civilized societies? If it is and we cannot see it, it is because we have been misled by an ideological fixation: *"the rabble hypothesis."* We are blind to group structure.[12]

The now classic Hawthorne studies,[13] in which Mayo participated, seemed to bear out his contention. The researchers concluded that workers work not as socially isolated individuals, each out to maximize his own self-interest, but as members of groups. Such groups, or cliques, emerge regardless of management's wishes. Usually they are antimanagement in their philosophy, and they more or less systematically restrict output in order to protect themselves against overwork and underpayment. They tend to be antimanagement because the individual's bosses treat him as a machine or an animal or an errant child. He does want care, but with respect. If he does not get it he feels bereft and may withdraw. Then his work suffers. He becomes perfunctory in his performance; he engages in "obsessive reverie" and looks for fantasy satisfactions in place of the real ones he has given up hope of finding.

The worker needs psychic nurture from the work group *but also from management*. If he does not get it he may become ill or resentful—either way he grows less efficient—or even rebellious, in which case he may form antimanagement unions and demand higher wages. (It is essential to bear in mind that this research was done mainly in the twenties, before independent trade unionism was supported by law and widely established.)

The practical import of Mayo's view is that the enlightened manager will devote a good deal of time and energy to making sure that worker cliques are allowed to form, are even fostered, under conditions such that the members are not bitter and resentful against management but essentially content. This calls for the cultivation of "human relations skills." Making people happy is a good thing in itself, but what is more to the point is that it has a dollars-and-cents payoff: happy workers are productive workers.

Systemic integral groupism

Follett and Mayo, pioneer theorists of the organization-as-a-society perspective, exemplify in their work the bent of the whole vanguard school of the twenties and thirties. Actually there were two schools: a "Follett school" emphasizing coordination as a problem, and a "Mayo school" emphasizing cohesion. In common they took issue with individualistic rationalism, the perspective of the organization-as-an-economy, and proposed in its stead an image of the essential character of the organization that may be called "systemic integral groupism" (an embarrassing bit of jargon, but it does have the virtue of precision).

Mary Follett saw the organization problem primarily as coordination, because her concern was with how the manager-administrator, the high-level functionary of the organization of whatever sort, would put together these marvelous energies she saw immanent once they were released into a unified whole. She is a *Gestaltist* in style of thought, one who sees the totality of a thing as having a separate order of reality than the sum of its parts. How is a higher organizational unity to be achieved out of a body of separate and quite possibly antagonistic parts? She offers no sure formula for a way out; but the important thing is to pose the problem, and that she did.

Mayo's insight is that the logic of the new, rationalized technology runs counter to one of the oldest and most durable of human propensities: to do one's work in the company of peers, and to do it as an expression of group loyalty to achieve a group objective.

Most work acts are a product of sentiment, Mayo argues, *group* sentiment, not individualistic rational calculation of advantage. Therefore, the organization problem is primarily cohesion. How is the integrity (and thus the cohesion) of natural groupings, or cliques, to be fostered while at the same time the advantages of technological and functional rationalization are realized? Unlike Mary Follett, Mayo does have a prescription: more and better "human relations skills." But what this means is not very clear, and in practical effect Mayo leaves us dangling.

It is clear enough how the groupism of Mary Follett and Elton Mayo is integral, for both emphasize the integrity of the group as a precondition for the effective functioning of the individual and the organization. Action in the organization is group-centered; at any given moment the sociologically real component part of the organization is the group, not the individual. And the group's bent is to maintain itself as it is, unchanged. It is in that sense "integral." It is "systemic," additionally, in that the meaning of the group's activity is functional. In this view, activity is either functional or dysfunctional, that is, its meaning can be judged in terms of its effect on the needs of the enterprise as a whole, as a system of objectively interrelated parts. Neither Mayo nor Mary Follett spelled it out, but from the standpoint of the history of organization theory, the postulate is implicit in their scheme.

THE BEHAVIORALISTS

Researchers and theorists interested primarily in how the individual adapts himself to the organization; how he learns to play his role and eventually how he plays it in fact; how he relates to others, interacts with others, accepts the direction of others, or gets others to accept his bidding; how he communicates and receives communications; how he decides what to do (makes decisions) and actually does it (carries out decisions)—in short, researchers and theorists who take the individual human act as the strategic datum for understanding the organization contribute a body of work I call *the behavioral strand*.

The following writers exemplify the type: Kurt Lewin, Chester Barnard, Herbert A. Simon, and Chris Argyris. They have in common a view of the organization as a society. They emphasize problems of coordination rather than cohesion (when they examine cohesion it generally is in order to get at the problematics of coordination), and have an important secondary interest in the organization-as-an-economy, with the accompanying commitment to raise questions about rationality and control.

Lewin

Kurt Lewin is not ordinarily thought of as an organization theorist. But he is universally acknowledged to be one of the founders of modern experimental social psychology and of the new specialty called "small groups theory." [14]

Lewin and his co-workers demonstrated in the mid-thirties, with unparalleled clarity, that an important segment of individual behavior is a function of the kind and intensity of his group affiliations. The German sociologist Georg Simmel had laid down the essential groundwork of concepts and postulates a generation earlier. Lewin was an emigrant from Germany to the United States, and was influenced by Simmel, but in one sense he went further, since Simmel's analysis lacked the empirical closure that has since come to be regarded as essential if research is to qualify as science. Lewin set up experimental situations and found that the individual's beliefs about truth and falsity and his sentiments, his feelings about what is good and bad, right and wrong in conduct, are conditioned by a "group climate" of opinion; in general, his actions are a manifestation of "group decision." Moreover, "group climate" (of opinion) and "group decision" could be treated as experimental variables under certain conditions—in plain language, they could be manipulated.

The significance for organization theory of Lewin's research, and the research he inspired, is the postulate that the structure and functioning of the organization cannot be understood without taking account of the "group factor," or, more precisely, "the group dynamics factor." The way the individual feels and thinks and acts is neither rational nor irrational, but nonrational. He acts and reacts as a member of a group: he takes his cues about what is real and what is important from others who form an informally organized social environment and a social matrix in which he is embedded. What he does he does as the enactor of a group-sanctioned and group-supported role, an informal, unofficial role. The way he performs his formal, official role (his organization role in the conventional sense) is heavily influenced by "group climate" and "group decision." The experienced and effective organization functionary will take these factors into account and will bear in mind that he has the power to influence them, sometimes even to use them. Thus he may find it expedient in a given instance to work indirectly, to secure compliance by manipulating the group as a means of manipulating the individual.

Barnard

Much of Chester Barnard's importance stems from the fact that he is an "original," a business executive (at one time president of the New Jersey Bell Telephone Company) who wrote a scholarly treatise out of his own experience. Of course, he had read Weber and Simmel and other academic sociologists; still, his work bears the mark of a man seeking to classify and arrange the facts he knew firsthand, and to analyze them and grasp their meaning for himself. Arid and difficult as *The Functions of the Executive* [15] is to read, it has been seminal for organization theory. The complicated abstractions Barnard devised for his own convenience stated a point of view and defined a set of problems which are still very real a quarter of a century later.

Barnard, unlike Lewin, looks at the organization from the top down and from the outside in. Thus he takes a macroscopic rather than a microscopic view, and the features of the terrain he sees as important are hierarchical and functional divisions and their interrelationships. (Lewin worked with a two-level system: the quasi-self-enclosed group and the manipulator-"outsider.") The organization is a system of communications—up and down status positions, through strata, and across functional boundaries.

In Barnard's scheme the important questions have to do with how the organizational apparatus (hierarchical and technological differences in status and function) on the one hand promotes and on the other hand interferes with the initiation and transmission of information. Social differences make a difference in how communications linkages work—that is Barnard's point. The novelty is that he sees the individual as occupying a place in the organization which gives him a considerable amount of discretion in how he does his duty. It goes far beyond a simple choice between compliance and noncompliance. Directives flow "down the line" and information about performance ("feedback") flows up the line. The individual may eagerly seek direction or information, interpreting it, piecing it out as it passes through his hands; or he may be indifferent and neither help nor hinder the flow; or he may be hostile and delay it, change it, or even deliberately sabotage the communications function.

Barnard calls for "leadership." Organization functionaries at all levels should be aware of "the functions and pathologies of status systems" (the title of one of his essays); they should act to promote the functions and guard against the pathologies. The chief functionaries, executives on the policy-making level, should be ever alert to the possibility that the officially prescribed relationships among offices ("formal organization") will have to be changed from time to time in order to break up unofficial channels of communication ("informal organization") which hamper their effectiveness and freedom of action. At the same time they must recognize that such channels are normal, within limits, and that a strategic part of the executive's job is to explain current policies, interpret the mission of the organization, and accordingly reconcile the necessities of the immediate program, and in this way encourage the largest possible extension of the "zone of acceptance" of legitimate directives.

Simon

Barnard's treatise has never directly inspired extensive research on organizations; its impact has been theoretical and conceptual rather than empirical. Scholars have found it useful as a point of departure rather than as a route map showing where to go and how to get there. It does not in itself lay out a program for research, and it does not define the scientifically problematic, at least not in the sense that it pinpoints gaps in our knowledge of organizations. The tenor of the discussion renders "leadership" as a kind of mystique, and this hardly encourages those who want to make it the subject of factual inquiry.

Herbert Simon's *Administrative Behavior* [16] is designed to remedy this limitation. The aim of the book is to help place the scientific study of organizations on a firm empirical foundation. It is as if the author has set out to accomplish for macrocosmic analysis the equivalent of Lewin's feat on the microcosmic level: what Simmel was to Lewin and the small-groups theorists, Barnard was to Simon and the positivistic systems theorists.

The subtitle of *Administrative Behavior* is "A Study of Decision-making Processes in Administrative Organization." Conceptually the book owes a great deal to Barnard's earlier work (which is duly acknowledged). Most of the topics discussed (communication, hierarchy, authority) are straight out of Barnard, and others are closely related. But they are treated in quite a different spirit. (Different but not irreconcilable: Barnard wrote the introduction to the book, and he said then and has said since many laudatory things about it.) Barnard was a practical man trying to make sense out of the world and its workings as he experienced it, somewhat in the fashion of the "armchair scholar" or "philosopher" of an age now gone. Simon was an academic political scientist, a specialist on public administration, who was greatly intrigued by the possibility that an empirical "administrative science" might be ripe and ready for development. He was an important figure in a movement in political science, particularly strong in the immediate post–World War II period, to modernize that venerable discipline in the image of "behavioral science."

Besides the Barnardian topics mentioned, Simon takes up rationality, efficiency, organizational equilibrium, and the value-fact problem. These additions reflect his determination, as a scientist in the spirit of classical positivism, to seek scientific solutions to practical problems as the ultimate goal of research—that is, to build a technology of administration with a scientific foundation. This program calls for de-mystifying the "decision-making process"; and the way to achieve that goal is to carry out research that is truly cumulative and generic—rigorous in method, exact in execution, and quantitative to the fullest extent possible. These programmatic directives make it necessary to think systematically and psychologically. The primary datum must be the individual human act, and the frame of reference in which the act has meaning must be the organization conceived as an equilibrium-seeking social system.

Argyris

The work of Chris Argyris is something of a synthesis of the microcosmic and macrocosmic approaches to contemporary organization theory. Argyris' first book was published in 1957. By that time, some of the messianic zeal of the immediate postwar school of radical behavioralists had worn thin. It had proved enormously difficult in practice to carry out the kind of research on the decision-making process which Simon and the others had called for, and the results achieved were not very impressive. The more rigorous they were the more they became a sort of twentieth-century version, still just as sterile, of medieval scholasticism. The really interesting researches were the sloppy ones. This was as true of the small-groups theorists (microcosmic) as of the systems theorists (macrocosmic). When what they had to say was indisputably true it was uninteresting, and when what they had to say was interesting it was only speculative. (This is not to say that research activity dried up. Far from it. It fructified. But still it lacked the pristine *élan* of that of Lewin and Simon.)

The title of Argyris' book is *Personality and Organization*.[17] It states the theme not only of his first but of all of his subsequent writings. Taking his cue from earlier successful studies of work relationships in industry (such as those of Mayo, Warner, Jacques, Walker, and Whyte),[18] he cast his researches in an unpretentious, clinical case-study format. The basic postulate is a simple one: the individual and the organization each has needs which often conflict. The researcher must try to establish in a given case what these needs are, how and why they come into conflict, and how the conflict is resolved, or at least contained.

A novel feature of Argyris' approach is that he takes "the boss" (usually a plant manager, or a middle-level functionary with a similar degree of autonomy) and his immediate lieutenants as his research subjects rather than the foreman or group leader and the work gang in his charge. The implicit hypothesis is that working relationships in the middle and higher administrative echelons are problematic in both the scientific and the practical sense; through research perhaps we can understand them better and improve them, make them more productive. Like Lewin and Mayo, Argyris assumes that there is a group dynamics factor in much individual human conduct in the large organization, but unlike them he thinks it applies to leadership as well as operative echelons. Like Barnard and Simon, he thinks status differences and the uses of authority inhibit free communication and rational decision-making. Unlike them, however, he does not treat the decision-maker as uniquely free and rational but locates him in a group situation and explains his actions as a product of group pressures, just like those of everyone else.

In spite of his relative lack of interest in doing rigorous, quantitative research with generic significance, Argyris is in the behavioralist tradition. His primary datum is the individual human act, and he conceives of the organization as nothing more than an elaborate network of communications. When it is "healthy" and functioning well, it transmits the results of individual human acts (information in the form of directives down and feedback up). When it is in a pathological state and functioning poorly, it blocks such transmission. Healthy or sick, the organization has no past, no future, no character. It is just machinery, manned by individuals whose actions are nonrational insofar as their unmet need to be accepted and psychologically nurtured by the group makes them so.

THE INSTITUTIONALISTS

The group of theorists and researchers whose work constitutes what I have called the institutionalist strand (the names James Mooney and Alan Reiley, Berle and Means, Peter F. Drucker, Philip Selznick, Alvin W. Gouldner, and Wilbert Moore will serve to sketch in its outlines) [19] take the opposite tack. They see the organization as more than inanimate machinery. It is more like a conscious organism, with a history and a fate and a character uniquely its own. Organization is a process which produces an apparatus, an established set of arrangements for carrying out joint action. These arrangements become institutionalized in the course of time, which means they take on value and acquire momentum and thus become more or less autonomous component parts of the situation occupied by the individual. In the Durkheimian sense they have a reality of their own (as social facts they are exterior to the individual and constrain him in his actions) [20] and function as independent sources of causation.

The institutionalists raise questions which emphasize change, meaning, and conflict.

Change is of interest in the sense that any organization (or any type of organizational apparatus, such as a bureaucracy) is viewed as a product of its history, altogether apart from the intentions or the technical excellence of the men who have led it.

One must look to the past in order to understand the present, and the phenomenon of institutionalization must be taken into account.

Meaning—*subjective* meaning, the meaning of action and events from the standpoint of the participant in them—is studied by the institutionalists because they see it as important and factually problematic. The researcher cannot know what any given situation of action means (or meant) to the people in it without inquiring. And yet he ought to know because it has an important bearing on what happens and why: "situations defined as real are real in their consequences," as W. I. Thomas succinctly put it. Is the domination exercised by wielders of power in a situation "legitimate" (i.e., as defined) or not? It makes a difference in how things get done. Men do not willingly subordinate themselves to others unless they see the relationship as lawful, and the conduct of the holder of authority as falling within the limits of his rightful discretion.

Conflict concerns institutionalists because in the flux of circumstances the individual continually finds himself involved in it. His group's interests drive it into collision with another group. The stratum of groups, of which his is one, collides with another stratum and all the groups comprising it. Or he himself, as a lone individual, finds his "material" or "ideal" interests,[21] or both, propelling him into conflict with other individuals or groups, including his own. A large organization cannot exist without some measure of "imperative coordination," [22] which means that those in authority must apply force or its equivalent to resolve potentially disruptive conflict. Conflict suppressed is still conflict, however. Driven underground it can result in groups and individuals becoming disaffected or alienated, perhaps to the extent that they engage in casual sabotage or even frank conspiracy to destroy the whole operation.

The behavioralists are interested in many of these things, too, but ordinarily they do not research them. The reason is that it is hard to get very far with studies of such phenomena as bureaucratization, legitimacy, and alienation if one clings to the methodological premise that the individual human act is the one and only acceptable primary datum, and that this act has meaning—objective meaning, not subjective—only in the context of the static, equilibrium-seeking organization. The effect of these positivist canons and the program of research they engender is to treat levels of reality above the individual or the immediate, face-to-face group—institutions, for example—as not really "real": somehow they are either just fictions or else derivatives. Similarly, phenomena whose existence cannot be directly observed (subjective meaning, most temporal processes) but must be inferred are treated as unreal because they are assumed to be beyond the reach of scientific inquiry.

The positivists pay a heavy price for their rigor. In their program, change is studied only to show that it can be studied. Legitimacy is ignored because it consists of nothing but "the subjective evaluations of individuals." The ties that bind the individual to collectivities larger than the work group are defined as nothing but discrete "attitudes"—for example, those a person has toward the work, the work group, and the work supervisors. W. I. Thomas' careful distinction between attitudes and values *in* the situation [23] is ignored. One is treated simply as a function of the other.

In order to hold the discussion within manageable limits, I have chosen the following writers as exemplary of major aspects of the institutionalist strand: Mooney and Reiley, Selznick, Gouldner, and Moore.[24] The first two are *normative* in their approach to organization theory and research; the second two are *clinical;* and the last, Moore, combines features of both.

Mooney and Reiley

In the late twenties a medieval historian (James D. Mooney) and an economist (Alan C. Reiley) collaborated on what was perhaps the first scholarly interpretation of the giant corporation and its problems in the spirit of the new managerialism. It was published in 1931 under the misleading title, *Onward Industry!* The book is a good deal more serious and solid as a work of scholarship, despite its obvious bias, than such a sloganized title indicates. Read today against the background of the lively and continuing discussion [25] of whether or not the corporation has a conscience, or is developing one, or should develop one, it seems remarkably prescient.

The book was written in a spirit of unabashed normativism. Very much unlike the positivistically minded behavioralists, the authors were not inhibited by the value-fact problem and took it for granted that a proper object of scholarly inquiry is: what should our policy be? What interested them was the unformed state of the new corporation executive, or manager. What was he? Who was he? What should he do? And how should he do it? The ambiguity in English grammar of the imperative "should" in this context seems not to have troubled them at all. Clearly, they assumed that the ethical should ("this is what you must do and the way you must do it because it is right") and the pragmatic should ("this is what you must do and the way you must do it because it works") are fundamentally in harmony.

The manager must seek coordination, but in modern times the way to coordination is through the engineering of consensus. (The historical progression in Mooney and Reiley's analysis is from "domination" to "compromise" to "integration.") The problem of the modern corporation is a "moral" one. There is a need for "constitutionalism," and yet clearly it is lacking. The "cultivation of the sense of mutuality" is conspicuously deficient in modern society. The result is "misunderstandings, distrust, and hatreds"—in a word, conflict. The manager is in the last analysis a coordinator, but he must use "the technique or method of handling people." He seeks "psychic correlation" of all the human forces within the organization, and he achieves this by fostering the "consciousness that, beneath all of the different group interests, there is a greater common or mutual interest." The expertise he must cultivate for this purpose is "the science of humanics." When successfully applied it can translate "passive harmony into an active and truly efficient harmony."

Isn't "humanics" just a question of propaganda, manipulating appearances? Not at all, say Mooney and Reiley. First there must be a change in reality and *then* the application of humanic "science."

"Organizing," which is what must be done in order to change reality, is logically prior to "managing," although they overlap in time because organizing is a continuing process. Organizing involves "formal" or "structural" correlation; managing is "psychic correlation." First, the structure of the organization must be laid out, which means dividing up the work to be done so as to realize advantages of specialization, routinization ("functional differentiation"), and centralized direction. Then people are assigned to jobs and thus placed objectively in relation to each other and to the organization as a whole—and the trouble ("misunderstandings, distrust, hatreds") begins. Organizing, then, must yield to managing as a focus of executive activity; once structural correlation is carried as far as it can go, it must be supplemented by psychic correlation. If this is successful the immediate result is "horizontal correlation," the resolution of conflict.

The end result is the "unity of thought" absolutely necessary if decentralization, a central feature of the strategy of functional differentiation, is to be carried through.

> Unity of thought in organization simply means that every member of the organization, whatever his responsibilities, shall be thoroughly indoctrinated in the best thought of the organization, not as a finality, but as a condition necessary to his own constructive thinking and planning. To state the matter practically, the indoctrinated man is the only man who can safely be trusted with that relative freedom of action which is essential in a decentralized organization, and to make such indoctrination universal it must flow through channels additional to the single one of line command.[26]

Horizontal correlation is the functional equivalent of "tight" versus "loose" supervision. "Indoctrination" both reveals a structural reality and makes it work.

Management must "preserve central control" even while pushing decentralization to the furthest possible limit by fostering psychic correlation. Partly this is a matter of technique, but only partly. There must be a goal, which necessitates a commitment to basic values. What do you tell the indoctrinated man, aside from generalities about "mutual interests" and "work in the nature of social service"? What do you point to in order to make credible the version of reality you want to propagate?

Just as there is a structural reality in the organization, there is also a constitutional reality, because the modern corporation has a "moral problem" corresponding to its "economic problem." It is a question of rights. Does everyone have rights or just the boss? If "the boss" is also an employee like everyone else, which is the case in the modern corporation, by what right does he hold his authority? What is his warrant? Good answers to these questions must go beyond sloganeering and describe something real. And unless good answers are found, psychic correlation cannot be realized. This is the moral crisis of the corporation: with the passing of family capitalism and the splitting of the atom of property, how is the legitimacy of authority in the modern productive enterprise to be established?

Mooney and Reiley say there must be constitutionalism, a government of laws and not of men. It must be either based directly on function or else fashioned in such a way that it is congruent with it. The "administrative function" (decisions on basic goals and a watchdog power of review over the conduct of the enterprise) belongs to the board of directors. The "management function" belongs to the chief executive and his subordinate officials. This division prevails because it is functionally logical, and therefore each party has the right to exercise the authority he holds formally on grounds of both "logic" and "law." The rules of operation come before individual whim; in effect, the promulgator of the rules guarantees to respect them himself and exercise his authority accordingly.

The effect of these arrangements is to endow each individual with a set of rights (including the highly significant "right to a career"). Constitutionalism means that "certain ideals, certain aims and objects, are concreted in company policies until they possess the force of law, superior as such to any individual will or whim." [27]

Selznick

Philip Selznick's approach to the study of organization is clinical rather than normative. He is less interested in laying out correct doctrine for managers to follow than in analyzing actual doctrines. Unlike Mooney and Reiley, he does not want a "science of humanics"—a technique for managers—but a science of organization, or, more precisely, a scholarly discipline devoted to the scientific study of organizations and problems of leadership within organizations. Selznick wants to better understand the organization as a locus of natural phenomena. Social scientists ought to cast themselves in the role of botanists first, and only then, very warily, as healers.

What places Selznick in the institutionalist rather than the behavioralist tradition, predominantly, is his emphasis on the molar or collective act as a primary datum, on time as an indispensable variable, and on subjective meaning as an essential category of analysis. He also accepts certain positivist canons of research methodology: the directive to phrase research results in the form of universalistic rather than nominalistic propositions; and the directive to work with and from a concept of the collectivity such as system theory provides.

TVA and the Grass Roots, published in 1949, is Selznick's study of the changing organizational structure of the Tennessee Valley Authority. His objective was to identify and then explain the emergent "character" of the organization by attributing it to "commitments" made in the course of adapting to a changing political, social, and economic environment.

"If democracy as a method of social action has any single problem," Selznick writes, "it is that of enforcing the responsibility of leadership or bureaucracy. A faith in majorities does not eliminate the necessity for governance by individuals and small groups." [28] This is the Michelsian dilemma: how is democracy possible when the instrument through which policy is made and administered is a self-interested minority? Michels' interest was in voluntary associations—labor unions and socialist parties—bent on gaining political power as a means to bring about radical social change in the interests of the industrial proletariat, and in the puzzling fact that as the workers' organizations grew stronger they became less militant.[29]

Selznick saw some close analogies in the history of the TVA. Created in 1933 in the spirit of the New Deal as an agency "with the power of government and the flexibility of private enterprise," and "charged with the broadest duty of planning for the proper use, conservation, and development of the natural resources of the Tennessee River drainage basin and its adjoining territory for the general social and economic welfare of the nation," [30] by 1943 it had become securely established—and incapable of carrying out its full mandate. Was there a connection between these two facts? Selznick theorized that "the Authority's grass-roots policy as doctrine and as action must be understood as related to the need of the organization to come to terms with certain local and national interests; and that in actual practice this procedure resulted in commitments which had restrictive consequences for the policy and behavior of the Authority itself." [31]

What happened? We must remember that "the tools of social action" are universally "recalcitrant." In the instance of TVA, the price the agency had to pay for survival was conditioned by the fact that "ideology," in particular the doctrine of "grass-roots democracy," had become "a resource in the struggle for power."

Like the "successful" but tamed revolutionary German Social Democratic party Michels had studied—tamed by its own success —TVA after ten years was a captive of doctrine it had evolved in order to keep going. Was the price it paid a tolerable compromise or outright organizational surrender?

The Tennessee Valley Authority was to be a showcase of the New Deal's welfare-state concept of "positive government." Except for a short honeymoon period it was faced with continuous and severe political challenge. Private electric utilities and other natural monopolies saw it as a mortal threat: it seemed nothing less than a paradigm for nationalization. Local institutions and community power structures throughout the Tennessee Valley feared they would be bypassed and deprived of their constituencies and functions. The local institutions and the private utilities had powerful spokesmen in Washington and found a common ground in opposing "big government." They were antagonists, however, on the issue of cheap power and federal help in conserving and developing natural resources.

This division of interests gave TVA its chance to establish a constituency and work toward an accommodation with some of its powerful enemies. Under the leadership of two of the original three commissioners, Dr. Harcourt A. Morgan, president of the University of Tennessee, and David E. Lilienthal (soon to become chairman of TVA), the Authority developed the bedrock premise of its claim to legitimacy in a democratic society: the theory that while "centralized administration" is a functional necessity, "decentralized government" is both feasible and desirable. What this meant, in practical effect, was that in two of the really vital programs of the Authority, rural electrification and cheap fertilizer for "test demonstration" use, the distribution was to be handled by local user cooperatives with TVA functioning as a wholesaler. The grass-roots doctrine was that the people themselves should "govern" (manage?) to the fullest extent possible those activities which most directly affected their lives and well-being.

Selznick points out that the organizational function of decentralized government was to "absorb new elements into the leadership or policy-determining structure . . . as a means of averting threats to its stability of existence." In short, TVA traded off some of its functions for support and recognition of its right to exist. This is the process of cooptation—bringing outsiders into the leadership structure to obtain other benefits.

Such benefits are of two distinct sorts. "Formal cooptation" is the sharing of responsibility—but not power: people are involved in the forms of policy determination but not the substance. This is what happened in the case of TVA's electric power distribution program. The local cooperatives had very little real discretion in making decisions; their functions were technical rather than political, and the prestige, such as it was, enjoyed by members of the governing body was based on myth. The fertilizer program, more broadly the agricultural program, was quite different. The governing boards had real power; the ostensibly technical decisions they made (which farmers were suitable recipients of free demonstration-project fertilizer) were readily politicized into a form of patronage. This inevitably ramified into and throughout the whole power structure of local institutions, with the prime beneficiary being the Agricultural Extension Service of the land grant colleges. Cooptation of this sort is "informal"; it was not the forms of power that were shared but the substance, under an innocent guise. The Authority needed the support of the Extension Service, and this is how it got it.

The means through which TVA implemented its concept of grass-roots democracy determined the ideological content of its program, and over time the content became frozen into doctrine. The decisive commitment was to work through established local institutions and not bypass them. By allowing expediency to dictate the choice of procedure, the organization inadvertently chose its character; henceforth its choice of ends would reflect its commitments to a particular set of means and to the operating doctrine that rationalized it. The most serious consequence was the curtailment of the free play of functional rationality, so that decisions made on ostensibly technical grounds were in actuality doctrinal. TVA thus acquired a vested interest, a vested *ideal* interest, in its version of "grass-roots democracy." Its character was formed.

As we have seen, Selznick views the organization as an instrument of human action in its design; but it ends up frustrating human action because of its undesigned acquired capabilities and limitations. Leadership in the organization can find itself hemmed in and even directed by the logic of its structure. In the extreme case, he who is supposed to be responsible for the organization and to it ends up being used by it. This is the "tragedy of organization": goals get displaced, means become ends, the mission of the organization is transformed even though no one intended it that way and perhaps no one is pleased that it turned out that way. This is shown most strikingly in Selznick's study of the American Communist party, *The Organizational Weapon: A Study of Bolshevik Strategy and Tactics.*[32] Again, Selznick makes it clear that the doctrinal commitments and institutionalized procedures of the organization shape its character and conduct. What it does is largely a function of what it can do and therefore must do.

Nothing could be further from the ebullient rationalist optimism of Mooney and Reiley than the gloomy existentialist pessimism of Selznick. He sees the motives of men, the individual and joint motives that propel the organization on its course and at the same time reflect its movement, as iceberg-like. Only a tenth of their substance is above the surface; the other nine-tenths are perpetually obscured, to be known only by inference and then with great uncertainty. The other two theorists see motives simply as territory which is as yet only partly explored. Knowing it and controlling the subjective factor is just a matter of studying it carefully and developing an appropriate technology (a "science of humanics").

Selznick's clinical bent comes out, finally, in his later work, *Leadership in Administration.*[33] It is a book addressed more to sophisticated laymen than to social scientists or other academic specialists. At first reckoning it looks more normative than clinical, but this is misleading. The author does seek to draw from his study of organizations some practical conclusions that ought to be of value to managers and others in leadership positions. But they are not prescriptive do's and don'ts; the book does not tell managers what they ought to do but what they ought to look for and think about. Selznick recommends a strategy of "institutional assessment" and self-diagnosis, not a method or plan that is bound to work if only applied properly. In Selznick's view, leadership is action that has an inherent element of moral responsibility. There is no "One Best Way," no single technique to follow. One does not seek to maximize rationality but rather to minimize irrationality, and the only way to do this is through self-study—"self" being understood as one's organization as well as one's individual self. The whole process is something like psychoanalysis, with an implied role for the sociologist as a sort of organizational psychoanalyst.[34]

Gouldner

Alvin W. Gouldner is a much more explicit theorist of "clinical sociology" than Selznick, and he means something rather different by it. *Patterns of Industrial Bureaucracy* and *Wildcat Strike* [35] report the results of an intensive study of a gypsum mine and an attached plant manufacturing building materials located in a small town in the eastern Great Lakes region. The study is in the institutional rather than the behavioral tradition because it takes institutional patterns rather than individual human behavior as primary data; it treats time as a key variable; and it admits subjective meaning as an important category of analysis. Like Selznick's *TVA and the Grass Roots,* Gouldner's work is a case study in depth, with the researcher trying to understand what happened, and why, in order to develop universal propositions.

Gouldner wondered how an industrial establishment adjusts to a change in leadership. What happens when the plant manager dies, retires, or is replaced? How does the new manager establish his authority? How do the manual workers and the lower echelons of management and the technical groups react to his efforts? The new boss cannot simply pick up where the old one left off; he must learn how to control the organization, and he must get the "consent of the governed," gain recognition as a legitimate authority, if he is to do it effectively and efficiently. Does Weber's monocratic model of bureaucracy fit the real world well enough to provide a guide to changing it?

Gouldner found that the wallboard manufacturing plant and its attached gypsum mine were severely jarred, as an organization, by the changeover in management following the death of "Old Doug." His regime had been easygoing, with an "indulgency pattern" of control. The new man, sent out by the "front office" located some distance away in an urban center (the plant studied was one unit of a complex of several), resorted to a "punishment-centered" type of impersonal, bureaucratic control.

Workers in the manufacturing plant resented the tightening up, as did the subordinate managers, or most of them; but the miners, with their elite status and strongly developed bonds of group solidarity, went beyond resentment and revolted. Their right to be autonomous, to make their own work rules in the name of "safety," was challenged, and so they walked out, not bothering to use contractually established grievance machinery. They carried the plant workers with them in their wildcat strike and quickly won the sympathy of most of the townspeople, including most of the lower managers and supervisors.

Gouldner's conclusions turned mainly on his interpretation that the new plant manager's insecurity and isolation led him to adopt an excessively formalistic "punishment-centered pattern" of bureaucratic controls. He was under pressure from the front office to show results, but the plant community was such a tightly knit organization informally that it was in a strong position to resist quick and arbitrary (unlegitimated) changes in patterns of authority.

One of the major differences in approach between Gouldner and Selznick is the empirical focus. Selznick researched the impact of a decision freely made—it could have gone either way—by top leadership upon *external* (organization-community) relationships; Gouldner, taking *internal* (management-labor) relationships as problematic, sought to trace out the consequences of a decision unfreely or reactively made by an insecure new middle-level manager as one episode in a succession crisis.

Selznick's holistic, quasi-organismic concept of the organization thus grows out of and is suited to a particular set of research interests: how organizational character gets formed, how the arrangements for joint action interfere with original goals and may even change them. This model would not have served Gouldner's research interests at all. He needed a concept of the organization which would identify and differentiate between "right" and "wrong" ways of acting, whether the action analyzed is establishing authority, installing new methods and machinery, or winning a strike. This prescription was fulfilled in the strategic distinction between "representative" and "punishment-centered" patterns of bureaucracy and the propositions that follow from it.

Thus we see that the theorist's concepts and his research interests are interrelated. The clinical approach covers a broad spectrum of interests in research and theory. Selznick's image of the organization leads him to emphasize the urgency of the need for enlightened and effective leadership, but it also causes him to draw pessimistic conclusions about the prospects of achieving it. Gouldner, on the other hand, sees leadership as mostly just good technique. There is no large uncertainty about it; ultimately it can be taught and learned, and so a posture of optimism about the prospects of clinical sociology applied to problems of large-scale organization seems reasonable.

Moore

Wilbert Moore does not write as a counselor to management, nor does he diagnose the ills and failures of management practice—at least not explicitly. The thrust of his work is not exactly clinical, in the sense that Selznick's and Gouldner's are, with all their differences. Nor is it quite accurate to say that Moore offers a doctrine for management like Mooney and Reiley, although his major work does lend itself to that use.

Is he then not a clinician but a "normativist"? The normativist sees the policy problem as the important one. He looks for an objective answer to the question, what should we do?—"we" being the central actor in the analytic scheme, such as the manager. The clinician wants to know how and why things go wrong, in the hope that the miscarriage of intentions can be avoided in the future through study and the improvement of technique—better "know-how"—that can be expected to be its natural byproduct. The normativist leaves open the question of ends and focuses on means.

By these criteria Moore is neither the one nor the other, and yet somehow both. Moore's earlier work on organization theory appears in his *Industrial Relations and the Social Order,* first published in 1946 and revised in 1951.[36] Although designed as a text for courses in industrial sociology (in 1946 still a barely recognized specialty), it is in substance a treatise on modern industrial society. Most of the book discusses "industrial organization" explicitly or touches on it in one way or another. As the first influential book in a rapidly growing field, Moore's work defined industrial sociology as being properly concerned in large part with the study of complex organization from the standpoint of management problems. The whole treatment reflects the impress of the work of Mayo and his school, and the earlier school of "scientific management" associated with the name of Frederick W. Taylor.[37] It is in the institutionalist rather than the behavioralist strand of organization theory, however, because Moore is less interested in positivistic rigor than in raising and coping with large questions of the impact of modern industry on the social order.

Like Mayo before him, Moore was impressed with what he calls "the Durkheim problem": *interdependence does not mean integration,* even though functional interdependence is increasing. Any society, let alone one that is highly interdependent (the greater the level of interdependence the greater the need for a high degree of integration), presupposes cohesion if it is to continue to function on a certain minimum level of integration. The conclusion is not drawn—neither is it disavowed—but the whole tenor of the discussion points to it: in Mayo's sloganized interpretation of Durkheim, in modern industrial society *"collaboration cannot be left to chance."*

This normative concern with the possible weakening of the fabric of society (cohesion and consensus, integration) is much more explicit in a book of Moore's written seventeen years later, *The Conduct of the Corporation.* In this informal treatise the author takes a bemused, urbane attitude toward the conceits and foibles of management in the big industrial corporation. As he has been a consultant for General Electric, one can infer that he draws in part upon his own observations and experience.

The book's subject is legitimacy, or rather the current illegitimacy of management authority in the very large business corporation. Since the large-scale industrial enterprise is a key institution in our society, so the unstated normative proposition runs, something we need and which can remake us all through its impact upon our social environment, it follows that anything wrong with it is wrong with us. If the social order is to be preserved in a healthy and desirable state, so must the corporation; and that means a rationale must be found for management. We must discover how the corporation works and then use this knowledge to establish the rule of law throughout the organization.

According to Moore, who takes up the theme set forth earlier by Mooney and Reiley, industrial management confronts a "moral crisis" because of the passing of family capitalism. The private-property legitimation of authority in the enterprise no longer makes sense. It is too obvious that managers are not really accountable to stockholders, regardless of the persisting legal fiction. There has been an irreversible separation of ownership from control, and this is as it should and must be. It would be both outrageous and technically infeasible to claim the near absolute "rights of private property" of the small proprietor, and run the giant corporation on the principle of maximum short-run profits —and "the public be damned." Instead, the new calculus of self-interest demands that "the public be cultivated," not damned, and considerations of long-run stability and growth must override short-run profit-taking.

Those who conduct the corporation, the executives, have a functional need for their power, but as yet they do not have an established and credibly justified right to it. Because they are accountable to no one they are in a position to abuse their power. At the same time they lack the warrant in law and custom to do the things they feel they must do in order properly to perform their function, and so they are subject to abuse for using their power in ways that are "right" in substance but "wrong" in our presently illogical moral understanding of the matter. The logic of their situation calls for institutionalized restraints on the one hand and supports on the other. As functionaries they must be made secure; at the same time the public interest must be protected.

This is the institutionalist side of Moore's analysis. The behavioralist side comes out in his anatomization of the corporation. How does the corporation work as an organization? Moore strikes a keynote when he observes how "miraculous" it is that in the organization there is cooperation without anyone being consciously cooperative, and goals are achieved without anyone consciously seeking them or willing them. This happens because within the enterprise there is a sociologically real entity, a "bureaucracy" (but here called "administrative organization" to avoid pejorative connotations) which functions according to its own laws.

The administrative organization governs such things as how individuals are hired, fired, promoted, downgraded, transferred, remunerated, and assigned work and directed in the performance of it; how jurisdictional lines are drawn reflecting the hierarchical delegation of authority and the functional division of labor; how rules are promulgated, established, implemented, and changed;

how coordination is effected through communication up, down, and across all of these lines; how line and staff functions are divided and then recombined; how the organization relates to its various constituencies outside; and how informal organization plays a role in all these activities. Everyone has a role to play, from "relations experts," who establish and maintain liaison with outside constituencies, to "administrative generalists," responsible to the whole for the whole.

Two features stand out in this analysis: Moore uses Weber's conceptual scheme, in a special version that ignores time and emphasizes "system," as a guide to posing questions about administrative organization; and he abandons the "Durkheim problem" that bothered him earlier by simply assuming that "miraculously" people *do* cooperate and goals *are* reached.

Max Weber formulated his conception of bureaucracy as an ideal type. Its purpose was to clarify what we mean when we speak of "bureaucracy" and call this or that "bureaucratic"; it was to lay bare a certain kind of institutional logic, not to describe concrete reality but rather to provide the terms of such a description. Its use in research, as Weber saw it, was to serve as a conceptual frame of reference for making historical and cross-cultural comparisons of institutional structures. What interested him was the tendency for industrialization and urbanization to produce a massive trend toward bureaucratization of modern society as a whole.

Moore's interest is quite different. He wants to show that "the modern corporation," or at least the part he calls administrative organization, is a bureaucracy. He does not show that all kinds of factors in any given situation act to help or hinder the growth of bureaucracy, or deform the course of its development. Which modern corporation is he talking about? The big one or the small one? The old one or the new one? The one that is closely held or the one loosely held? Under progressive or old-fashioned management? In utilities or services or manufacturing?

Moore or any other scholar who makes use of Weber's concept

of bureaucracy is under no obligation to follow his procedural canon as well and use it to ask only historical or comparative questions. Nevertheless, the Weberian canon ought to give us some critical perspective on how the concept of bureaucracy is used and, in the strictly logical sense, misused.

Moore undertakes a generalized description of "the modern corporation" as a bureaucracy. Thus he ignores bureaucratization as a process, and he does not distinguish among different degrees and kinds of "bureaucracy" in actual business corporations. Is there anything wrong with this? No, if the point is to produce a rough-and-ready first approximation; yes, if the point is to produce facts bearing on the normative question of what should be done about it. The author's whole inquiry is normatively oriented; his bias is that the big business executive's position ought to be made legitimate. The facts he cites are often interesting and insightful in themselves, but what they add up to is an assortment chosen to illustrate this preconceived thesis.

The source of the bias is Moore's desire to describe "the modern corporation" generally as "a bureaucracy." Because he ignores the process of bureaucratization, he is not interested in different kinds and degrees of "bureaucracy" to be found in actual business corporations. This makes it possible for him to develop some interesting and useful insights into the workings of bureaucracy in modern corporations, such as that the new "relations experts" are "two-faced" (they face "inward" and "outward" at the same time), and that the "promotions ladder" is really an "escalator" ("it takes a positive effort to get off"). But he plays the game of finding out how and why the corporation faces a moral crisis with a stacked deck. No matter how Moore deals the cards, the result makes sense only in relation to the question of how the authority of top management can be made legitimate. The question of whether or not it *should* be made legitimate is foreclosed by the way the problem is presented.

Moore's abandonment of "the Durkheim problem" of cohesion and integration is related to the way he understands and uses the concept of bureaucracy. He says in effect that in the real world things work out so that collaboration really is *not* left to chance, and the reason for this is that managers are doing their job. This accounts for the "miracle" of cooperation without cooperativeness, and goal achievement without goal achievers. The novelist and conservative moralist Herman Wouk has one of his characters describe the U.S. Navy as "a machine designed by geniuses to be run by idiots." Moore's system theory version of the Weberian concept of bureaucracy is the same sort of thing. There is nothing wrong with the system, so the assumption goes, it's only the lack of a credible rationale for the legitimacy of authority that makes the "idiots" restless. And not without reason, for the holders and exercisers of authority cannot quite know what they are doing and will sometimes act irrationally or irresponsibly without such a rationale. A rationale will keep the troops quiet and the commanders straight.

Max Weber, Karl Mannheim, and many others have pointed out that propositions in the social sciences are inevitably value-relevant because the formulation of the problem, the choice of conceptual tools, and the way these tools are used in trying to solve the problem all have a bearing on the main values and public issues of the time. All are relevant to current values, and the values are relevant to them. Thus the ostensibly neutral instruments of scientific study are subtly influenced: the men who do the research and the setting in which they do it are affected by cultural values and material interests. It is hard to deny the core of truth in the Marxian proposition that "the ruling ideas of the age are the ideas of the ruling class."

In Moore's conceptualization of bureaucracy in the corporation, there is no provision for the play of power. Power not discussed is power taken for granted. The underlying assumption, held consciously or not, is that existing arrangements are fundamentally just: those who have the power ought to have it, and those who do not should not. Here, then, is the value-relevance of Moore's proposition that the modern corporation faces a "moral crisis."

There are, to sum up, two main strands of organization theory.

The behavioralists take the individual human act as the primary datum; they view the organization as a system of communications; and they emphasize problems of command and control as the locus of things that need explaining. Some work with the microsystem of small groups within the organization, others with the macrosystem of the whole organization.

The institutionalists take institutionalized patterns of behavior and their subjective meaning as the primary datum; they view the organization as essentially an organism with its own unique life history and emergent social character; and they emphasize that the process by which the organization is established and the legitimacy of authority secured is especially problematic. Some are normativists in that they assume the objective validity of certain key value judgments. Others are clinicians: they assume that some states of the organization are pathological, and that the task of the social scientist is to devise a technology of meliorative intervention analogous to medicine.

ORGANIZATION, POWER, AND RESEARCH BIAS

Even the purest concept in the social sciences has an ideological dimension, because it is built upon abstractions; and abstractions are made not in a vacuum but from one of a number of possible points of view. The concept is reliable and useful as a tool only if its roots are real and not fictitious, if they embody the ideal and material interests of real people in real situations. It follows that any concept is biased both in its source and in its consequences. A particular way of construing reality, if it is to have any human use, inevitably hurts some people's interests and helps others'; it makes out "the truth" to be one thing and not the other. Appearances aside, who *really* has the power? The "factual" answer depends in large measure on who raises the question, and from what point of view. And, in any case, establishing what *is* inevitably raises further questions of what *ought to be*—justice.

Organizations are instruments of human collective action, so it is not surprising that social science analysis of organizations is inclined to reflect the viewpoint of those who favor maximum efficiency and effectiveness. As this is also the attitude of managers and top executives, much organization theory supports their efforts to legitimate their authority. Organization theory is more than managerial ideology, but it is notoriously prone to being used as managerial ideology.

Barnard and Simon, for example, see the organization primarily as a system of communications. If things go wrong it must be because of a "communications failure"; somehow people have not understood one another. This conception portrays conflicts over the uses and kinds of power as a symptom rather than a root reality: fix the communications system and you solve the problem. Argyris, Whyte, and others of the "human relations" school take a similar tack when they treat "conflicts of interest," or even direct challenges to authority, as the result of a technical defect in the way human relations are ordered. The people involved in such conflicts "have problems" and "need empathy training." Or perhaps the formal-informal structure creates "strains" which can be eliminated through redesign.

The behavioralists, in general, set up their analysis in such a way that the authority of management is never called into question. It is treated as a given, a "system parameter." The complaints or rebellious acts of individuals and groups are symptoms of defective management technique, not a demand for justice. Justice simply is not a factor in the behavioralist scheme. The effect is to legitimate authority implicitly by denying that there can be any question of the abuse of power.

Mooney and Reiley see the organization as a legal and moral system of human relationships, and this is true of the institutionalists generally. Management is responsible for achieving a "correlation of social forces," "coherence," and a harmony of interests. There is never any question of "rights"; management has the responsibility to lead and therefore the right to exercise authority. Peter F. Drucker pushes the harmony argument to the point where he all but denies the right of trade unions to exist because they are without function—or they soon would be if management did its job.

Gouldner is not very different. He sees unions as reactive: when the workers go on a wildcat strike it is because of management's ineptness. There is nothing mysterious about leadership: it is just good technique. Management has a function which is societal, not just organizational; regardless of the quality of the individual performance, the function itself is legitimate.

Selznick and Moore are much less confident that "science," or management technology, will save us. But they do see a generalized, society-wide management function; and they wonder about its legitimacy, although in different ways.

Selznick sees management, or leadership, in an open-eyed *realpolitik* perspective: there is a need for leadership and in that sense a leadership-management function. But he is less interested in how management ought to behave than in how it actually does behave. One of its most important functions is to look after its own interests, as a group in relation to other groups.

Moore is less neutral, more "helpful" as it were. The message between the lines is that management is inevitable because it serves an indispensable function—not just in any one organization but in society as a whole—and so it is in the interest of all of us to help it over its current legitimacy crisis. Individual managers are often shortsighted about their own true interests and do not realize that much of their present trouble lies in the fact that many people find their use of power overbearing, selfish, and socially destructive. They need their power, but unless they earn the right to have it, unless they legitimate their authority, they are in for more trouble. Moore offers managers a good deal of advice on what is wrong with them and what they should do about it.

Gouldner and Selznick are two of the very few theorists and researchers in recent years who have tried to raise and answer significant questions about power in the large organization. This seems odd because there certainly is no lack of a sense of need for better understanding, as one can see in the large body of informed speculation about power by political journalists and others. For example, specialists in the art of "Kremlin watching" or "Sovietology" draw ingenious inferences from relatively flimsy data, indicating a good deal of sophistication about the formation, uses, and effects of power in big organizations—at least in the Soviet Union. In the United States, newspaper columnists (Drew Pearson, Joseph Alsop, James Reston) "watch" the White House and the federal departments, including the Pentagon, all of which are in the public sector, but they pay little attention to the big corporations that constitute the private sector.

Academic social scientists in America pull back from studies of power in big private bureaucracies primarily because it is hard to get financial support, hard to get access to the organizations, and hard to get really good, solid data even after you get access. Some smuggle in a study of power relations while ostensibly doing other research, but then they face the ethical question of violating confidences, stated or implied. Some study power structures and relations from a distance, in the style of a Kremlinologist (C. Wright Mills did this in his book *The Power Elite*), but they face the problem of reliability of evidence. Most turn away out of timidity or reluctance to get involved, and study aspects of organization that have nothing to do with power, or else they study the uses of power and the managing of power as pure technique. Studies of "the decision-making process" are a good example; the purely rational component can be the formal focus of analysis, leaving the sociologically much more interesting but "tricky" and "messy" element of power to be observed at best unsystematically and unobtrusively, and reported only to trusted colleagues, informally, never published.

What can be done? If we are to understand the functionary in the organization we need a clearer picture of power relations within the organization. But private industry is reluctant to let "outsiders" in to "snoop around." (Public institutions and organizations are just as reluctant, but unlike the private corporation they often cannot legally keep the researcher out.) Bureaucracies always have a vested interest in secrecy. A particular organization has a lot to lose and nothing to gain, or so it believes, from the presence of a sociologist who will probably find closets full of skeletons in the course of his research. Perhaps some device such as the five-year clause now written into employment contracts, to protect the company against having its secrets exploited by a former employee, could be written into a research contract. Perhaps an industry-university committee could be established to open some doors that are now closed. Perhaps foundations could provide seed money.

One thing is clear. Organization theory and research presents its subject in a biased perspective today because it systematically plays down the aspect of power. Unless we have a chance to get to know the functionary in one of his most significant and characteristic roles, as a man of power, elitist and occupational archetype of the new society, he will take his place as culture hero without our quite knowing what to expect of him.

Part Two

3

The military

The first functionaries were soldiers, priests, and government officials. In these spheres, organization and organizational discipline
first became strong enough to foster functional rationality as an
ethic and as a mode of thought.

Military men have been in this vanguard because of the unique
importance of discipline in their work. In the moment of truth in
combat, the military professional must conduct himself in a way
that will bring credit to his family, his clan, his lord, his city, his
order, his regiment, his commander, his comrades in arms, his
nation—even to the universal brotherhood of fighting men every-
where, friend, foe, or alien, which cuts across all other identities.
He feels bound in honor to perform well in the face of death.
The worst disaster he can imagine, far worse than being killed, is
to exhibit bad judgment, panic, or cowardice.

The logic of the military work situation demands the subordination of ego, which is what discipline means. The military professional is always the functionary because he always acts in the
service of an organized collectivity. He is always under orders.

He is an instrument with a certain sinister beauty, and that is his glory and his pride.

Much of this is true of church and government functionaries as well, allowing for differences in degree. The military man must be prepared to risk his life, quite routinely, while the other two types rarely have to go that far. Their professional honor is tested by the temptation to be disloyal or to abuse their official prerogatives for personal gain. The military man has the opportunity to exploit his position, too, but the character of his work makes such deviation less salient as a test of his discipline and honor.

Other things being equal, the soldier is also more typically the functionary because his work situation requires him to be a "specialist on violence," as Lasswell puts it.[1] He must be prepared to risk both physical and moral disaster, so while he is inclined to be socially conservative he is under continuous pressure to be technologically innovative.

The rare instances of really flagrant technological conservatism among military men in high places underscores the point. It is shocking, for example, that one of the top American field commanders in the Pacific during World War II refused to believe the atomic bomb would work until it was actually exploded over Hiroshima in 1945. More recently, Admiral Hyman Rickover, "father of the atomic submarine," had to go to Congress to leap a wall of skepticism and indifference put up against his proposal by Navy chiefs. They would not permit development of the underseas missile-launching vehicle until forced to.

The air of scandal surrounding such incidents is due to the sense that unwillingness to foster new technologies is intolerably illogical. This kind of moral indignation is not generated as frequently by conservatism in government or the church. There is less at stake.

The military man approximates the ideal functionary because the logic of his situation demands a high level of discipline and a high degree of openness to technological innovation. He thus offers a particularly good example for analysis. It will be useful to gain some historical basis for comparison by reviewing a few of the major types of military men, and then tracing the impact of bureaucratization and functionalization upon their work and upon the military establishment.

MILITARY TYPES

The tribal warrior

The encampments and villages of hunting and gathering peoples and primitive agriculturists were places of defense against marauders and staging areas for military action against enemies. Every able-bodied male was a fighting man, and every able-bodied female was involved in providing the warriors with food, shelter, nursing care, and menial services such as carrying gear on the campaign trail or looking after the gardens and domestic animals during the warriors' absence.

The unit of military action was the foray, which lasted a few hours or days, or the campaign, which might last months. The strategy of the foray was to hit hard and run fast, carrying off trophies and booty. The campaign was different. Sometimes its purpose was to counter a threat or to stop harassment. Sometimes it was to gain territory; occupants were expelled, exterminated, or enslaved. Sometimes (rarely) it was to impose suzerainty upon a weaker people and make them tributaries. The conquered were let alone as long as they accepted overlordship and paid their dues; sometimes a second campaign was necessary to crush a rebellion and punish the rebels.

The foray was carried out by a small band of warriors with minimum supplies and equipment. The campaign was large in scale, long in duration, and required logistics support, so the warriors were accompanied by their wives, camp followers, or even the whole tribal unit.

The warrior prided himself on his strength, skill, and bravery as an individual fighting man. He fought as part of an undifferentiated mass rather than as a unit or subunit of a formally organized collectivity. There was a war chief, or commander, and sometimes several subchiefs, but otherwise there was very little evident division of labor or specialized expertise. The war chief himself was expected to lead, quite literally, by staying up front where he was visible and where the fighting was fiercest. He directed the joint endeavor and maintained the cohesion of the group more by deeds than by words; he was the living example of what each individual was supposed to be doing. If he fell, the others would break off the engagement and withdraw, if they could, not so much out of fear as uncertainty.

A functional division of labor of a gross sort did exist between the front echelon of warriors and the rear echelon of women, children, and old men. Thus there was an operations function, a support function, and a rudimentary command function. But functions do not necessarily make functionaries. Rationalization does, and there was none in operations or support. The war chief was a dim approximation of a true functionary, one who thought of himself and disciplined himself to act as the instrument of an organization; but he was temporary, a dilettante in office and not a specialist, and his powers of command were highly limited.

The patrician militiaman

The first cities were fortified centers of commerce, government, religion, and agriculture. Every able-bodied man who was a citizen, that is, who belonged to the elite stratum of families who had political rights, was a member of the urban militia.

The Greek city-state of the Hellenic period provides the best example. The young patricians were not full-time professional soldiers, but their first obligation to the city was to keep themselves trained, outfitted, and prepared for a call to defend it or to go forth and punish its enemies. They were part of a privileged leisure class, but much of their leisure was taken up with civic duties, and military service was the most important.*

The patrician militiaman was a whole man, not a specialist. His first identity was patrician and citizen; he was a military functionary or subfunctionary only part time and episodically. But his training was hard and thorough, he fought often, and he took a keen interest in weaponry and in military science and tactics. This made him something of an organizational and technological innovator. For example, the Greeks invented many tactics which called for careful timing and close teamwork, such as the phalanx (still used today as the "flying wedge" in riot control). The militiaman was heavily armed and highly skilled in the use of a variety of weapons. Battlefield tactics called for a good deal of movement and for close coordination among different fighting units. The captain was an important figure, therefore, and there was a considerable place for generalship.

The Greek scheme of military operations involved a fairly extensive division of labor, although much of it was *ad hoc* because it was based on differences in tactical mission rather than on specialist expertise made necessary by complex weapons technology. This created the need for a sophisticated command function. But command, as well as the logistics function, was limited in its development by the fact that most campaigns were relatively short and took place not far from home. (This seems to have been generally true. The Battles of Thermopylae and, centuries earlier, the siege of Troy were spectacular exceptions.)

* Later city states and quasi-states, such as those of medieval times, also maintained a citizen's militia for the common defense, but it was of a different sort. The call to service was not limited to the patrician stratum but included all "burghers," or free men of the city, who constituted most of the population. Moreover, the core of the militia was a body of full-time mercenaries.

The empire soldier-bureaucrat

All empires are characterized by the rule of alien peoples by an aggressive, expansionist state that is militarily strong and (usually) technologically advanced. The conqueror offers the conquered a choice between annihilation or enslavement if they continue to resist, and limited autonomy if they agree to cooperate with the imperial power. Cooperation means the surrender of sovereignty and the acceptance of subject, tributary status under the symbol of empire (the Roman Imperium, the Ashanti Stool, the British Crown).

The Roman empire is the clearest example. The Roman city-state brought the whole known civilized world under its hegemony by the time of Christ, and held it for nearly half a millennium. To accomplish this it established a military dictatorship at home, under the emperor, and established a military bureaucracy to manage empire affairs in relation to subject peoples. It succeeded by setting discipline and organization above everything else.

One consequence was that Rome was able to open the ranks of its citizenship to all who could qualify on the basis of merit and service, regardless of national origin, and military service offered the surest way to achieve it. The Roman Legions recruited men from virtually all of the subject countries, with the promise of citizenship and a plot of land upon retirement from the service. Moreover, in theory the Roman soldier could rise through the ranks to the very top of the militarized bureaucracy of the imperial government.

The Roman soldier was also a career man, a regular, full-time member of the service regardless of his duty assignment status at any given moment. He thus acquired a new identity, one which set him off altogether from the civilian. He cut his ties with the past irrevocably: he was born again. The whole gamut of his life interests was bound up thereafter with his fate in the Roman military establishment.

Finally, the Roman military bureaucracy was relatively receptive to innovation in weapons, tactics, and organization. Rationality was the fundamental guide to action, not legality which incorporates tradition (and recognizes a body of law over and above "reasons of state"). This is dramatically evident in Roman works of engineering and architecture, most of which were carried out under the aegis of military-bureaucratic authority. A strong bent toward functional rationality is the understandable result of a supreme emphasis on discipline—every man a functionary and nothing but a functionary. As it was practiced, substantive rationality reflected the cosmopolitanism of the bureaucracy, its freedom from civil authority, and the simplicity of the predicate upon which it was based: all legitimate goals and priorities are identical with the interests of Rome, and the interests of Rome are defined as the interests of the imperial bureaucracy.

The purely technical division of labor in military operations was not carried very far by modern standards. Different missions were pursued separately by different armies, however, and this sometimes created conflicts in priorities and jurisdiction. In weapons technology there was continuous refinement, but not many really fundamental changes.

The greatest impact of technology was felt in the support function, especially in logistics and communications. Large forces were able to operate for years at long distances from Rome, their ultimate base of supply and strategic information. This had important effects on the command function. The continuous movement of goods and personnel along the highways and rivers and by ocean-going ship made it possible to keep the top commanders in close touch with the field situation, and to rotate personnel and local commanders often enough to discourage the development of regional fiefdoms and satrapies.*

Bureaucracies and functionaries existed before Rome, but in a

* This policy was only partly successful, however, and sometimes backfired—disaffected field commanders not infrequently marched on Rome and deposed the emperor. Julius Caesar's triumphant return from Gaul was the prototype of such maneuvers. He was assassinated by senators who tried to forestall military dictatorship and save the republic, but the most they accomplished was to buy a little time.

sense the Romans invented them both because of their system's unparalleled emphasis upon rationality and the scope they allowed for its exercise.

The feudal knight

The Roman empire gradually collapsed in the course of the fifth century A.D. Its vast social cosmos was replaced by the monastery and the castle. The monastery was militarily secure because it threatened no one, contained very little of value, and offered no more resistance to marauders than could be provided by high walls and barred gates. The castle was secure, relatively, because it was elaborately fortified. Because of its architecture, a few defenders could stand off an assault force of moderate size for a considerable time.

The monastery and the castle were very nearly self-sufficient economically as well as militarily, since each was the seat of a large farm, or manor, worked by monks, bondsmen, or small free-holders in alliance with the bishop or lord. The economic surplus was sufficient to maintain the lord and his staff of retainers. These included the artisans and servants necessary to run a large house-hold, but also the human means needed to administer justice, maintain an armed force, and, as there was no functioning state apparatus, carry on "foreign relations" in commerce and diplomacy.

The lord's armed forces consisted of spearmen, bowmen, and horse cavalrymen called knights, whose armament, weapons, and mobility were so effective that generally speaking the only match for a knight was another knight.

The knight's training and equipage were too expensive to be within the reach of the ordinary man, and so he was typically the brother, son, nephew, or perhaps the cousin of an enfeoffed nobleman; he was of the aristocracy, a "gentleman." Thus he was typically not a mercenary (although some knights were) but a proud professional who entered freely into a contract of vassalage with his lord and could just as freely terminate it. In principle,

his services were performed not for a fee or salary but in fulfillment of his part of the feudal bargain: the lord made him a
member of his household and provided him with the means for
maintaining a style of life in keeping with the dignity of his name
and position; the knight in turn did his lord's bidding and treated
his interests as his own. If the relationship prospered and the lord
enjoyed good fortune in his ventures, he might reward the knight
eventually by dividing his estate and granting him the usufruct
of part of it (this act of sub-enfeoffment involved a further division of the functions of sovereignty, not merely the use of land).

The knight was not a functionary. He did the lord's will, to
be sure, but he was not continuously responsible for carrying out
or overseeing any activity that was coherent enough to be called
a function as we use the term in this book. The unit of joint
action was too small and unspecialized for a significant division of
labor to develop. The knight was a skill specialist and did specialized work, but the important thing is that he was not part of an
organization and so his skilled work had no *functional* meaning.

And yet the knight was highly disciplined. He had a touchy
sense of honor and felt obliged to fight to the death to uphold the
sacred symbols of that honor: first, the emblem of the lord's
house in whose service he was, and second, the good name of the
half-mythical knightly "order" itself. This order had no officers,
no recording secretary, no dues, no membership roll. But to be
knighted by an enfeoffed nobleman committed one to its ethical
code, chivalry. Like the soldier who entered the service of Rome,
or the monk who entered the service of God, the knight was
"twice born."

Discipline was self-imposed (reinforced by the attitudes of
peers and comrades), because the order was not an organization.
Those who failed and broke the code and fell away, however,
became known as "black knights," outcasts, living examples of
the evils and torments of heresy.

The absolutist infantryman

Knighthood failed [2] in late medieval times for reasons of technology and social organization. The great baronies became so big, for one thing, that the knight could no longer sit in fellowship with his lord and master at the "round table" (its roundness is a symbol for the fundamental equality of men-at-arms, whatever their rank). A hierarchy emerged in the great houses and eventually grew into a fully developed quasi-bureaucracy of the patrimonialist type. More and more the knights took on the character of mere courtiers.

The second development that hastened the knight's demise was the superior military effectiveness of infantry. The Battle of Agincourt demonstrated this once and for all. Knights fought individually and at close range. Infantry fights in platoons, with horse cavalry as shock troops, but they go into action *in units,* not individually; and by the fifteenth century infantrymen had learned to prepare their advance by laying down a barrage of missiles—first armor-piercing arrows, and later bullets and shot. Concentrated firepower could destroy any knight or group of knights, no matter how brave and skillful, before they could get close enough to engage the adversary.

Infantry requires organization; the knightly order of combat relied on individual skill. In effect, infantry expropriates individual skill and builds it into the organization. Infantry has the great advantage, furthermore, of being able to seize and hold a piece of territory. This is something knights cannot readily do. Infantry has the disadvantage, however, of being expensive. Knights trained and equipped themselves and were maintained in the lord's household. Most knightly combat was sporadic, short term, and involved numbers of men that could be counted in the dozens. The infantryman is trained, equipped, and maintained at the expense of the lord (or the king) whose service he is in. And he must be paid, in cash: most of the enlisted men under absolutism were mercenaries. Moreover, the infantryman is best suited for a campaign lasting months or years and involving hundreds, thousands, even tens of thousands of men. And just about the only way to make productive use of him when he is not in combat is to put him on garrison duty.

The expense of infantry, together with their unlimited capacity for conquest, given enough men and material, led to the expropriation of private armies by the new absolutist states of the sixteenth century. Henceforth the "King's Peace" would be enforced by the "King's Men."

The situation of the enlisted man was little changed by his serving the king instead of a baron, but the social character of the officer was changed completely. He became a functionary— in fact, if only very slowly in spirit.

Unlike Rome, in which the imperial military bureaucracy overshadowed the notables, the European absolutist state curried favor by reserving the commissions and warrants of officership exclusively to the stratum of notables: first the titled nobility, then the gentry, or subnobility (the "knights of the shire"), as well. Enlisted men were drafted, impressed, bribed, or hired into the service. Their character was half serf, half mercenary. They were not themselves functionaries because they were not entrusted with significant responsibilities, with the exception of noncommissioned officers, who were minor functionaries or subfunctionaries.

The absolutist officer *was* a functionary—though not a very satisfactory one because he had the notable's mentality. The logic of his situation confirmed his split identity and the conflict in roles he suffered. First, he had his commission because he was of aristocratic lineage, not because he was qualified on grounds of technical skill or leadership ability. But in exercising the authority of his office he was expected to command, that is, to enforce discipline, more than to coordinate or consult, and so he ruled by petty terrorism. As he saw it, his main task was to "keep the rabble in line." A good part of the time he was either on garrison duty, which meant that sergeants ran the operation and left him little to do, or else he was on extended leave.

The officer's role conflict grew out of the fact that while on duty he was subjected to an impersonal, organizational scheme of discipline that ran counter to the caste style of the aristocratic notable. His inability to resolve the conflict was manifested in an exaggerated *"machismo"* [3] sense of personal honor and a propensity to engage in the only sort of "heroic exploit" ordinarily available to him: drinking, whoring, brawling, and dueling.

The citizen soldier

There are many reasons for the phenomenal success of French arms under Napoleon, but it is clear that one of the most important ones was the "curse of rotten aristocracy" that sapped the strength of Europe, Russia, and Great Britain at the close of the eighteenth century. Napoleon conquered everything he could reach—he was barely stopped at Moscow, and for years Britain lived in fear of invasion—because he was able to organize and direct the immense forces of the emergent nation-state against regimes that were in varying degrees decadent. He did not succeed in burying absolutism, but he dealt it a wound that would not heal and so hastened its fated end.

The Napoleonic military differed from its predecessor in organization, tactics, and the use of technology, and this accounts for its new strategy of total victory. Absolutist military organization had been built upon a sharp and virtually impassable line between commissioned and noncommissioned ranks. Considerations of merit and technical competence had had little effect on recruitment, promotion, and the right to command. Generally speaking, officers became corrupt courtiers and willing participants in a system in which promotions and choice assignments were handed out as a form of patronage, while enlisted men became "stupid" and brutish. Napoleon (who had himself been a corporal) and the men around him were convinced that the old system was not only unjust but inefficient. They abolished the caste line and elevated men to command on the basis of what they could do, not who they were. Everything depended on performance, in theory, and in order to perform effectively the new commanders had to win the allegiance of their men and devise tactics to make the best use of that allegiance.

Command is imposed; leadership is won. Command implies a top-down structure of authority; leadership implies a bottom-up structure. All bureaucratic structures make use of both principles, but the emphatic shift in Napoleon's time from command to leadership was exhilarating because it expressed the new spirit of the nation-state.

The logic of the situation of the Napoleonic commander was that he had continually to validate and revalidate his right to command by proving to his men that he could lead them to victory. One effect of this was that because his fate was in their hands, in a way the men supported him by trying harder themselves for a successful outcome; their success and his success were bound up together. Another was that everyone, the commander and every officer and man down the line, was under pressure to free himself from tradition and shibboleth and attempt daring new schemes. With all eyes fixed on success, with pragmatism the rule of mind and faith in reason the rule of spirit, as the legacy of the French Revolution, conditions were ideal for subjecting tactical canons to the most thoroughgoing rationalization, whether they concerned the deployment of men and weapons or the development of logistics technique.

A famous example is Napoleon's use of artillery. Up to his time it was accepted doctrine that field guns were best used when attached to infantry units. When an advancing column came to a fortified emplacement, it would bring up its big guns to clear it. The Napoleonic commanders saw this as a failure to exploit the capabilities of artillery as a softening, spoiling, anti-personnel weapon. Properly timed and placed, a concentrated artillery barrage could play a uniquely valuable role as the battle developed. To accomplish this, however, it was necessary to effect a sensitive organizational change: artillery had to be detached from infantry and formed into its own units with its own tactical autonomy. Otherwise it could not be massed and coordinated to mount an effective barrage. Infantry officers generally resisted the innovation because it reduced their tactical options, and it threatened to reduce infantry's prestige ("queen of battles"). The credit for victory might go to artillerymen instead of to infantrymen who really take the ground.

The massed artillery barrage is generally acknowledged to be one of the more important Napoleonic innovations in military tactics. It is paradigmatic, from the point of view of this analysis, because it shows that the citizen soldier as a type was far more receptive to rationalization in military organization and tactics than was the absolutist officer whom he supplanted.

Was the citizen soldier a functionary in social type? Certainly he was in the minimal sense: he was the conscious and willing instrument of higher officials who gave him instructions in the name of an organized collectivity. And, unlike the absolutist officer, the citizen-soldier officer did not suffer from the role conflict of being both a notable and a functionary. Nevertheless, if he defined himself as a citizen, as a member of the national body which was the one true sovereign, he must have been troubled about national goals as they were defined by higher officials, and about the often inevitable conflict between national goals and the means that seemed dictated by rationality.

The citizen soldier was not yet ready to live and do his professional work by the principle, "My country, right or wrong," and so he lacked an essential ingredient of the complete functionary: passionlessness in his work.

The technician soldier

A few years ago Sigfried Giedion wrote a book called *Mechanization Takes Command*.[4] With some qualifications, that slogan would be an apt subtitle for this section. The citizen soldier made sense in the context of the newly emergent nation-state. Now, since World War I, and especially since World War II, the significant unit of social organization has become what is best called "mass society."

The mold in which we cast the social order still is the nation-state, but more and more the substance of sovereignty—the effective right to determine one's own fate as a polity—has drained out to leave a hollow form. The official logic, the conventional wisdom by which we arrange our social relationships, is no longer the operative logic. Nuclear weapons, superstate systems, and a world tide of revolution that is universalistic in ideology (however nationalistic in practice) have combined to destroy the pre–World War I polite fiction of a world community of sovereign states based on nationhood. Even the superstates, the United States and the Soviet Union, with their junior partners and satellites and clients and protectorates, are sovereign only in the legal sense: if either one were really free to do what it wanted to do, thought it should do, and was indubitably capable of doing, it would inexorably pull the trigger in a game of Russian roulette in which the revolver has a cartridge in every chamber.

The image of total destruction offered by nuclear weapons was presaged by World War I and was foreseen well by students of that dreadful and mostly senseless conflict. (Hundreds of thousands of men slaughtered by machine-gun bullets and artillery shells, and gas, as they crawl out of muddy trenches and try to gain a few yards of desolated ground . . .) It was elaborated by World War II and the new strategy of mass terror-bombing of civilians. A single raid, using conventional high explosives or fire bombs, could kill twenty thousand people or more; a single atomic bomb, as the United States demonstrated at Hiroshima and Nagasaki, could kill over 100,000; a single five-megaton Titan ICBM thermonuclear warhead could create a firestorm ranging up to eighteen miles in diameter; a single "doomsday machine" could be built with the power to destroy all life on the planet.[5]

The new technician soldier is not a joyful innovator of technique in organization, tactics, and weapons, as his citizen-soldier predecessor was; that is a matter for expert technologists. The citizen soldier was responsibly involved in determining ends as well as means, and this set limits on his practice of functional rationality and made it humanly bearable. The modern soldier cannot allow himself to be concerned with ends any more than he can with the logic of means. They are too complex, too remote, not so much inhuman as *un*human—again, a problem for the experts. The modern soldier feels he has neither the knowledge to understand them nor the power to affect them, and so they simply do not concern him. The logic of his situation demands that he keep his eye on the ball, that he stay on duty constantly, that he run through his operating procedures in simulated game situations again and again and again until he knows precisely what to do in the face of every contingency. He makes minor innovations in his job ("Scotch-taped procedures"), but ordinarily the best he can do is to learn the function of his unit—almost always he works as part of a team operation—and his role in it, and to learn other roles (through "cross-training") complementary to his own.

The modern soldier's attitude toward his work is, "It's a job. Let's get it over with and go home." Interestingly enough, this is true of both career men and draftees, but for different reasons. The draftee finds little joy in his work because conditions are at times so miserable, so long and drawn out, and seemingly so senseless. He gets a degree of satisfaction—at times a manic joy —in "making the thing go," even if it involves mowing down helpless men, women, and children from a helicopter gunship in Vietnam; but the adrenalin soon runs out and he wishes he were home.

He is a functionary in that he must exercise responsible discretion, as an individual, in performing the role and using the techniques he has trained for and knows. He must have skill and judgment, and he takes some pride in the fact. But for the most part he is rather like a semiskilled factory operative.*

The military career man, usually a commissioned or noncommissioned officer, has had time to learn the lore and think through the substantive implications of his function. Moreover, since he is of higher rank than the draftee, his technical repertory of skills and roles and his appreciation of the substantive as well as the functional meaning of his work is greater.

The career technician soldier comes close to being the perfect functionary, especially if he is a commissioned officer.[6] Does he see his work whole, that is, does he see his activity as part of a function that contributes to a certain goal? If so, does he feel responsible for that goal? There seem to be three possibilities: (1) he does see the goal and takes a willing share of responsibility for what the organization is doing; (2) he sees it but feels detached, alienated from his work (even though he may do it very well); or (3) he is an "idiot" (in the sense that Marx spoke of the mindlessness or "idiocy" of rural life), meaning that his functional imagination is undeveloped—he cannot see beyond the immediate necessity to "be a good soldier" and do his work to the best of his ability, taking a kind of mindless pride in his excellence in the functional equivalent of what used to be called craftsmanship.

BUREAUCRATIZATION

A functionary performs an activity that is responsible, continuous, involves the application of specialized skill, and derives its meaning from its integral part in some public or quasi-public venture.

---

* The difference is that the industrial worker usually likes his work better in proportion to his functional knowledge and imagination. The technician soldier likes his work less the better he understands his role as functionary, or subfunctionary, because a larger vision makes him at least morally responsible substantively, and not just functionally.

A bureaucracy is a body of officials; a bureaucrat is a member of such a body.

The difference between the "bureaucrat" and the "functionary" is that the former refers to the authority the individual has, while the latter indicates the kind of work the individual does. Both are abstractions. In reality, neither is distinct from the other.

The bureaucrat holds a position which carries with it the right to exercise a certain amount and kind of authority. The functionary occupies an organizational "slot" that defines him as being responsible for carrying out activities that contribute, ostensibly, to the performance of a vital function. Both have titles. In the limiting case, the bureaucrat's reveals nothing but his place in the hierarchy, and the functionary's tells only his place in the scheme of the division of labor.

Not all bureaucrats are functionaries, although many are, and not all functionaries are bureaucrats, although, again, frequently they are. There is a good deal of overlap.

In some types of organization, bureaucratic authority is justified and allocated as a necessary means to a (functional) end. In others, functions are created—quite literally "dreamed up"— to justify the creation or continued existence of certain offices. In still others, usually of the more archaic sort, there is a bewildering lack of congruity between the authority structure and the functional structure. In this last case, the reason is not hard to find. Authority means rank, and rank means social honor, even extending outside the organization. Authority *may* be necessary to get things done. But it is equally true that the "things that have to be done" may be pure fictions, goals whose only meaning is that they make it possible to "pay off" an organization notable by awarding him rank. Such rank is in substance honorary, although it masquerades as operationally rational.

In this section we consider how, in the light of these propositions, the concept of bureaucracy contributes to a better understanding of the military types set forth above. The categories of analysis used here (hierarchy, specialization, abstract rules, impersonality, technical qualifications, and tenure) are adapted from Max Weber's theory of bureaucracy.[7]

Hierarchy

An organization is hierarchical if, at its core, it has a body of officials arranged pyramidally in graded ranks. It is a ladder-like structure of nearly equivalent levels of authority. One can always tell, in principle, who outranks whom.

The Roman soldier-bureaucrat was very much the hierarchical man. The very term "rank," which originally meant nothing more than the placement of a line in the order of battle, e.g., "first," "second," and "third" in relation to the enemy, was first used by the Romans as a metaphor to indicate the relative importance of the higher commanders. Earlier military formations—Egyptian, Persian, and Greek—had instituted rank differences as a matter of fact, but it remained to the Romans to systematize it, rationalize it, and give it formal recognition in the logic of organization.

Feudal Europe fell heir to Roman civilization but bent old concepts to suit the new needs of the times. At first, differences in rank came to mean differences in the size and wealth of the fiefs and in the scope of the prerogatives of the fiefholder. Later they came to mean nothing more than differences in the "nobility" of one's lineage, a matter of titles and time. By this calculus, some were "more noble" than others. Thus the Roman function and meaning of rank became distorted to mean differences in the degree of social honor which a notable could credibly claim, thoroughly divorced from any organizational context.

The corrupt, derationalized legacy of feudalism undermined the effectiveness of the absolutist officer corps and made the way easier for the citizen soldier as a type to supplant it. Pointing to the "curse of rotten aristocracy"—functionless rank—the Napoleonic commanders made a fetish of divorcing rank from incumbent and of reintroducing a rationalized, systematic character into the command hierarchy.

The modern technician-soldier takes it for granted that the

rank hierarchy is rationalized and that it corresponds, except for staff positions, to graded differences in command responsibility.

Specialization

Specialization is realized within an organization to the extent that jobs are unique, or fall into unique classes, and therefore are not interchangeable. Ideally, everyone is a specialist, but practically this is never realized. The degree of specialization actually achieved is indicated by the number of job categories that are different enough, in the level and kind of skill they require, to make ready interchange of personnel among them impracticable. Specialization results from rationalization applied to the division of labor, just as bureaucratic hierarchy is the result of rationalization applied to the systematic arrangement of officials in graded ranks.

A high degree of rational specialization in the division of labor makes probable a correspondingly high degree of hierarchical rationalization, for each new specialized task added to the scheme complicates the problem of control and coordination. If there is an optimum ratio between the supervisor and the number of men he supervises ("span of control") for each type of organization, for example, it follows that a greater lateral spread—which is what specialization implies—inevitably creates the need for a taller hierarchy, more levels of command.*

This is evident when we consider that in Roman times the ratio between commanders and on-the-line fighting men was relatively low, even with Rome's elaborately developed, empire-wide military bureaucracy, compared with modern military organization. The massive investment of capital in modern armies, in the form of

---

* It does not follow that the converse is true, however. A tall, narrow hierarchy is sometimes found with a low level of specialization, although it is obviously irrational. One thinks of the Parkinson's Law phenomenon, in which "work expands to fill the time available for its accomplishment." See C. Northcote Parkinson, *Parkinson's Law, and Other Studies in Administration*, Boston, Houghton Mifflin, 1957, p. 2.

technology, equipment, and the training of technician-soldiers, has created a greatly expanded need for coordination, which has been met by greatly elaborating the logistics function and the command structure. (Part of this expanded structure is surely due to a technological lag: computers can eliminate a good many middle-echelon command positions.)

Abstract rules

Operating procedures are rationalized to the extent that their underlying logic can be stated succinctly in the form of an abstract rule, one so formulated that it fits together smoothly with other abstract rules on the same level. Ideally, all such rules can be deduced from general, logical canons of efficiency and effectiveness which form the constitutional basis of the organization. In principle, every rule is capable of being articulated with every other, first horizontally and then vertically.

Again, the Romans must be given credit for this bureaucratic innovation. They were able to do it—one might say they had to do it—because they needed clear communication between Rome and the remote outposts of the empire, among the outposts themselves, and between the proconsuls and the local populace. They needed a standardized operational code. Otherwise, distances in time and geography, differences in heritage and identity within the polyglot military bureaucracy and between the Roman garrisons and their subject populations, could make communications difficult and unreliable if not virtually impossible.

The modern technician-soldier has a different kind of need for abstract rules. The source of ambiguity in communications is not so much time and cultural distance as it is social distance. The involvement of many different occupations, based on skill, professionalism, and varying concepts of the overall mission of the organization, creates a problem of communications, coordination, and control, which makes necessary a universal language in the form of abstract rules.

Impersonality

One of the most important things a new recruit in military basic training learns is that "you salute the uniform, not the man." A bureaucratic organization incorporates impersonality to the extent that the individual learns to relate to superiors and subordinates in the authority structure as the embodiments of roles, not as whole human beings. If a man has the right to wear certain insignia of rank, you salute the insignia, the symbol of rationality, of graded and systematized authority, not the man wearing it. And you expect—demand, even—stylized deference by subordinates to the symbol of rank you wear, in the form of a salute or equivalent demeanor, not as balm to your ego but as a continuous legitimation of the authority you bear. This is the logic of the relationship between superiors and subordinates.

Stylized, impersonal deference works to render innocuous the clashes of personality that often occur in a big organization in which there are large and complex differences in function. This is especially true of the military because of the life-and-death importance of close coordination in time of crisis.

We know little about impersonality in the Roman military; we do know that this mode of bureaucratic discipline tended over time to lose force on the upper levels, undermined as it was by the "cult of personality" fostered intermittently by the emperor and by regional commanders. In the modern military establishment based on the technician-soldier, impersonality seems to be taking a different form under the influence of the technicist ethos. The underground attitude, which is surfacing more and more, is to show a certain contempt for the spit-and-polish emphasis of the old military and to see command rank as nothing more than a necessary evil. The tendency is to relate to a fellow soldier more in terms of what he can do and not so much who he is, regardless of his formal rank in the hierarchy of command.

Tenure and technical qualifications

Tenure is not really an important consideration in the military, except in the case of men who are overage in rank, having been passed over for promotion too many times, or who have reached the "seniority plateau"—in the Army, the rank of colonel. To move from colonel into the ranks of general officer a man must have something special going for him: advanced work in the War College, or equivalent achievement in the field or in administration or staff work. Simple, unblemished seniority can float him up to a colonelcy but not beyond it.

Technical qualifications apply, over and above seniority, to advancement in rank in the enlisted grades, and to "jump promotions" in the officer grades (in which seniority is brusquely overridden). Seniority counts, but merit "overcounts," as it were. And merit ordinarily means demonstrated proficiency in the development and application of technique.

This is precisely the area in which the modern military differs fundamentally from the military establishments of earlier times. The organizational problem for the Romans grew out of slow communications (although they were fast by contemporary standards), cultural heterogeneity within the armed forces, and the localist propensities of regional units and commanders. (Technology, relatively static, was not a problem.) Organizational difficulties led to the erosion of bureaucratic discipline. Corruption, feudalization, and instability of political authority at the top grew more severe with each successive generation after the Augustan age. Seniority and merit became less important than loyalty—identification and solidarity with the "right" faction in the fluid context of bureaucratic politics. The Roman soldier had service tenure, but it did not count for much during the organizational convulsions—today we call them purges—in the middle and upper echelons, in which hundreds, sometimes thousands, played the game of politics and lost; were tried, found guilty, and put to death for treason; or else were simply assassinated.

Technical qualifications were not very important as a practical matter in late feudal and absolutist times. Men were knighted, commissioned, promoted, and given choice assignments as the result of success in the game of court politics, either directly or through a patron, as much as on the basis of proven merit. For a while this policy worked, but it proved disastrous to military organizations in the late eighteenth and early nineteenth centuries. Absolutist officers were not only foppish, overbearing, and brutal, but technically incompetent as well. The rapidly growing effectiveness of military technology gave disaffected enlisted men a tool for mutinous inclinations.

Citizen soldiers in the new nation-state installed technical qualifications as a major consideration for promotion and command assignment, but leadership charisma was just as important. Napoleon himself epitomized the ideal. He was no well-turned-out expert (although he did found the École Polytechnique to ensure a supply of experts in the future) but a shrewd, alert, practical man who learned fast in a technical sense without forgetting the ancient axiom that the commander must dramatize himself and inspire faith in his intuition as well as his expertise.

Flamboyant self-dramatization can still be found in the modern military—MacArthur with his corncob pipe, Patton with his jodhpurs and twin pearl-handled revolvers are examples from World War II. But the new technician-soldier has little need for leaders who can fire up his courage or terrorize him, if it comes to that. The content of his work is such that he needs good training, a cool head, a reliable and efficient teammate at his side, and leadership that is more consultative than inspirational. This reflects the logic of the new, complex, immensely powerful technology in military operations. The danger for the modern soldier is not that he will lose heart and run, but that he will lose his mind—freeze with panic—and stop functioning.

FUNCTIONALIZATION

Bureaucratization is hierarchical rationalization. Functionalization, a broader and more comprehensive concept of specialization, is the process of applying rationality to the division of labor.

Hierarchy presupposes a division of labor, but not necessarily one which is either substantively or functionally rational. No scheme for the division of labor, rational or not, is viable without coordination, and if the job of coordination is sufficiently complex and extensive to require more than one level of officials, the result is hierarchy.

Rationalization of the division of labor, functionalization, occurs in three modes: optimizing of sub-unit *size;* optimum specialization by sub-unit in regard to operational *mission;* and optimum use of *technology* throughout the organization.

Size

A social organization grows through "quantum leaps." At each new size level, the social character of the organization unit—an army, for example—changes. The size of a unit, in the typical case, increases gradually and evenly up to a certain point and then pauses. A sense of crisis builds. There is oversaturation of the communications net, increasing remoteness and inaccessibility of key functionaries, lessening of the clarity and force of the mission as it has been defined, weakening of loyalty to the values that yield a common sense of identity, and other ills.

It becomes clear to some, at least, that any further growth demands a pretty thorough restructuring of the organization's internal arrangements. This means a different organizational character, a different work environment, a different mission capability. The question becomes, is it worth it? The answer depends in large part on what it takes to accomplish the mission—to get the war won, the dam built, the volume of output up to the level that makes the product competitive. If the organization is not free to choose its mission but has it thrust upon it, as in the military or in some government agencies, or if its only choice is between expansion and bankruptcy, as in the case of an uneconomically small manufacturing plant, its fate is sealed. It must "die" in the form it has assumed in the past, and be "reborn" in a new form appropriate to its revised and expanded mission.

Sometimes the organization has the option of preserving its present size and character by redefining its mission to suit its limited capability. For example, a small liberal arts college might place such great value on keeping itself to "human scale" that it gives up plans for a graduate program.

The organization may have another option: to choose colonization as an alternative to expansion. For example, anthropologists have observed that population increase in peasant societies does not increase the size of the village unit indefinitely. When the number of people reaches the level of fifteen hundred to two thousand, the tendency is to propagate a daughter village nearby rather than to allow the resident population to go on growing. Villages of more than three or four thousand are distinctly rare. If they do grow larger than that, they take on a new, nonvillage character. Similarly, Greek philosophers of the Hellenic period, speculating on the size of the ideal city, generally agreed that the number of citizens ought to be limited to the number that could comfortably see and hear a single orator. That would be in the order of ten thousand, they thought.

It is interesting that the Romans, who were of course greatly influenced by the Greeks, also hit upon the figure ten thousand as the optimum number of fighting men in a fully self-contained unit in the field. The smallest unit large enough to have a tactical mission was the century, one hundred men. The legion composed ten of these units, each commanded by a captain and supposed to be able to function autonomously for a considerable period of time in the field.

The deployment of armies (an army was an indefinitely large number of legions), legions, and centuries, each with its appropriate strategic and tactical mission, became a highly developed art with the Romans: generalship was rationalized and technicized, in part based on the assumption that the unit of military action ought to be adjusted to the "quantum leap" factor in social organization. The Romans' unique awareness of the fact that new qualities emerge as the organization grows larger is reflected in their overriding concern with rational discipline and with effective communications throughout the military bureaucratic establishment that ran the empire.

The citizen-soldier armies of Napoleon and, a bit later, of the two sides in the American Civil War gave some attention to the factor of optimum size. By that time, however, the new technologies of weaponry and communications made size more of a dependent than an independent variable.

Operational mission

The "human wave" tactics used by the Chinese against the Americans in the Korean War in 1952 called for a single tactical mission to be assigned, initially, to a large number of company-sized units. The strategic objective was to shock and demoralize U.S. forces—which by then had overrun most of North Korea—so that the American drive would lose its momentum. Individual soldiers and small units would then feel justified in "bugging out" as fast as possible. For a time the Americans were driven into a pell-mell retreat; the Chinese objective was realized.

At the other extreme is the example of a "sapper squad," about a half-dozen N.L.F. (Vietcong) frogmen who attached explosives to the hull of a Swedish freighter unloading in the harbor of Saigon, South Vietnam, and did considerable damage to it at the height of the Tet offensive in February 1968.

The point is that a tactical mission may be assigned to a force of six men or 600,000, depending on conditions.

Rationalization of sub-unit tactical missions, based upon division-of-labor principles, was probably initiated on a significant scale by the Hellenic Greeks. The state of the art was advanced little until the outnumbered, outgunned, and generally outclassed British Navy won a spectacular victory over the Spanish Armada in the sixteenth century. Historians generally regard the tactical ingenuity of the British to have been the decisive factor.

Tactical ingenuity means technical effectiveness in the art of deploying attack units, and in timing their movements in such a way that each makes a functionally specialized contribution to the overall plan of battle—but functionally specialized in the purely tactical sense.

Functionalization of the tactical aspects of planning a battle—by deploying units (warships, for example) of more or less equal capability, by conceiving of a battle as a "game" in which space and time as well as the gross balance of strength are calculable variables—gradually obsessed military and naval men. *Movement* became the thing, movement and timing. This created an emphasis on purely tactical specialization and rationalization which culminated in the shibboleth that "the Battle of X" (it hardly mattered which, as long as it was victorious) was "won on the playing fields of Eton." The great vogue of games of all sorts—polo for the infantry and cavalry, chess for the navy men, and Kriegspiel, or three-dimensional chess, for the civilian war analysts and planners at "think tanks" like the RAND Corporation or the Institute of Defense Analysis in the mid-twentieth century—testifies to the enormous impact on military thinking of the possibility of a "science of tactics" (really a technology, not a science in the proper sense).

Technology

Functionalization of technology, again in the context of the military organization, refers to the development and rationalization of man-machine weapons and logistics systems, but primarily weapons.

Technological rationalization was a factor in the Napoleonic wars, when organizational and cultural restraints on the optimum use of known technology were removed. But not until the American Civil War was technology allowed its head. And World War II (except for its "rehearsal" in the Spanish Civil War) was the first in which technology was not just freed but yielded to as a leading force. Industrial research and development in America has been "in uniform" ever since. Seymour Melman calculated recently that $15 billion of the $20 billion spent annually in the U.S. for research and development is for military purposes.[8]

An early example of functionalization of military technology was the division of command between sea and land forces in late Hellenic Greece. The military mission of the Greek Navy at that time was relatively minor. It was really more of a police force—analogous to the Border Patrol or the Coast Guard in modern times. It had no weapons that were specifically naval. Such autonomy as it had came not from weapons technology but from logistics: its unique capability to move large quantities of men and supplies fast and over long distances. It was autonomous because of the logic of its operations in that sphere. Technology was a factor only in that shipbuilding and ship operation were developed into highly specialized and esoteric arts.

Eventually, in the early sixteenth century, naval vessels became true military units in themselves, not just carriers of fighting men and their equipment and supplies. Ship design accommodated itself to the new function of the warship as a seagoing platform for heavy guns, with their devastating firepower at close range, and innovations in organization and tactics followed in due course. It is interesting to note, however, that after its initial dramatic success technological innovation in naval weaponry moved at a slow pace until the famous encounter between the *Merrimac* and the *Monitor* during the American Civil War. In this classic sea battle the combination of steam power, ironclad armor, and turret mounting of guns opened up a whole new vista of possibilities for naval ship architecture, ordnance, organization, and tactics, and even an imperialist political strategy for the projection of "seapower." [9]

Another example of technological functionalization and its

effects on military organization, and even on the role of the military in society and in the nation, is the use of land armor and mobile heavy firepower. The prototype vehicle is the tank, conceived as a miniature battleship operating on land. Too toughly armored to be easily stopped, heavy enough in firepower to engage most dug-in artillery and machine-gun positions, the tank was thought to be the answer to the stalemated and frightfully destructive trench warfare of 1914–1918. It would introduce the tactics of a "war of movement" on the model of naval battles. By reintroducing a new and better "cavalry," it promised to make generalship meaningful once again. Much of this promise was realized, as shown by the success of the German *Blitzkrieg* tactics early in World War II.

A third example is airpower. The German Army in the 1930's, ideologically receptive to technological innovation because of its unlimited fascist pragmatism, introduced the supreme anti-tank weapon, tactical aircraft such as the Stuka dive-bomber, at the same time it developed its *Blitzkrieg* tactics of a war of movement based on heavy armor and motorized infantry. Destruction of the enemy's base of supply and ultimately of his will to resist—so-called "strategic bombing" of industrial and population centers—was also a German innovation in the use of manned aircraft as an attack weapon, although, like the use of tactical air support for ground action, the Allies adopted the German innovation and achieved new levels of efficiency and effectiveness in exploiting it. The British carried out the unprecedented fire-bombing assault on Dresden, and the Americans fire-bombed Tokyo and Osaka. The culmination of the strategic bombing offensive was an American achievement: developing and dropping the world's first atomic bombs.

For our purposes in this book, the significance of air power is that first the Germans, then the Russians, Japanese, British, and finally the Americans made its technology and operational needs the basis of a third autonomous military command, parallel with the army and the navy. Later, the displacement of manned bombers by nuclear-tipped ballistic missiles with intercontinental range (ICBM's) created a lively dispute among the three forces as to who should have jurisdiction over them.

We see that in the modern age, technology determines organization, but not without a good deal of jockeying for position by vested military-bureaucratic interests. Functionalization based on technology never occurs in a vacuum. Social forces affect its content, direction, and pace.

CONCLUSIONS

The military man's work has evolved in ways that show the impact of bureaucratization and functionalization on the logic of his work situation. His social identity and his role as a functionary must be understood in relation to the matrix of organizational relationships which holds him. The meaning of his work, the logic of his work, and how he relates himself to others and to the larger collectivity are all products of these forces, which are beyond his control and mostly beyond his recognition.

The military man closely approximates the ideal functionary because, however egoistic his motivation in a given instance may be, the core meaning of his act is that it has nothing to do with the individual or with private goals and everything to do with the collectivity. Like it or not, realize it or not, he is close to being a pure instrument of a collectivity embodying a public purpose. In many ways he is the prototype of all functionaries in all organizations in the modern world.

If the private motive does become detached from its public purpose (which is unlikely because of organizational discipline), the soldier takes on the character either of a brigand or of an armed madman. But there is a third possibility. The logic of his action may be such that, knowing it or not, he seeks the real public good in place of the false representation of it that others accept. In that case he is not a brigand or a lunatic but a revolutionary.

We considered a number of historical types: the warrior, the patrician militiaman, the soldier bureaucrat, the feudal knight, the absolutist infantryman, the citizen soldier, and the modern technician soldier. One thing that emerges from this review is that the division of labor operates from the very beginning: however rudimentary, there is always an operations function, a support function, and a command function. At the same time, regardless of his personal motives, a man cannot accurately be called a functionary unless he is a specialist, devotes full time to his work, and is subjected to some sort of organizational discipline. Those military types who do not meet these criteria (the warrior, the militiaman, the feudal knight, and some of the absolutist officers) may be called *proto-functionaries*. The logic of their situation is such that they cannot feel the full force of functional rationality as the ground of their personal ethic. A man in such a situation who disciplines himself according to the norm of functional rationality is simply out of touch, an eccentric, because he does not respond to social forces that really exist.

Another finding is that rationalization of authority and hierarchy (bureaucratization) and rationalization of operations according to function (functionalization) do not necessarily go together in the military. Bureaucratization is the more independent of the two variables, although it is hampered by and subject to corruption by a parallel power structure of notables who exploit military rank, when they can, as a mark of distinction. Bureaucratization *can* promote functionalization in the military, although there is no inherent reason why it must.

Functionalization, on the other hand, is the "material factor"—that is, the way it works and the force with which it works are relatively unhampered by cultural norms, values, and individual attitudes. The hard facts that promote functionalization in the military sector of a society, regardless of that society's values, are the "quantum leap" phenomenon that determines the range of sub-unit size; the advantages of the rational division of labor for the mission specification of military sub-unit; and, most important of all, the logic of technology that in the modern world ultimately dictates the spirit and structure of the whole military establishment.

The new technician-soldier is more inclined to be a slave to technology than its master. He is of a social type which evades questions of substantive rationality and resolves them, in effect, by endlessly elaborating functional rationality. But, in all fairness, what is he to do? He has two options. He can speak out against the current "overkill" policy of endlessly stockpiling nuclear weapons and of emplacing greater and greater numbers of "strategic" —meaning city-killing—missiles, in which case he is accused of assuming the civilian prerogative of deciding ultimate military policy. Or he can remain silent and be accused of dereliction of his duty as an expert to educate the public to the terrible risks of nuclear devastation.[10]

It is hardly surprising that most high-ranking military men avoid both of these uncomfortable alternatives and instead play the functionary's role to the hilt. Their job as a soldier, as they see it, is to be guided by the ethic of functional rationality. In context this means building a better and more credible rationale for not only keeping but expanding the scope of their particular function. If this results in substantive "overkill," [11] or wars against peasant people which have no sense or end and border on the genocidal, the quite sincere rejoinder is, "But that's not my department." They dissociate themselves from questions of substantive rationality because their proper sphere, as they see it, is the application of functional rationality. It is an austere soldier's code, and in its own terms it is perfectly logical and perfectly ethical.

4

Government

Industrial workers who have access to tools and materials—machinists, for example—sometimes use company time to do things that are productive in substance but not for the organization—not *functionally* productive. They make hunting knives, toys for children, gadgets useful around the house or for the car. They do it not to make money, although sometimes they sell the things, but in the spirit of playful "goofing off," "beating the system." With lighthearted irony they call it "government work."

Since the beginnings of the industrial revolution, it has been part of the conventional wisdom to assume that government is inherently unproductive and parasitical, however necessary such functions as law enforcement, adjudication of civil disputes, and maintaining the apparatus for waging war have been recognized to be in practice. The laissez-faire attitudes of the nineteenth century, continuing into the twentieth, made suspect public works, public education, care for the needy, and even the regulation of commerce. The sociologist and Social Darwinist Herbert Spencer contended that publicly supported fire departments, poor farms, and even lighthouses should be turned over to private enterprise. If there was a real need for them, he said, the costs should be borne by those directly concerned.

No one can get an audience anymore to listen seriously to claims that the government should get out of the business of regulating commerce or maintaining aids to navigation or seeing to it that citizens have adequate police and fire protection. But the demand is heard occasionally that the United States Post Office should go out of business and turn over the function of providing mail service to private enterprise; and, just recently, the once dead issue of universal and compulsory free public education has been exhumed and propped up for review. The most serious specific challenge in the twentieth century has been directed at the right of an autonomous agency of the federal government, the Tennessee Valley Authority, to be in the business of electrical power generation, transmission, and distribution. The measure of success of the attack is indicated by the fact that there have been no "authorities" like TVA established since. The only agency that manufactures anything that might be called a commodity is the Atomic Energy Commission, and its product, radioactive substances of various sorts, is so severely restricted in its availability for sale that it is a very special kind of commodity indeed.

Government work is work done by people employed by the federal or by state or local governments. With rare exceptions they produce nothing of market value, although what they do certainly has value in substance. People are willing to pay taxes and to elect legislators who appropriate money to maintain government employees and for the facilities and materials they need for their work. Moreover, there is nothing inherent in government which makes the work done by its employees unproductive of value even in the market sense. This is shown by the success of TVA, of manufacturing plants owned and operated by government agencies in wartime, and by the virtually unanimous acceptance in every country in the world outside the United

States of the principle that public ownership and operation of railroads and other essential utilities does work and is a good thing.

On the other hand, there is a grain of truth in the claim that government work is unproductive. For one thing, the most distinctive and characteristic government functions (collecting taxes, granting licenses, enforcing laws and regulations, keeping records, operating the courts, carrying on diplomacy, and so on) clearly are not directly productive of things which have value in the sense that one could put a price tag on them, even though they have indirect value because production and commerce could not flourish—perhaps not continue—without them. For another, the newer, welfare functions of government have in common with the older ones the problem that their relative value cannot be calculated, either because there is no conventional market for them or because they are protected from the market. One thinks of education and social work, for example. Each has a small "private sector," but the public sector is so overwhelmingly large that it is not of much use in determining the "objective" value of educating a child for a year, or of "handling a case" in social work.

There is no way to calculate relative values in government work, and so there is no rational way to allocate priorities or choose ends. The scope for practicing substantive rationality is limited to deciding whether or not a proposed project is likely to yield "benefits" in proportion to its cost (cost-benefit analysis). This does not directly affect functional rationality, however, which is why the government functionary and subfunctionary are not very different from their counterparts in private industry.

Government work is thought to be unproductive because it is carried on through what Anthony Downs calls "nonmarket bureaus" instead of "market bureaus," [1] which are in the private sector. Agencies of government do things which have value, but the value is hard to determine with precision. This hampers rationalization—functionalization and bureaucratization. It will be instructive to examine the various spheres of government operations from the standpoint of the question of how and why functional rationality is fostered in some instances, impeded in others. Government functions are of three types: core functions, regulative functions, and general welfare functions.

CORE FUNCTIONS

The powers of government in the modern state include, at minimum, the right to define and secure the rights of citizens, to enforce contracts, to make laws defining criminal acts and to punish lawbreakers, to carry on necessary relations with foreign powers, and to provide for the common defense.

Maintaining security and enforcing contracts are of primary importance. A state which will not or cannot do these things, both of which follow from "successfully claiming a monopoly of the right to use force in a given territory" (Max Weber's definition of the state), is not a state in the sense the term is used today and has been used since the sixteenth century.

The "government functionary" is familiar enough as a social type. The fact that the term still carries with it some odor of contempt reminds us that the governments of early modern states made use of "little men," "petty officials" (or "mere officials") to carry out its functions. The rising authority and the sheer proliferation of these "king's men" ruffled the hauteur of noble aristocrats and earned the officials the disdain of the gentry and the patricians. Each of these notable types took a fierce and touchy pride in "being one's own man." Threatened politically by the king's men, they retaliated culturally and socially by scorning the type of man who bore the awesome powers of government but was still no more than the instrument of the sovereign's will.

Government functionaries of the seventeenth and eighteenth centuries served warrants, issued summonses, collected taxes, adjudicated claims, oversaw expenditures, assessed values, collected and recorded information, and served ministers of state as advisers and executors of policy. Collectively they constituted a career service and a bureaucracy. They evolved their own ethic and their own sense of professional identity, partly as the basis for developing skill in their work and for a workable doctrine of operations; and partly as a defense, grounded in the mystique of expertise and in strong bonds of occupational solidarity ("the service"), against powerful notables in the general public and in the top echelon of appointed or elected officials (noncareer men —those holding "exempt positions," in modern parlance, meaning that the conditions of their appointment and tenure are not bound by civil service restrictions).

The bureaucracy of functionaries in the early modern period, when work in the area of the core functions constituted most of the activities of government, was not very "bureaucratized." It rested for its legitimacy only in part on the rational-legal principle that pervades the spirit and structure of modern bureaucracy. The sovereign, whether speaking through king, prime minister, or president, had to delegate authority in order to get the rapidly increasing work of government done. He did not have to delegate it rationally, however, and often he did not because he did not know how. He did not yet appreciate the gain in efficiency and effectiveness to be had, nor did he have the means to accomplish these ends—accounting and budgetary techniques, communication and information-processing technology.

Rationality had a hard time of it, moreover, because the need to appoint and promote on the basis of merit, technical qualifications, and achievement was accepted and built into the system only very slowly. The government bureaucracy was frankly both political and nepotistic in most of the Western world until not much more than a century ago.

Bureaucracy means, at minimum, that there is delegation and subdelegation of authority, and at least some functional division of labor and rationalization of official jurisdiction. True delegation of authority, which specifies an office and an incumbent who is "vested" with the right to take official actions (not only *of* the bureaucracy but *for* the bureaucracy) on his own initiative and over his own name and title, was rare for a long time. Most of the early functionaries in the core sphere of government operations were not really officials, or not quite, if we use the term in its restricted sense. They acted "in the name of" someone else, a true official, rather than in their own name. They were emissaries, agents, retainers. This undermined their dignity, as well as their efficiency and effectiveness. With time and the expansion of operations, initiative fell to them more and more by default, and approval by their overworked superiors became perfunctory. Accustomed to act on their own, in substance if still not yet in form, the functionaries gradually took on the character of true officials.

This perfunctory endorsement of subordinates' initiative created the conditions for the rationalization of the authority structure. It was objectively in the interest of both parties to subdelegate, and routinized subdelegation protected the interests of both, for it made it necessary to specify precisely the points of linkage in the chain of command in order to minimize ambiguity. It was necessary to know just where one official's jurisdiction left off and another's began.

In the realm of the core functions, rationalization of the authority structure, bureaucratization in the limited sense, was fostered by the need to free operational functionaries to act on their own and the need to pinpoint responsibility for any given action. Thus it was a way to optimize both freedom and control. But rationalization of operations, or functionalization, developed little impetus until much more recently because there was no technological imperative. The core functionaries could and did claim empirical expertise, but not technological expertise. The division of labor remained loose, unanalyzed, guided by common sense and tradition. Functional rationality, in the U.S. State Department, for example, has not been much of a force even up to the present moment.

REGULATIVE FUNCTIONS

The modern state has never restricted its activities even in theory to the core functions. Pressure from special-interest groups, the virtually universal recognition that there are certain things "for the public good" that only the state can do because of its residual powers as sovereign, and more recently the demands of the new technology for central coordination have caused government to expand the scope of its operations again and again.

Adam Smith observed, in 1776, that the wealth of nations was a function of their industry and commerce. The nation whose businessmen were energetic and intelligent, and unhindered by legal restrictions mistakenly designed to secure a favorable balance of trade, would be able to produce and sell goods in the open market at a lower price and still make a greater profit than those less favored. This was the royal road to riches, contrary to the mercantilist thesis that a net surplus of gold in the state treasury must be ensured through a system of licensure, legal monopoly, franchise, and control of imports and exports through quotas and duties.

Smith and the theorists of laissez faire prevailed. They destroyed the credibility of the mercantilist policy and forced the removal of many restrictions on business. But government regulation of the economy did not come to a halt; there were too many vested interests at stake. Businessmen wanted "free enterprise" but not totally unprotected enterprise. In their view it was in the public interest for government to limit imports, encourage exports, and in general to provide incentives and create the best possible climate for investment in commercial and industrial enterprises.

It is a fundamental premise of modern political theory that law is not "the will of God" or "part of Nature's plan," as used to be thought, but nothing more nor less than the command of the state. Now, if law is not something revealed or discovered but instead something made by men, it follows that law is the instrument through which the economy can be regulated (in addition to the regulation of individual conduct in general, through criminal law and the law of torts, or civil law). The regulation of commerce and industry through law, for different ends and by different tactical schemes, constitutes a second sphere of government functions and is carried out by a somewhat different set of government functionaries.

The management of government's fiscal, legal, and foreign affairs, as we have seen, was and still is carried out by a body of functionaries who gradually moved up from the status of emissaries or agents to become true officials. Their type of bureaucracy tends to be rationalized hierarchically, but not functionally. They were and remain empirical experts, not technicians and technologists. The content of their work still has the character of "state business"—the charisma of the sovereign is close at hand.

Regulative functionaries have been more pragmatic, more matter of fact and unceremonious from the beginning. And they bear the style-imprint of the technological expert, even though they may not be such themselves (some are). This is because in the nature of their work they deal with practical men and use the law primarily as an instrument rather than as a source of legitimacy for their own actions. They must negotiate, they must improvise, they must make little informal emendations and exceptions in order to come to terms with cases. In order to be effective they must understand the logic of the body of regulative law they work with and the objective it is designed to achieve. They cannot just memorize chapter, verse, and letter.

Regulative functionaries deal with business and businessmen, sometimes as the bearers of gifts (subsidies) or as helpers in other ways, and sometimes as investigators, enforcers, prosecutors —what is good for business as a whole is not necessarily good for one particular businessman. They also deal with farmers, trade unionists, and occupational and commercial groups of all sorts. Regulative law, originally limited to matters of economics in the narrow sense, commerce and industry, now applies to virtually everyone insofar as his interests may conflict with another's. Its object is to promote the interests of all groups whose activities are consistent with the public interest, and at the same time to secure equity when interests come into conflict. In large part it is a matter of setting priorities and of laying down what are essentially "traffic regulations" governing the use of scarce resources which are public rather than private. The Forest Service regulates the use of the national parks and forests. The Labor Department makes ground rules for the conduct of labor disputes and provides a staff of mediators. A large number of semi-autonomous boards and commissions, on state and local as well as federal levels of government, oversees air, sea, river, rail, and highway transportation, radio and television broadcasting, management of harbors, bridges, and interurban transit systems, conduct of water, power, and other utilities—the list is endless.

Regulative functions differ from the core functions of government in that they invoke an image of the state as helper and facilitator (a traffic policeman or labor-dispute mediator) rather than as a stern instrument of state sovereignty (a soldier, sheriff, or judge). Law is still important to the functionary in this field, but less so and in a different way. For the core functionary, the law, or *raison d'état* (interest of the state), which amounts to the same thing, is sacred. It is what his work is all about. For the regulative functionary, law is a statement of public policy objectives and a set of more or less flexible guidelines for reaching them. His concern is not with the will of the state in any immediate sense but with the public interest as it is codified.

The regulative functionary is in the career civil service, typically, like the core functionary. But this is more a legal than a sociological description. The regulative functionary is less likely to stay for life, for example. He is less likely to feel "in the service" and totally committed to it, because the farther one is from the direct exercise of sovereign powers, the less the work has a special character. It is more mundane, more secular, less character-defining as government work. The regulative functionary is closer to the world of practical affairs, and his skills and experience are more easily transferrable to the private sector. Whether or not he is a technological expert, his expertise is only to a limited degree of the empirical, esoteric sort that has no value in the market, and so he is not priced out of it—he is not "hooked on the pension system."

The work environment of the modern regulative functionary is relatively less "bureaucratic," in the pejorative sense of the term, than that of the core functionary. There is less emphasis on rank, less of a sense of the stuffy presence of high officialdom, less calm deliberation of weighty matters best left undecided if there is doubt about what to do. Less importance is attached to The Judgment. From the top looking down, there is less need to pinpoint responsibility; from the bottom looking up, there is a good deal of operational freedom and less chafing at the bit about the need to "get clearance" before acting.

The reasons for this different outlook are partly historical, partly technological. Government performed regulative functions from the beginning of the modern state, but it was not until the second half of the nineteenth century that they began to grow into a major field of activity. Commerce and industry rather suddenly became superpowers, threatening the integrity of government itself, let alone the public interest ("The public be damned!"). Conservation of natural resources, control of traffic, and the need to restrict the runaway freedom of business tycoons, able to control the economic and even the social life of whole states and foreign countries, provided all the rationale one could ask. Since that time even businessmen have accepted the need, in principle, for some degree and kind of public regulation. It is unimaginable that a large municipal airport, for example, could operate without stringent, disinterested, and thoroughly expert air traffic control.

Thus the need for quick, on-the-spot decisions which ground their legitimacy on functional expertise has stamped its character on the regulative bureaucracies and the regulative functionary. Unlike the core functionary, he must cope with a work situation that neither rewards nor even permits dodging responsibility in most cases. He is less the state official and more the public servant. The clientele he serves is powerful, knowledgeable, and quite capable of bringing political pressure to bear on the superior officer of a man who delays action by referring too many matters "up the line" for approval. His authority is functional at least as much as it is official, as an instrument of government; he must see that the laws are applied, but at the same time he must not interfere with the movement of traffic except as a last resort. Under the circumstances, it is not surprising that he cultivates a "can do," businesslike expertise which distinguishes the manner and spirit of his work from that of his colleague in government service, the core functionary.

GENERAL WELFARE FUNCTIONS

The United States Constitution reflects eighteenth-century conceptions of the state and the functions of government. Nonetheless, it captured the spirit and the logic of the newly emergent republican state so well that many of its essential propositions have been adopted by modern and modernizing national states ever since. (This is true even of communist countries.) The industrial revolution and the urban revolution have made much of it obsolete in detail, but the part that remains is still impressively cogent.

From the Civil War to the great depression of the 1930's, most social legislation was justified by the commerce clause of the Constitution. Faced with an unprecedented crisis, President Roosevelt's New Deal relied first on the commerce clause and then shifted to the general welfare clause as the basis for legitimizing the expansion of government functions.

One of Roosevelt's intimates and close advisers was Harry Hopkins, a professional social worker. To him, and to FDR, as it turned out, the immediate fact that one-third of the breadwinners in the country were unemployed meant that existing federal government regulation of the economy was not enough to deal with the crisis. Many local and state governments were fiscally unable to cope with the widespread distress through the traditional dole or county relief system. New Dealers contended that the federal government had the power and responsibility to see that imperative social needs were met, even if this meant outright planning of the economic and social life of the nation.

The New Deal program encouraged the organization of business to maintain prices, the organization of labor to maintain wages, and agricultural organization to maintain farm income. The able-bodied unemployed were offered jobs created by public works programs, and the unemployable indigents were given direct relief in the form of food stamps and cash payments. Massive government spending was supposed to have a "pump priming" effect on the economy, and was to be phased out as prosperity—always thought to be "just around the corner"—returned. But much of the emergency apparatus became permanent. It survived the war boom of the 1940's and the halfhearted efforts of the Eisenhower administration in the 1950's to dismantle it. Finally, there is no longer a doubt that in the United States, just as in Europe during the same period, a whole new set of welfare functions became established as a legitimate sphere of government operations.

The new welfare functionary often works for state and local governments, or dispersed governmental units, like hospitals and school districts, but the best single clue to his social type is the kind of "home" he has in Washington. One thinks of the two newest cabinet-level agencies: Health, Education, and Welfare, and Urban Affairs. But in order to get a sense of the range of these new activities, several others must be mentioned. The new, glamour agency (now in serious trouble) is the Office of Economic Opportunity, charged with the mission to carry out a "war on poverty." Less conspicuous are agencies tucked away in old-line departments: the Office of Vocational Rehabilitation and the Office of Manpower Retraining and Development are examples. Somewhat different in character are the Bureau of Indian Affairs, the Veterans' Administration, the Farm Security Administration, the Social Security Administration, and the U.S. Employment Service; and, finally, with the mission of projecting welfare activities abroad, the Agency for International Development.

Certain conclusions can be drawn, even from this partial list, about the social character of the welfare functionary and the logic of his work situation. First, welfare functions are not new in any categorical sense. Publicly supported facilities and services for the poor, the sick, and the abandoned (poorhouses, county hospitals, orphan asylums) have existed since the beginnings of the modern state, although, like schools, they were established and initially supported for the most part by churches and other private charitable institutions. Government aid was generally limited, stingy, and a last resort. The reform movements of the 1840's and 1850's changed this concept, most dramatically in the case of the schools. The opportunity for all children to get at least a minimum education at public expense gradually became an established social right throughout the Western world. This was paralleled by the growth of a *de facto* right of indigents to minimum subsistence and health care. Even the new Agency for International Development has its precedent in the venerable Bureau of Indian Affairs. Both are concerned with the problems of modernizing "backward" (the euphemism is "underdeveloped," or "less developed," or "developing") societies, with the unstated premise that the welfare of these peoples concerns us because they eventually must be assimilated into the community of nations.

Second, the content of the welfare functionary's work varies a good deal. Some receive claims, determine eligibility, and authorize government action (typically in the form of disbursement of funds). This is true of the Veterans' Administration and the Social Security Administration, for example. Like his colleague, the regulative functionary, who adjudicates essentially economic rights, or the core functionary, who adjudicates civil rights, the welfare functionary of this type adjudicates social rights.

Others work as service professionals: teachers, doctors, social workers, lawyers, public health experts, and so on. Still others are professionals and technicians whose skills are not specific to the welfare function but who are needed to carry it out effectively. One thinks of social scientists and natural scientists doing research and development work, and librarians, archivists, editors, and computer and laboratory technicians.

These welfare functionaries are as different as one can get from the core functionary. They have civil service status, but it is viewed more as a fringe benefit than as a mark of identity. They have little sense of being "in the career service," and none at all, typically, of having their work touched by the magisterial dignity of the state. Their commitment to the job is low and their mobility is high, for their involvement typically is with The Profession rather than The Service.

Third, the welfare functionary has a greater chance of being a program entrepreneur (or perhaps a member of an entrepreneurial team) than does his counterpart in the regulative or the core sphere of government operations. This is because the family of welfare functions is less settled in its logic, more fluid in its technology, more expansive in its ideology than are the other two. Welfare operations are frequently on the frontiers of proven technology. Many welfare enterprises—the more usual term "program" does not convey the element of challenge—turn out to be pipe dreams because of a faulty technological assumption, but, after all, that is inherent in frontiersmanship and adds spice to the venture.

Functionalization, of both operations and management, has the best chance of succeeding in the old, long-established welfare functions like those of the Bureau of Indian Affairs and the Veterans' Administration, and their newer counterparts, the Social Security Administration and the U.S. Employment Service. Thoroughgoing functional rationality ought to meet the fewest obstacles in this sector, fewer even than in the sphere of the core functions, because most decisions can be routinized and decentralized, being neither irrevocable nor very weighty, and because there is plenty of room for the direct application of information-processing technology.

Welfare functionaries in these areas are professionals, overwhelmingly, on both the operational and management levels. Professional people, usually, are organizational conservatives insofar as any proposed rationalization threatens what they take to be their legitimate prerogatives in respect to autonomy in work. They are progressives, however, in respect to schemes to achieve organizational decentralization and the reduction of "bureaucracy," meaning layer upon layer of officials above them. This means that they accept limited functionalization of operations, provided it does not reorganize their work routines too drastically, and they positively welcome it if it brings operational policy and decision-making closer to operations itself. They want a voice in making policy, and they consider it their right as professionals to have it.

Welfare functionaries in the "hot" new fields of antipoverty operations,[2] manpower management and training, vocational rehabilitation, and urban problems generally do work that does not lend itself to rationalization, in either operations or management. Very often their efforts go into "demonstration projects" which are designed, quite frankly, to get experience as much as to achieve a practical objective. They are really a type of research; their purpose is to field-test known but unproven techniques, develop expertise, try out a few "blue-sky" ideas, and hope that the project will "stimulate fresh new thinking" about the whole problem. There is a certain amount of bureaucratization in that there is a budget to worry about, and a time schedule, and operational guidelines and evaluational criteria as set forth in the original proposal used as the basis for funding.

There is at least a short hierarchy of officials in these experimental ventures, and they are expected to conform to minimum standards of functional rationalization. In the nature of the case, however, it is understood that both the management structure and the organization of operations will be loose, even "sloppy."

CONCLUSIONS

Government work is nonmarket work, typically. When government agencies produce and sell things of immediate value in themselves, it is because the market does not work or cannot work, or because if it is allowed to work the results are socially undesirable. Utilities are either owned or closely regulated by government because they are natural monopolies. Government directly enters manufacturing during wartime in order to minimize profiteering and to keep costs and prices down. In time of depression, government expands its public works programs to keep prices up. (Government may deliberately create a competitive market situation, however, by requiring or encouraging the entry of new firms into a highly monopolized field, such as aluminum production, or it may even enter into direct competition with established firms in the private sector through its own agencies, such as the TVA.) The significance of the nonmarket character of government work is that, in general, it fosters bureaucratization and inhibits functionalization.

The government functionary works in a nonmarket situation which makes it difficult—not impossible, but difficult—to determine how well or how poorly any given individual or organizational unit is performing. (Defense Secretary Robert McNamara introduced cost-effectiveness analysis into the Department specifically to help remedy this problem.) As a result, the powers of the official are magnified at the expense of the technical expert's prerogatives. The standards used are top policy decisions made on the basis of ultimately political considerations, reflecting subtle shifts in the power structure and in conceptions of public policy (known in the beginning only to privileged insiders), and not the result of objective assessments of market conditions made by experts whose judgments are available to anyone. Lower-ranking government officials and functionaries generally find it hard to practice functional rationality, to functionalize their operations and organization structure, because of this element of irrationality built into nonmarket work situations.

Markets can be simulated through the use of computers, however, and there is no doubt that such techniques can be of great help in forecasting and planning in quasi-market situations—those in which the market is a factor although a remote one, as in the case of oligopoly. The same applies in situations in which, for purely practical reasons, the real market is not a factor, as in the case of utilities. But it must be borne in mind that market simulation as an aid to rationalization makes sense only when the market either is or could be a real factor in decision making, even though only one among others. In most government operations the technique would be no more than marginally useful, because the market is excluded from playing a role by logic and not merely by technical infeasibility.

The second prime source of the impetus to functionalize is technology. Technology as applied to the production of things which have value in the market, goods and services, is very far advanced; technology as applied to functionalization, that is, to human organization in operations and management, is much less so. Moreover, the technology of functionalization meets resistance in government operations because it is often hard to get a clear picture of what the goals are ("What is the name of the game?"), and even harder to do the personnel reshuffling and retraining, the respecifying of jobs that any serious degree of functionalization requires. Civil service people are naturally reluctant to see their comfortable skills and long-established work routines made obsolete, and they are somewhat less vulnerable than their counterparts in the private sector to being uprooted and relocated in the name of progress.

The logic of the functionary's work situation in government is not ideally conducive to functionalization, yet the functionary as a social type has his origins in government. Functionalization manifestly is a force in government operations, even though lack of the market and lack of a relatively unhampered technological thrust makes for unfavorable conditions. How can this be?

We talked about three rather distinct types of government functions and thus of government functionaries: the core functionary, the regulative functionary, and the welfare functionary. In order to explain functionalization in government, it will be useful to make a further distinction: between the *traditional* and the *rationalized* functionary. Both do work whose meaning, in the case of government, is that it helps fulfill a responsibility vested in an agency of the state. It requires skill in that it calls for knowing the routines and being able to give reasons for action. The difference between the two lies in the nature of the routines and in the reasons for them, in how they were worked out to begin with, and in the spirit in which the work is done.

The traditional functionary follows work routines that are unanalyzed. His reasons for them are abstracted *from* routines established originally for all sorts of reasons, rational as well as irrational, instead of being the logical basis *of* the routines. The whole thing is very much like the application of Anglo-Saxon common law. Decisions made case by case come to constitute a body of lore and precedent with a sacred character. Viewed as a whole, the corpus is full of anomaly and paradox; but a thorough knowledge and mastery of these logic-defying peculiarities, and ingenuity in getting around them to achieve something approximating substantive justice, is "the name of the game." Technical skill consists in the know-how that comes only from long experience in achieving the best possible result with the limited and terribly cumbersome means at hand.

The rational functionary's work routines ideally have nothing to do with tradition, rule-of-thumb, and sacred precedent. They are explicitly the result of an analysis of the function itself in relation to complementary functions and to the whole. Man-sized units of work are packaged and "specified" for optimum efficiency and effectiveness. The work of individual men is designed to realize the greatest possible benefit from operational and organizational technology. The functionary describes and defends the particular things he does and the way he does them by citing abstract rules of procedure from which his routines are derived.

The whole corpus of work routines and procedures are rational in that they constitute a coherent, articulated whole. Instead of the traditional functionary's bemused attitude toward the anomalies of antiquated principle and procedure he must work with, the rational functionary reveres the perfectly harmonious and elegantly integrated procedural canons that guide his conduct. He counts his skill not as pragmatic ingenuity but as technological expertise.

The traditional functionary is most often found in the core functions of government, but his style stamps the character of the older bureaus in regulative and welfare activities as well. The rational functionary is predominant in the newer bureaus, partly because they are less burdened by tradition, partly because they are more secularist in spirit. Moreover, the content of their work is the sort that lends itself to the exploitation of the latest technologies.

Finally, we can conclude that functionalization and accompanying functional rationality grow more prevalent in government operations generally, even though there are forces which hinder it, because more and more the people attracted to government work are already imbued with its logic. They themselves insist on modernizing operations, which means rebuilding the often antiquated organizational structure of agencies and respecifying tasks to incorporate the spirit and substance of the new technologies. It is, rather than an immanent development, a case of cultural importation, an invasion, an attack by a new social type bent on rooting out and supplanting the old.

5

Business

The businessman-as-functionary appeared only when the arche-typal business firm became a large-scale organization. The growth of the stock corporation, with its tremendous potential for acquir-ing new capital, necessarily separated ownership from control. Instead of the old proprietary entrepreneurs, managers with dif-ferent interests came to do different kinds of work. In turn, the need arose for management technologies of command and control.

Commerce, in retailing or wholesaling, did not enter such a process until quite recently. Before the growth of the large de-partment stores and the chains in the 1920's and 1930's, and more recently the supermarkets and supermarket chains, overhead costs were not a major factor in the management of capital. In business of any sort, it is only when overhead costs become large that administrative organization gets complicated; when business-men start worrying about keeping costs down, they suddenly see organization as a problem in itself. This happened first in industry, then in commerce, then in the service industries, where the proc-ess still has a long way to go.

INDUSTRY

The industrial revolution began in the late eighteenth century in cotton textile manufacturing, which first converted from the putting-out system (tools and materials were "put out" to the workers in their own homes) to the factory system. There had been earlier "manufactories," in which hundreds of workers and machines were assembled together under one roof (notably in Russia, in the state-sponsored armaments industry), but none that were entirely under private auspices and had to face open-market competition. Followed soon after by France, Belgium, and the United States, British entrepreneurs cut the costs of production of textiles dramatically by bringing a large work force of men and machines together in one building (the word "factory" derives from the French *factorerie,* which means warehouse), where the flow of production could be more easily scheduled, directed, and monitored.

Better work discipline and more uniform quality of product brought an immediate payoff in higher profits—*rationalization began at this point and it has never stopped.* It was quickly evident that foot- and hand-powered machines wasted energy, and it became economical, as the technology developed, to shift to wind, water, steam, and eventually electrical power. Machines were redesigned and workers' tasks respecified. The art of machine design to maximize efficiency and effectiveness developed into the highly sophisticated technology of mechanical engineering. By the mid-1880's the design and redesign of better production facilities, a continuous process, was routinized; it was safe to turn the mechanization of production over to the technologists, and to save entrepreneurial energies and talents for other tasks.

Frederick Winslow Taylor, known as the father of scientific management, noticed at about the same time an element of futility in designing better machines alone, because their operatives, the workers, were generally "lazy" and incompetent and used them at far less than capacity. The new machines had made the old handicraft skills obsolete, but the workers resisted the need to change their work routines and adapt to the requirements of the machines. Taylor set out, with the point of view of the mechanical engineer who sees the machine-operator as an extension of the machine, to "redesign" the worker. This new technology, the new "science" of management, would pick up where mechanical engineering left off, pushing production costs down to ever lower levels.

Taylor's technique of time-and-motion study to find the "one best way" of performing any given production operation did not in itself give birth to management technology, at least not directly, because it overlooked the problematics of human organization. But it pointed the way. It laid down the premise that the rationalization of work *functions* is necessary and desirable.

Early administrative organization

Until and even beyond the time of Taylor's early work, manufacturing was comparatively small scale. The typical large factory, or "mill," employed two or three hundred workers. A few employed several thousand, but even they, like the smaller plants, had a simple plan of organization. The owner, or the owner's agent, his deputy, assisted by a handful of key men, directly oversaw the work of anywhere from a few to as many as several dozen foremen. (In large plants there was an intermediate layer of superintendents between the two groups.) The foreman was essentially a labor contractor. He fixed wage rates, hired and fired, and kept his own records, if any. The "higher-ups" or "big bosses" usually left him alone if he got the work out. The front office staff was small.

The whole system was patrimonialist, personalized, not bureaucratic. This was possible because the small number of "bosses" made for short lines of communication and a great deal of face-to-face interaction. Men prided themselves on "knowing men," not routines; and there were not that many routines to know. As circumstances changed, procedures were adjusted pragmatically; if the usual way of doing things did not work, the fact was quickly evident, and a new method could be improvised by rule of thumb. There was a certain amount of division of labor, of course, but only as the artifact of countless improvised arrangements, bit by bit over time. The division of labor was not functionalized— that is, it was not thought through, seen whole, reduced conceptually to a system capable of being easily understood and of providing guidelines for evaluating procedures and devising new and better ones.

In short, because the system was not functionalized it was not rationalized, and it was not capable of being rationalized. There was room for task rationality but not for functional rationality. And, needless to say, without functional rationality there can be no functionaries.

The case of the railroads

World War I provided a vast stimulus to expanded production. This, and the cost-price squeeze which followed the war during the financial crisis and recession of 1921, jolted American manufacturing into functionalizing its organization. Long before that, however, the railroads had found it expedient to draw upon the experience of the military and to bureaucratize and functionalize. Most of its people who held operational and supervisory responsibilities by the time of the war were functionaries.

The railroads of the 1880's and 1890's were not a great deal larger than the nation's larger industrial plants in terms of the total number of employees. Some were quite small, in fact ludicrously small by modern standards: a few dozen miles long. But even the small roads had proportionately a heavy investment in capital; fixed costs were high absolutely and high in relation to direct production costs. Thus the railroads sought to economize their capital—perhaps even more than their labor costs—and to rationalize their operations.

The other impetus to functionalization was the extraordinary importance of communications. The communications problem was created by two circumstances peculiar to the railroads. First, the initiators and recipients of messages were ordinarily at some distance from one another and could not talk face-to-face. They had to rely on mail, telegraph, and eventually telephone. Second, in order to make optimum use of capital, roadbed, and rolling stock, the information contained in the messages had to be accurate, precise, and complete. Faulty scheduling of train movements, for example, could cause wasteful delays, confusion, and even accidents costly of human life and property. In the typical factory of the time, by contrast, most communications were face-to-face. The consequences of misunderstandings or lack of information by operating personnel were rather easily remedied and were much less frightful in their effects even if, through oversight, they stood uncorrected.

The case of the automobile industry

Functionalization entails bureaucratization, although bureaucratization, once it is firmly under way, turns about and fosters a further degree of functionalization. This proposition describes one step in the evolution of industrial organization generally. The sequence, first functionalization and then bureaucratization, need not be experienced by each plant in each firm in each industry. Once the precedent is established in one industry—which is what the railroads did, looking to the military for their model—other industries can be expected to follow as soon as they are ready and the need seems great. Then bureaucratization can be initiated and set on its course at the same time as functionalization, or it can even come before functionalization and serve as its midwife. This seems to be what happened, by and large, in the automobile industry.

Heavy investment in fixed costs did not occur in the automobile industry until the mass production stimulated by World War I. Several technological breakthroughs, in tires, glass, and metallurgy, and, most important of all, the moving assembly line, made it possible to produce cheap and durable automobiles for the first time, and Henry Ford showed that there was a huge domestic market to be tapped after military needs were met.

The shift from small-scale, handicraft production to mass production, which "deskills" the worker and builds production skill into an ever more elaborate man-machine production system, could not have been accomplished without a certain amount of piecemeal functionalization. The changeover in the automobile industry proceeded so rapidly, however, that the pace of functionalization lagged behind the needs created by technological advance and the logic of a production system distinguished by its heavy and intensive use of capital.

The stage was set for crisis, and it came with the sudden, sharp recession of 1921. The era of mergers and "management reorganization," which meant functionalization and bureaucratization, began and lasted throughout the twenties and into the thirties. The number of independent firms engaged in automobile manufacturing dropped from something over three hundred to less than fifteen by 1935. The wheeler-dealer financier, such as Sieberling, Willys, Leland, or Olds, was supplanted by the deliberately self-effacing, cool, rational manager, such as the new chief of the General Motors combine, Alfred P. Sloan, the very model of the modern tycoon who carries his modesty to the point of subtitling his autobiography, "Adventures of a White-Collar Man."

There can be no doubt that Sloan, Paul W. Litchfield of Goodyear, Owen D. Young of General Electric, and a number of similar men in the twenties were "engineers" in Thorstein Veblen's sense, as distinct from "robber barons," "captains of industry," or financial tycoons. They intuitively grasped the logic of modern industry, made it into a quasi-religious faith, and spent their lives not only propagating it but actually living it with an almost monkish fanaticism. Like their not-so-distant ancestors of early New England, they sought to build Jerusalem here, now, in the organizational sense. They saw functional rationality as a new ethical system: the individual must live totally for the Cause, he must not only accept but embrace the discipline demanded by the logic of the new industrial system. He must efface himself and ask others to do the same, all the way down the line.

The lesson taught by the crisis of the automobile industry was that the individual at all levels must learn to *think functionally*— to obey guidelines, to treat his superior as a consultant and not a "boss" in interpreting them (and to play that role himself in relation to his own subordinates), and to pour all his energy into innovating ways and means of performing that function more efficiently and effectively. The measure of his success as a functionary is the Better Methods he finds and installs. His job, regardless of the level of output and of market conditions, is to conserve labor, materials, and capital so that the cost of each unit of the product is pushed down toward the absolute minimum.

But what about Henry Ford? Ford, the maverick who pioneered the development of mass-production technology, lagged so in modernizing management that the Ford Motor Company as recently as 1948 was a museum of administrative antiquities, an organizational fossil losing $10 million a month. The fact is that Ford was superb at functionalization but hopelessly inept when it came to bureaucratization. He was the supreme modernist, brilliantly effective in grasping and implementing *technological* functionalization. But he obstinately refused to see that it could not work, it could not be sustained in the long run, without *organizational* functionalization as well. He insisted on personal management to the last—"There is only one title in this company, and that's president; and I'm the president." As sole proprietor of a billion-dollar enterprise, he could get away with it (although it cost him probably another billion dollars to do so: the company was worth less in 1946 than it was in 1926).

The railroads invented the industrial functionary, out of the needs of operating management, from the ground up, as it were. Detroit took the big step from personal, financially oriented management to a management of functionaries, because of a double crisis growing out of helter-skelter expansion to meet a booming

mass market: uneven and unarticulated technological development, and financial crisis growing out of the rapid shift to a mode
of production that required very heavy investment in capital.
Other manufacturing industries took their cue from the "General
Motors plan" of management and operational decentralization,
and turned over management to the new breed of functionaries.

It is worth remembering that military organizational doctrine
provided the model for early railroad functionaries, and later,
indirectly, for the full-fledged industrial managerial functionaries
of the twenties and after. Because of this, to this day they have a
hybrid character: half authoritarian, half consultative.

COMMERCE

As a field of business enterprise, commerce has a much longer
history than industry. But it has lagged behind industry in recent
years—let us say, since the post–Civil War period—in organizational development. It still is possible to find houses of commerce
that are essentially unchanged, in the organizational scheme which
reflects the logic of their operations, since the invention of double-
entry bookkeeping in the fifteenth century. Like the Ford Motor
Company in 1948, they are living fossils. Other companies, of
course, have taken full advantage of the computer revolution and
have cybernated everything in sight.

Commerce is business in its pristine form, before the survival
and welfare of *the enterprise* (something with an identity and a
reality of its own, over and above the entrepreneur) became a
factor to be reckoned with. The logic of the commercial venture
is very much like the logic of the military campaign: you win or
lose, you prevail or you are beaten back; you count time in ventures, each one a success or failure. The organization, such as it
is under these conditions, is nothing but a simple tool, easily
grasped even though it may have been fashioned with art, finesse,
even genius. Once the governance of the enterprise itself becomes
a factor, as it has been almost from the beginning in the industrial

sector, the game gets more complicated. The skill and energy of the entrepreneur then must be divided between gathering intelligence and maneuvering in the market, on the one hand, and continuously building, improving, and renewing the indispensable instrument of action, the enterprise, on the other.

In commerce, traditionally, the investment in fixed capital is low in relation to operating capital, and communications are simple. Neither of the two thrusts toward functionalization, as posited by the theory put forth here, is very strong. Without technological functionalization there is no need for organizational functionalization, and so there is little bureaucracy. The spirit and structure of organization are patrimonialist. And the traditional model is still viable in some fields. However, the modernizing commercial enterprise not only exists, it threatens to wipe out the traditional commercial house by realizing economies of scale and integration not available to it—for example, by reaching back, through vertical integration, all the way to the manufacturer himself. When it is successful, as in the case of the great chain department stores like Sears, Roebuck, it either obliterates the traditional commercial house or relegates it to a marginal role.

In the past, big commerce was wholesaling. The retail outlets were local "mom-and-pop" stores. Gradually the larger stores began to shift their basic logic of commercial activity from cornering staples to cornering customers: first the big department stores and chains, like J. C. Penney, specializing in dry goods and "notions," then the big supermarkets, stocking everything from apples to cold cream to zebra skins imported from Africa. The important thing is not the market, in the classic sense of Adam Smith, but the clientele. Will people buy or not? They cannot be trusted to be rational, so they have to be pre-sold through advertising.

Functionalization makes little sense in a commercial house whose business is limited to importing tea and spices and rum; the dollar value of the turnover may be quite large, but the entire staff may consist of two dozen people, including agents in various parts of the world. Business is done deal by deal, not continuously. Functionalization makes a good deal of sense in a commercial enterprise of the chain department store or chain supermarket type. Capital investment may involve hundreds of millions of dollars. Employees may total several tens of thousands in number. The products—thousands upon thousands, with almost as many brand names, and each brand with its own clientele of pre-sold customers—are so varied and voluminous that technologies of warehousing, inventory control, shelf management, customer relations, building maintenance, promotion, planning, personnel, and so on proliferate without end. And each produces its own specialized technicians, technical managers, and idea men who demand the attention of the store manager. This functionalization makes it necessary for him to create one or more strata of assistant managers to coordinate activities. And he himself finds that, as the chain expands, he must deal with a superior who is one or two levels removed from the final executive authority.

Functionalization creates specialized expertise, which in turn must be guided by layer upon layer of management specialists. Lines of communication become longer and longer, more and more complex. The commercial establishment finds itself, organizationally, more and more like the modern industrial enterprise. Functionalization creates the need for bureaucracy, and bureaucracy fosters an ever more rationalized and schematic, an ever more thoroughgoing functionalization.

The modern commercial house is ultimately no different from the modern industrial enterprise in essentials, in its reliance on functional rationality as an operating creed, and on the indispensable functionary who bears it.

SERVICES

The service industries are the last redoubt of the handicraft mode of operations. Most maintenance, repair, and renovation work is still in the hands of craftsmen, many of them self-employed. The master plumber is an example. The picture is mixed in the case of customer-service activities which call for little technical skill but a considerable degree of tact, good judgment, and skill in managing interpersonal relations. Dry cleaning and laundry services, automobile service stations, hotels, motels, restaurants, bars, and nightclubs are examples. Some managers are proprietors, but they face increasingly stiff competition from franchised operators.

A wholly different type of customer-service industry—better called public service—is that represented by banks and utilities. There is no room for small proprietors or franchised operators in a field dominated by some of the world's largest industrial organizations (the American Telephone and Telegraph Company is worth more than $15 billion).

What are the causes, conditions, and consequences of functionalization and bureaucratization in each of the three types?

Craft services

People need their toasters and television sets fixed, their toilets and sinks unstopped, their houses painted, plastered, rewired, their cars repaired, their hair cut or curled or cleaned, their teeth straightened, their children given lessons in piano or painting or ice skating, their health looked after, their trees trimmed, their legal affairs untangled, and, finally, their mortal remains laid to rest. These needs make work for a great many specialists whose main capital investment is handicraft skill, and whose style of operations follows a logic that has remained essentially unchanged for thousands of years.

The self-employed craftsman, including professionals like doctors and lawyers in private practice, has been able to prevail so long in this type of service industry because it requires little capital and less organization. The division of labor is external rather than internal, so there is little or no work-related communications activity. Without the need to economize capital or rationalize communications, the conditions which create a demand for functionalization are lacking. The independent craftsman holds the field against the functionary.

The indications are, however, that the functionary will prevail, if not tomorrow, then the day after. The first reason for thinking so is that burgeoning technology is creating the need for greater and greater capital investment in order to perform these services satisfactorily and at low cost. Painters, plumbers, doctors, landscape gardeners, even lawyers are finding that new materials, machines, and techniques are making it possible to do some things cheaper and better, and to do other things that could not be done before. The second is that technological advance is cracking the atom of skill monopoly the craftsman once had: this means new, highly rationalized specialties on the one hand, and a greater need for helpers, or permanent subcraftsmen—not apprentices—on the other. As a result, "team practice" is making inroads in work formerly monopolized by individual practice, because for the first time an internal division of labor (intra-unit) pays off in significantly greater efficiency and effectiveness.

The third reason for thinking that the independent craftsman's days are numbered is from the other side: the nature of the demand is changing. The consumer of craft services today is, paradoxically, both smarter and more ignorant than his counterpart a generation ago. The mass media have made him familiar with services in general, with what they can do for him and what they cost, but at the same time they have made him aware of his own lack of competence in deciding, rationally, which among a variety of services and of individual purveyors is best, and best for him. He may ask the advice of friends and associates, but in an increasingly urban, mobile society he may not trust them, either. He feels vulnerable. He is afraid of being "conned." The easy way out is to run down to Macy's to get his watch repaired, have Sears, Roebuck send out a crew to remodel his kitchen, contract with a landscape gardening service to keep his lawn mowed and his hedges trimmed, and join a health plan and a burial society to avoid having to choose a doctor and a funeral director.

This type of consumer is not yet in the majority, but it seems probable that he will be soon. The increasingly intensive use of capital and an increasingly elaborate internal division of labor, with the problems of communication and coordination the new scheme brings, means that things are changing faster and faster. Functionalization and bureaucratization in repair, renovation, and maintenance services, still new and moving at a relatively slow pace, are bound to speed up.

Customer services

Craft services are occasional, imperative, and often involve substantial cost because they require individualized attention and a good deal of skill. Customer services are relatively more commercial, standardized, impersonal, deferrable, require less individual attention, and require the application of skills that may be simple or complex, but are quite intangible.

One of the striking differences between the two types of service is the way in which functionalization occurs. In customer services it takes the form of lateral consolidation (several units brought into a single chain); in personal services it results either from efforts by an established, multifunctional enterprise to diversify operations, or from the decision of a group of specialists to coordinate their work and work places (team practice) and provide one-stop service.

One reason for the difference is that the customer buying service of the sort offered by the gas station, restaurant, or hotel is rather more interested in convenience and reliability than he is in nuances of difference in skills purveyed, quality of materials used, or competence of the practitioner. Moreover, he cares for little more than the façade of individualized attention. After all, not much is at stake: if you have seen one gas station, or one "luxury hotel," modern style, you have seen them all. A person's skill as a consumer has been made superfluous through proliferation and standardization. The dwindling minority of people who like to show "good taste" in such humdrum purchases are either hicks or aristocrats; they certainly are out of step with the new logic of urban consumership.

The other reason for lateral consolidation has to do with the economies of scale that can be realized through more efficient use of capital and management technique in operations. Customer-service establishments ordinarily have a moderate to heavy investment in fixed overhead costs. Much of this goes for land use, because location is a key factor in success or failure. Real estate values are notoriously changeable, and this puts the "independent," the owner-operator, at a considerable disadvantage. No matter how effective he is in lowering his operating costs and increasing his volume, his gains can be wiped out overnight through an increase in his rent ("Lost Our Lease—Must Sell") or, if he owns his land, by a boom in values that makes it economically irrational *not* to close his business and sell. The independent also suffers because the franchised operator, who is his direct competitor, gets many of his materials and services at lower cost. This includes auditing, accounting, personnel and payroll services, and management analysis, training, and consultation.

The chain operation removes not quite but nearly all the risks of a customer-service establishment. (The franchised operator is liable, ordinarily, only to the limit of the price he has paid for the franchise. In effect, he is a man who "bought himself a job.") And it can handle these risks much more efficiently. Both the management of capital (real estate is usually the biggest item) and the management of operations can be rationalized, which is to say, functionalized and bureaucratized. The latest technologies can be tried, because capital and know-how are available. The franchised operator becomes part of a system in which he is freed from the risk of losing his capital and from anxiety over whether he is modernizing fast enough.

The chain operation in the customer-service industry permits and fosters functionalization. The effect is to push proprietors back out of the picture, both on the top-management level and on the operational level. The formerly independent owner-operator as well as the real estate financier becomes a functionary or is displaced by a functionary.

Public services

The service industries cater to more-or-less whole *clients,* or to individual but relatively standardized *customers* (they fall into homogeneous groupings), or to the mass *public.*

Public services, for one thing, are those which meet a vital and continuous societal need. Virtually everyone in society depends on having them available to use, whether or not he actually has occasion to use them for days, weeks, months, or even years at a time. Water, gas, electricity, and sewage disposal are services the urban dweller needs constantly. He may not travel by air or rail very often, or even by bus, but he would feel deprived if he did not have those services constantly available. If his telephone is not working, if his garbage is not collected, if the streets, parks, and highways are unsafe for lack of police protection, if the building he lives in is dangerous because of code violations or an ineffective fire department, if he cannot get his rights protected or collect damages for civil wrongs because the courts have backlogs of unfinished business that force him to wait months or years, if the public schools are unable to provide his children with a decent environment and effective education—if any of these vital services breaks down, the urbanite is tempted to withdraw from "the whole stinking mess" and move to the suburbs. He may even fancy becoming a hermit, living in a cave in the woods. (But even then he would be the passive beneficiary of public services: forest rangers put out fires, policemen suppress crime, the armed forces provide security against foreign aggression.)

We have seen that, broadly construed, public services range all the way from those items that are merely convenient from the individual's standpoint—"maybe society couldn't live without air travel, but I could"—to those things that are vital to health and safety and well-being. Since this chapter is about functionaries in business, not in government, it will be useful to limit the category of public service to those which the individual user pays for directly, and which may be organized as private business firms and corporations. This includes all of the utilities and, with minor exceptions, the transportation and communications industries. (Film, radio, and television count as one branch of communications. The other consists of telephone, telegraph, mail, and message delivery.)

In this narrowed category of public services, capital investment is extremely high in relation to operating costs. Partly because of this, these services are inherently monopolistic or quasi-monopolistic (the air lines, for example) and subject to a large measure of government regulation. The operating unit is large, and the division of labor is complex and far advanced: experts are used extensively, to cope with legal problems and government relations, and to consult with and advise operations and planning personnel in making the best use of technology.

Thus we find nearly optimum conditions for functionalization and bureaucratization in the public service industries generally. The counterrational factor of individual choice, which hampers functionalization in the craft and customer-service industries, is so low that it is virtually insignificant. This is true because there is only one purveyor of the service, as in telephone communications, or else because the several competitive purveyors, as in television broadcasting, are only marginally differentiated in kind and quality—the choice between "I Love Lucy" and "The Beverly Hillbillies" is not one that allows much exercise of rationality. Technology may or may not be complex and volatile, but even when it is not, as in natural gas service, for example, the heavy involvement of government in operations, "looking after the public interest," more than makes up for it in the demand for technical expertise.

The industrial functionary first appeared in the older public service utilities as well as in the railroads. The "bureaucrat," a certain type of functionary, is associated in the public mind with government. It is not surprising that the first industry to have its operations regulated by an agency of government, the utilities, is also thought of as a stronghold of bureaucrats.

To the extent that service remains a special kind of commodity, one which must be tailored to the needs of the client or customer and so involves the application of skills at the point of sale, there is less occasion for functionalization and consequently fewer "pure" functionaries. Conversely, in a nonmarket situation, when the commodity becomes a vital need and its purveying becomes an activity "affected with a public interest," there is not only the opportunity but the demand to install functional rationality in place of market rationality. The functionary thrives as a social type to the extent that the direct influence of the market upon operations is curtailed or even eliminated as a factor in the organization of the industry.

CONCLUSIONS

The picture of the functionary in industry, commerce, and the services varies greatly, but one conclusion is clear: functionalization has made tremendous strides in all fields of business in modern industrial society (with the partial exception of personal or craft services), and every indication is that it will continue to do so.

Why?

First, capital is relatively cheap, plentiful, and available for investment in high-growth industries.

Second, the explosive advance of technology has made both the implements of production and the sustaining organizational structure obsolete in the older, capital-intensive industries; at the same time it has made it possible for industries formerly light and sparing in the use of capital and dispersed in small units to become consolidated and capital-intensive.

Third, the shift from an operational logic of "high profits, low costs" to a logic of "cost-effectiveness analysis" has greatly lessened the influence of the market as a factor which directly affects operations.

Fourth, the elaboration of management and management-service structures has greatly complicated the communications problem.

Fifth, for all of these reasons, better capital management, usable technological expertise, and communications efficiency and effectiveness have become requirements that can be met only through rationalization; and rationalization, in the context of large-scale organization with a complex technological base, demands a strategy of functionalization, with its inevitable concomitant, bureaucratization of administrative relationships.

The businessman-as-functionary has already become the predominant type in the United States, having displaced the older financial tycoon, the classical owner-entrepreneur, the capitalist ruling through an agent, the patrimonialist, the dictatorial family patriarch, and the craftsman proprietor. The logic of functional rationality demands nothing less, and it is the prevailing logic of modern industry.

6

Voluntary associations

In organizations we have been describing up to now, organizations in the military, government, and business, the people in them are employees and officials appointed by higher authority. The special character of voluntary associations is that the people in them are members and officials elected by the members.

The difference is clear enough in industry: one is a "member" of the Foreman's Association of America, but "with" General Motors. A manual worker is a member of the United Auto Workers, but he is "at," not "with," GM. A white-collar worker or a manager is with the corporation, but it is quite unlikely that even the president really considers himself a member of it— loose, homey metaphors of the we-are-all-members-of-a-big-happy-family sort notwithstanding. Nor does the stockholder. A business corporation has no members, only employees. Some of them, the white-collar people, are with it because they are administrative and technical staff and have career jobs. The others, the production workers, are not. Whether or not they work and how much they work depends directly on production schedules, which in turn depend on the state of the market for what they produce. The blue-collar workers are neither of the organization nor with it.

The distinction is not as clear in the case of government and the military. A man in military uniform is a "member" of the armed forces regardless of rank, and he is "in" or "with" a branch, division, and so on down to the company unit, and "has" a rank and a specialty. A man who works for the government ordinarily is "in" the civil service, but it sounds quaint to say that he is a "member" of it.*

The member gets something special from the organization. It provides him with a significant new identity and with the right to have and enjoy certain goods and services not available to the nonmember. He is entitled; others are not. But the organization gets something special from the member as well: he puts aside the calculus of self-interest and stands ready to serve in ways that can only be called altruistic, to hold attitudes, to act so that he volunteers a part of the moral terrain ordinarily considered private to the collective, quasi-public interests of the service.

The voluntariness of voluntary associations inheres in the distinctive quality of the pact entered into by the association and the member, held in force as long as he is a member, and not in whether or not he is free to join or leave. The constitutional logic of that pact is that each gains from the other something worth having: honor, duty, protection, love, acceptance—quite intangible things over and above tangible ones like the right to use the club swimming pool. The association serves the member and the member serves the association; there is a mingling of interests and mutual support. The condition and consequence are the kind of social-psychological, even spiritual, metamorphosis that is found elsewhere in modern experience only in marriage.

---

* Certain ancient or otherwise special elite corps are an exception. An individual is a member of the Peace Corps or the Foreign Service, no quotation marks around the word member needed.

This is the constitutional basis, not necessarily the actuality. There are different types of voluntary associations and different degrees and kinds of involvement by members, functionaries, and leaders.

LEADERS, OFFICIALS, AND FUNCTIONARIES

Lyndon Johnson, Richard Nixon, Walter Reuther, James B. Conant, Fidel Castro, the late Cardinal Spellman—one thinks of these individuals as examples of men who, because of their place in society, are of the type we call leader. Some are officials, some are not. Among those who are, we find some elected, some appointed, and some self-appointed. Among those who are not, there are opinion leaders, influentials, spokesmen for a sect, an establishment, or The Establishment.

It appears that a leader is not necessarily an official, an official is not necessarily a leader, and neither of the two types can be called a functionary without implying that he is something less than what he is. But the fact is, leaders and officials have done and continue to do functionary work as part of their regular activities. The process of functionalization is never complete, and so the general-purpose man, the statesman, the decision-maker, always has a basketful of nonroutine unfunctionalized work to do. His routine work does not make him a whole functionary, but it does make him akin to the species; and it reminds us that work done by functionaries in voluntary associations is in essence work formerly done by the leader that was given over to specialists.

Leadership functions

There appear to be four basic leadership functions in voluntary associations. They are listed below, with the role and typical activity corresponding to each.

The leader of a small association (or movement, which is a sort of informal association) that prospers and grows into a mil-

Types of Leadership Functions in Voluntary Associations

FUNCTION	ACTIVITY	ROLE
1. Maintenance	keep, monitor, police	Apparatchik
2. Action	organize, mobilize, direct	Militant
3. Intelligence	plan, teach, explain	Intellectual
4. Command	administer, mediate, fight	Politico

lion-member giant is in somewhat the same position as the small proprietor who winds up simply one among several major stockholders and officials of a billion-dollar corporation. Each started out running a one-man show, and as the price of success, each had to take more men into his organization to specialize in doing things he formerly did himself. He delegates authority but he also allocates functions, and just as his control is progressively attenuated as layers of command build up, his virtuosity is circumscribed as he relinquishes one function after another.

There is a pattern in the process of functionalization, just as there is in bureaucratization. The first function to be spun off, typically, and assigned to a specialist is maintenance. The activities of monitoring the work of others, policing their activities in order to secure discipline, and keeping the sacred symbols of the brotherhood from being profaned through mishandling are rather easily reduced to routine and rationalized. And so the first functionary to emerge, in the natural history of a voluntary association, is the type I have called the apparatchik. He is responsible for what is called housekeeping, "the business side of things."

Action and intelligence are the next two functions the leader relinquishes as his work load gets unmanageably heavy. Planning, teaching, and explaining are not hard to routinize. They are suitable for assignment to specialists, because a highly developed technology is available for use in these activities, and there are plenty of technicians—intellectual functionaries—ready to be brought in and put to work. Organizing, mobilizing, and directing activities are much less easily given over to functionaries. The militant, the type who carries out the action function, is usually in short supply and inexpert. Moreover, like the apparatchik, with rare exceptions he must be found and developed from within.

Command is the one function that may be shared but not relinquished. Partly this is because command activities—administering, mediating, fighting—can be routinized only to a limited degree. The politico functionary is an operator, a technician with his own fund of expertise, and so he is a true functionary in type. It is in the nature of the game, however, that all the technique in the world will not help him if he lacks the personal style to make it work. The politico's predicament is just the opposite of the militant's. The militant may be enthusiastic, energetic, truly dedicated, even charming, and yet without technical expertise he cannot be effective.

Command cannot be handed over to functionaries because it resists rationalization except within narrow limits, as we have seen. But the larger reason is that command is the core function of the leader, particularly, although not exclusively, in voluntary associations. It is the mark of the sovereign. The leader who shares it too freely with his lieutenants, no matter how trusted, or fails for any reason to give his frequent attention to mending fences, neutralizing challengers, isolating hostiles, developing confidants, coopting militants, polishing his image, revitalizing his charisma, and renewing the coalition of political forces that constitutes his power base, eventually finds himself out of touch and left behind.

The game of power is played *with* functionaries but not *by* functionaries. Functionaries of the politico type, the lieutenants, do have a part in the game, but they do not play it for themselves and in their own right—at least not legitimately. They are still the king's men. The charismatic leader sets policy; the politicos show their particular style as functionaries by the combination of personal flair and technical expertise they muster in doing *their* part, which is to carry out the policy.

The pattern of functionalization depends a great deal on the kind of voluntary association in which it occurs. Obviously, there are large differences between the Westwood Country Club and the New York Karate Club, the Communist party and the Republican party, the Future Farmers of America and the American Medical Association, the United Auto Workers and the United World Federalists, the Audubon Society and the Hispanic Society, the National Association of Manufacturers and the National Association for Mental Health, the Moslem Brotherhood and the Brotherhood of Locomotive Engineers, to pick out a few. But each has problems of recruitment, indoctrination, record-keeping, financing, action-programing, factionalism, struggle against hostile outside forces—in short, problems of leadership. Leadership is too much for any one man, unless the association is very small, and so functions are spun off, as we have seen, by setting up an apparatus of officials and technical aides.

It will be useful to look at how functionalization works by considering it in relation to some major types of voluntary associations.

People come into voluntary associations because they have interests and needs that can be met satisfactorily in no other way. Following Max Weber's usage, I have tried to specify the prime *material* interest and the prime *ideal* interest the individual has in being a member. He is a member of a religious-type association, for example, because he and the group have a place in society that predisposes them to hold beliefs about the good and true and a vested ideal interest in personal salvation. At the same time, they have a stake, a vested material interest, in influencing others by demonstrating exemplary personal and corporate rectitude.

The same logic applies to the reasons why people join fraternal- and political-type associations. One joins a political party or movement because he wants to see society changed; he has a

Types and Characteristics
of Voluntary Associations

ASSOCIATION TYPES	MEMBERSHIP BODY	MATERIAL AND IDEAL INTERESTS	ARCHETYPAL FUNCTIONARY
1. Religious	faithful congregation	–influence (M) –personal salvation (I)	Intellectual
2. Fraternal	solidary brotherhood	–money (M) –sociation (I)	Apparatchik
3. Political	totemic fellowship	–power (M) –social salvation (I)	Politico

NOTE: The letter "M" in the Interests column signifies material interest, and the letter "I" signifies ideal interests.

vested ideal interest in "social salvation," and he sees that the way to achieve this is by going after power—that is his vested material interest. The member of a fraternal association wants the experience of sociation, being with and of the body of one's peers, because it is a good thing in itself to stand shoulder to shoulder and be solidary, to constitute a brotherhood. That is his vested ideal interest. His material interest, along with his fellows, is to gain protection for his livelihood (and a kind of private social insurance against the economic consequences of death and other severe personal hardships) through mutual self-help. Ideal and material interests are complementary. Each is a means to the other taken as an end.

The function of a voluntary association reflects the combination of ideal and material interests that draws and holds the members. Type of association is again the differentiating factor.

A religious membership body has the character of a faithful congregation, while its counterpart in a political association is better described as a totemic fellowship. If we bear in mind that these distinctions are relative and not absolute, we can see certain interesting differences. The political membership body, for one thing, is more secular, more activist, and more game-oriented than the religious body. The point is to win against a real, live, tangible earthly opponent in a contest for power. The totemic symbol (donkey, elephant, hammer and sickle, and so forth) defines and identifies oneself and one's fellows, reminds the individual of what the game is about, and boosts morale—like the flag on the battlefield in a Civil War movie. The religious congregation or community rests on a cohesive bond which is typically deeper and stronger. The individual knows much more about his identity because there is so much more to know—the body of lore is endless—and so much more latitude to care, because the whole self is engaged. Moreover, the congregation of communicants seeks not to win but to prevail.

A fraternal membership body has the character of a solidary brotherhood. The bond that unites the members is not as deep and reverential as the sense of mystic communion ("brothers in Christ," "children of Israel") felt by the congregation of the faithful, and less enthusiastic and activistic than the tie that holds the totemic fellowship together. It is more mundane, yet at the same time it is socially more encompassing and friendlier. Typically, there are more little social circles of people who have known each other well and for a long time—circles within circles, intersecting circles, and large circles which loosely include a number of smaller ones. The point is to be sociable, because this justifies and is justified by the overriding importance of solidarity of the "brothers" ("comrades," in old-socialist language). Members are more "brotherly" than their counterparts in religious and political associations because their reasons for belonging touch more directly on their central life-interests in modern society.

The intellectual, the apparatchik, and the politico are the archetypal functionaries, respectively, for religious, fraternal, and political associations. The archetypal functionary is one whose activities and expertise best exemplify the character of the organization. What *he* does is what *it* does, or does most characteristically. The intellectual is the archetypal functionary of the religious association, for example, because above all the member of the congregation must have his life and experience interpreted for him in terms of the doctrine he has been taught. The member of the solidary brotherhood of the fraternal association needs good, solid, reliable men to conduct the mostly routine business of the association. This is a prescription for the apparatchik as archetypal functionary. In a political association, the name of the game is political infighting and outfighting, and at the same time the creation, or re-creation, of associational unity through coalition government. This calls for the expertise of the politico.

The types and different characteristics of voluntary associations are quite abstract and rest on greatly simplified assumptions. We must not confuse typological analysis with empirical description. Just to take one example, it is obvious there are many subtypes of fraternal associations, and their functionaries engage in a far wider range of activities than the monitoring and policing of the apparatchik. He is not the only functionary type in them, and he is not even archetypal in some associations at certain stages in their development. Types are designed to tell us what we can expect to find when we consider some concrete instances of the three major kinds of voluntary associations in the sections below.

Religious associations

Religious associations come in all kinds of organizational shapes and sizes. There are churches, sects, denominations, cults, and movements, each with its typical structure of arrangements defining the relations between leaders and followers, functionaries and members. Nonetheless, any religious association has the character of a congregation or community of those who profess the faith and wish to be associated with their fellow communicants. Every religious association holds up a creed consisting of doctrines, more or less formalized, concerning the ultimate meaning of life, and sets forth a scheme of spiritual and mental discipline which follows from it. The individual is provided with the means to escape sin and find virtue ("salvation" as it is understood in Christian and quasi-Christian religions).

Christian churches and denominations, and their equivalents in the Jewish Orthodox, Conservative, and Reformed congregations, carry on the full range of functions characteristic of voluntary associations. The intellectual (the clergyman) is the archetypal functionary, but in some cases the apparatchik, the militant, and even the politico are to be found as well. The extent of personnel depends on factors such as size, wealth, and the way in which the church views its mission in the modern world.

The large, wealthy, urban congregation usually has committed itself long since to a doctrine called "the Social Gospel." Affluent and sophisticated people in the worldly sense lose interest in the mysteries of faith and seek redemption here and now. Philanthropy, social service, renewing old bonds of brotherhood and creating new ones, clarifying issues of civic morals, even engaging in direct political action are the activities that grip the largely secularized conscience of the individual member. The old rituals are kept, in simplified form, as symbols of respect for dead beliefs. They evoke nostalgia and are considered beautiful in themselves, but they have little to do with the real business of the congregation.

The effect on the organizational structure of the church of this emphasis on social service and community work is quite striking. The new activities expand to the point where they become routinized and rationalized into functions, and this generates a need for technical expertise and rationalization of the support, or housekeeping, functions. Here is a clear instance in which, in recent times, functionalization has led to bureaucratization: the proliferation of specialized staff functionaries (apparatchiks, specialized intellectuals, and a tamed and skilled type of militant) has compounded problems of control and coordination and so fostered bureaucratization. The "hierarchy," an opprobrious term in the Protestant world at the time of the Reformation, has returned in a different form in the major denominations. And the ancient, tradition-bound hierarchy of the Roman Catholic Church has recently been shaken to its roots by the modernizers, who are of course the functionalizers: the doctrines they propound constitute a rationale for the new, secularist activities of the Church.

The small, poor, rural or small-town congregation, if it is independent, has more of a sectarian than a churchly character. It sticks to "old-time religion" and tries to avoid community work as frivolous. The mass media have undermined its insularity and its authority, however, to the point that it feels compelled to have at the very least a youth program if it is not to wither away for lack of new members.* Generally speaking, however, the apparatus of action and administration is quite rudimentary and is staffed, except for the clergyman, by lay notables with no special expertise.

A sect that is not static and introverted but is still in its evangelizing phase is different. It has much more the character of a cult or movement. The so-called Black Muslims (the Nation of Islam) are a good example. The church has a number of branches (mosques), a school, several business establishments, a newspaper, and a youth club for girls and young women and another for young men (called "The Fruit of Islam"). The rather considerable staff, including the clergymen, or ministers, is recruited from within the organization. At the apex is the supreme leader, unchallenged and unchallengeable: Elijah Muhammad, Messenger of Allah.

The ordinary sect is administered by lay notables (usually

---

* The Youth Director is likely to be a traditional rather than a rational type of functionary, however, in order to minimize the contamination of secular influence. An instance of a compromise arrangement occurred in Idaho. A church hired a specialist in dance to manage its youth program—with the understanding that dance practice and instruction would be referred to as "rhythmic play."

called deacons or elders), and so it is unbureaucratic. Its few functionaries are lay dilettantes with a smattering of technical expertise. Only the minister is—or may be—formally qualified for the work he does, and even then his role is more that of the entrepreneur than the functionary.

The cult-sect is not just unbureaucratic, it is anti-bureaucratic. It venerates its leader and permits the apparatus to consist entirely of his personally loyal retainers. The only specialists who develop are the home-grown type who acquire their skills incidentally while carving out a role for themselves in the organization and learning to play it well.* Functionalization is perceived in the sect and the cult to be an even greater danger than bureaucratization, because it directly undermines the insularity a sect needs in order to survive.

A religious association of the movement type is too formless to have functionaries, or even a single leader or an organized leadership structure. Instead of members it has adherents. It is significant as an associational form, however, because it is often an embryonic cult-sect.

Fraternal associations

Fraternal associations include trade unions, professional associations, cooperatives, clubs, and orders. They have their historical antecedents in craft and merchant guilds; so-called "friendly societies" of common people who relied on one another for help in providing dowries and funerals; aristocratic dueling fraternities and social clubs; and secret societies in the form of secular cults. Some have survived, changed but still recognizable. Some have collapsed, their functions absorbed by organizations better adapted

---

* But personal entrepreneurship can be tricky and dangerous, because it implicitly threatens the monopoly of charisma claimed by the leader. Witness the fate of Malcolm X, who defected or was expelled from the Nation of Islam. He foresaw his own assassination, and events proved him a good prophet.

to new times. Some have declined and disappeared as social change made their functions meaningless.

Trade unions are the best single example of the major type of modern fraternal association, especially the industrial unions that make up the CIO (now merged with the AFL). The typical CIO union, the United Auto Workers, for example, preserves many of the old traditions passed down from the earlier, heroic period of trade union organizing. Old heroes are venerated, moments of valor in the face of outrageous persecution are recalled, and "Solidarity, Forever!," a sort of national anthem of the American trade union movement, is sung on ceremonial occasions. But the UAW has an old-socialist heritage as well, which the still vigorous Reuther brothers personify. The result is that even though bread-and-butter issues are still paramount—more money, better working conditions—the realization of welfare and justice and a more humane society are part of the union's mission. As the number of practicably organizable workers grows smaller, the functionary who was formerly a militant becomes either an apparatchik or a politico; or if he remains a militant he shifts the sphere of his operations from organizing and recruiting to welfare and social service.*

The older, more conservative craft unions that constituted the pre-merger AFL, plus a few independents such as the railroad brotherhoods, define the union's mission much more narrowly. They have little use for welfare, social service, and cultural activi-

---

* The militant may not care to become a "welfare worker" because it brings him into activities in which the intellectual functionary is preeminent —and he cannot realistically hope to acquire the intellectual's expertise. He may not care much for the apparatchik role, either, because it is highly routinized and rationalized. The politico's function is hard to get because so much depends on sponsorship and personal ties, who-knows-whom. If he becomes sufficiently frustrated, the former militant may rebel and try to become an opposition politico. This is a dangerous course because it means challenging the leader and the whole political establishment he has built.

ties, or programs of any sort, and so the militant as a functionary type belongs completely to the past. The organization is made up of a few politicos at the top, and the rest are apparatchiks. There is a small but growing place for the intellectual functionary, however, not to teach and explain so much as to assist in planning. Effective collective bargaining has become difficult without batteries of lawyers and accountants, and a few of the conservative unions even have regularly established research departments. All have newspapers, some have public relations men, and a few have speech writers.

Trade unions are not the only kind of economic interest association, but the others, consumer cooperatives and professional associations, for example, have a number of things in common with them. In all, the effect of functionalization has been to push the militant into eclipse, exalt the apparatchik, and cast the intellectual functionary in the role of rising star. The politico has remained an important type (although now he is concerned more with maintaining than with creating a coalition as the leader's power base), but just as he was once overshadowed by the militant, he must now accept the apparatchik as the archetypal functionary.

The second major subtype of fraternal association, the social club, is not really very sociable. Luncheon clubs—Rotary International, Lions, and the like—meet once a month so that members can see and be seen. Business and professional men need these contacts to carry on their work—informal socializing is a means to an end. Officially they constitute a solidary brotherhood, however shallow, which reflects the constitutional logic of the association. The archetypal functionary is an apparatchik, the secretary, because everyone knows that the president is a ceremonial figure who merely presides. There are a few militants, but they are come-and-go dilettantes and so cannot be called functionaries; similarly, amateur politicos and sojourning intellectuals are drawn in at times, but there is so little in the way of a real bureaucracy within the association that there is no significant functionalization.

Clubs with facilities offer their members the use of squash, tennis, and handball courts, golf, swimming pools, gyms, lounges, bars and restaurants, and sometimes lodging rooms in the manner of a hotel. Athletic clubs are mostly downtown, indoors, and exclusive (Union League Club, Racquet Club). Their membership tends to be old upper class (a few of the "best" still bar Jews), and men only. Country clubs are suburban, outdoors (they have golf and outdoor tennis, and usually an outdoor pool), mostly upper middle class in character, and familistic rather than masculine in social atmosphere. The membership has very little of a brotherhood character. Just about the only manifestation of the brotherhood that remains is the ease of sociability; one has the sense of being among peers. The functionaries of these clubs are not in themselves members, ordinarily, but hired staff. (The members elect a governing board which appoints a manager, who then assembles a staff.) There really is no place for the militant or the politico. The functionaries are apparatchiks and skill specialists—functionally analogous to intellectuals—like the golf pro, who teaches and coaches people who frequently are his social superiors.

The third fraternal subtype is the order, or secret society. One thinks of the Moose, the Elks, the Odd Fellows, the Knights of Pythias, the Shriners, and the grandfather of them all, the Masons. The order is a phenomenon of rural and small-town America. In its constitutional logic it is patterned after the illicit and subversive secret society the Masonic Order once was, and the craft guild of medieval times. Now, of course, the ritual secrecy and the elaborate hierarchy, corresponding to demonstrated merit and proficiency in knowledge and ability to practice the mysteries of the craft, are mostly play. But it is play taken seriously by a few, half-seriously by the rest. The new member gets in by being sponsored, and in the beginning he is subjected to a certain amount of hazing. In theory, to join the order is to take up a vocation: the new member must show he is willing and able to play the game. Again in theory, the membership is a close-knit brotherhood of fellow vocationers who look up to their elders, the notables of high degree, for advice and example that is both technical and moral.

The archetypal functionary in the order is an apparatchik of a peculiar kind. His activities are keeping (conserving, preserving), monitoring, and policing, and he brings a considerable measure of technical skill to his work. At the same time, he is a member and a notable, his work is part time and generally unpaid, and so he has the character of the dilettante as much as of the true functionary. The same is true of the intellectual. He is venerated and sought after for his ability to teach and explain the craft mysteries, but in all likelihood his office is informal and his work is part time and casual. There is no room at all for the politico, and very little for the militant (some orders sponsor lavish programs of social service—hospitals and the like—but they usually rely on outside professionals to execute them).

The spirit of brotherhood is in principle stronger in the order than in any other type of fraternal organization, yet it is the least bureaucratized and functionalized. Probably this is because the "craft" of the order is farthest removed of the three subtypes from the central life-interests of its members. The volatile, fast-moving life of the big city makes the order too portentous in style, more of a handicap than a social advantage. Small towns and small cities are generally rather static: the theory still is that what counts is who you are, not so much what you do. The warm sociability, the identity, the sense of trust in one's brothers in the order is what counts in terms of livelihood, because in the small town one likes to do business with friends, and one expects reciprocity.

Political associations

The range of political associations in the Western world includes three types of parties: (1) those which seriously seek electoral victory or participation in electoral victory, such as Republicans and Democrats in the United States, Laborites and Conservatives in Great Britain, and parties of the social-democratic or Christian-democratic type in Western Europe and the Scandinavian countries; (2) parties and groups with an ideological and sectarian character which may or may not run or endorse candidates, but mainly seek to influence public opinion ("third parties" such as the Progressives, Socialists, Dixiecrats, Prohibitionists, American Labor party, Liberal party, Americans for Democratic Action, Conservatives, and the new Black Panther party in the U.S., and their counterparts in Canada and Europe); and (3) parties that are anti-parliamentary and totalitarian (Nazis, Fascists, Communists), that operate legally or illegally, depending on circumstances, and have the character of a movement. Discussion clubs and "youth movements" (ephemeral associations of college students for the most part) should be classed with the second type, and overtly subversive organizations (the Minutemen, the Ku Klux Klan, the American Nazi party, the Progressive Labor party) are akin to the third.

Boundaries are hard to define in all types of political associations because the difference between supporter and member is blurred. The electoral party is more mythic than real most of the time for most of the people in it. Presidential elections in the U.S., for example, pull around 70 per cent of those qualified to vote into affiliating themselves nominally with the Republican or the Democratic party. But at best their preference is a crude measure of allegiance, because there is always a certain amount of split-ticket voting and a certain number of nonaffiliated voters, independents, who vote for "the man and not for the party." This is dramatically evident in the significantly smaller turnout of voters for mid-term and local elections. A great many people who consider themselves Democrats or Republicans actually come out and vote for their party's candidates only once every four years, when the drama and excitement of the presidential race activates their latent party adherence.

The party pros, those who work faithfully during every election and stay involved in party activities continuously, make a commonsense distinction among leaders, activists, regulars, and constituents—a rough scale of involvement ranging from high to low. Most people are constituents: the pros figure the party is doing a lot for them if they only knew it. They need the party—but they also need persuading, and so mobilizing them, getting them to see where their interest lies, and galvanizing them into acting on it is one of the pro's major activities between and during election campaigns. Functionalization of these activities creates an organizational need for the militant and the intellectual.

The militant and the intellectual are not the archetypal party functionaries, however, because mobilization of the followership is not as crucial as organization of the leadership. This is the job of the politicos. Their work, the work of coalition-building, is excruciatingly difficult and morally corrosive.* The politicos are the leaders, the experts on power, the ones who decide finally on the party's slate of candidates. If they are entrenched and high-handed—meaning they have alienated enough people to allow a significant opposition to develop—they are "bosses." If they err in the opposite direction and worry too much about popular support, they are "weaklings." Either way they are archetypal functionaries, or quasi-functionaries, and their activities and expertise make them politicos.

Political sects are stranger animals than electoral parties. It seems at first to be carrying typological license too far to place a moribund relic of a lost cause like the Prohibition party in the

---

* New York City's Mayor Lindsay's disparaging remark about "the power brokers," in connection with a transit strike in 1966, evoked deep echoes of concern among the pros in local politics and those who have some appreciation of the deadly imponderables of the game.

same class with a snappy, modern, effective organization like the Liberal party of New York, or the Americans for Democratic Action, or even the Conservative party, which has managed to show a good deal of electoral strength in New York in recent years. There is a common denominator, however: political sects run candidates or endorse candidates not in order to win elections but to muster opinion and use the currency they gain as a means of buying their way into the power structure. Moreover, in the logic of their situation as permanent third parties (a true third party is either a thing of the moment or else it seeks to displace one of the two electoral parties), they must be fiercely ideological in utterance but softly pragmatic as they play the game of power behind the scenes.

The relations between the political sect and the major electoral party to which it is most closely akin, as the ADA is to the Democratic party, for example, follow the same logical pattern of coalition-building that is the life of the electoral party. The alliance between the two, as it is normally concluded, is understood to be momentary and to have the character of an honest "deal," an arrangement in the interest of both parties because it reflects the real balance of political forces. The virtue of the political sect is compromised by such a marriage of convenience, but not without gain. If the electoral party wins, it pays off in the hard cash of power.

The sect has leaders, activists, regulars, and constituents, just as the party has. But its constituents are far fewer, much more dedicated, and generally expect a much more personalized relationship with the inner circle. The result is that the militant as functionary has a smaller role to play. The apparatchik is relatively more important, and the intellectual, as planner, theoretician, and expounder of ideological principles and doctrine, is absolutely more important because the sect's ideological commitments are fairly narrow. Its members and adherents are devoted to principle first of all; they play the game of power usually with reluctance and some disdain as a means to an end. "We've shown that opportunism works," as the top official of one of the more important political sects put it. He and his fellow politicos could not have done it, considering the ideological touchiness of the members, without the aid of the intellectuals.

The politico is the sect's archetypal functionary. He is the one who actually arranges the deals and manages the coalitions which the sect must enter into if it is to be effective as a political entity. The intellectual functionary helps plan these maneuvers and then portrays them to the rank and file as necessary to realize the association's mission, yet consistent with ideological principle.

Unlike the electoral party or the political sect, a movement has no membership, only a body of adherents. It is not itself a party, although typically it contains one or more parties in it that claim leadership and in fact represent the more militant elements in each of the several branches that make up the whole. To complicate the picture, the movement has spokesmen who do not affiliate with any of the parties or organized groups, such as committees, rallies, institutes, and the like, but take an independent line. The Abolition movement, the women's suffrage movement, the labor movement, the civil rights movement, and the contemporary peace movement are examples of what we usually mean when we speak of a political movement.

The movement has no membership and no leadership, at least not in the proper sense; but it does have followers, and the followers have leaders. Above all, it has a cause. Shapeless as it is, the movement must be considered a type of political association. Its cause is the functional equivalent of the avowed mission of the more conventional voluntary association. Devotion to the cause and action in pursuit of it, often cooperative, constitute the functional equivalent of membership.

The informal groups, or bands, that cluster around one or another leader have something of the character of a military task force, and at the same time of a political club. Quite often the informal band organizes itself into an association not very different from a stable political sect, such as the Committee on

Racial Equality (CORE) was until the departure of James Farmer in 1965 (which signaled a change in character and direction), and engages in sect-like political bargaining. Or it may go to the other extreme and become a revolutionary, semi-underground, paramilitary organization like the Communist party. The Progressive Labor party, the Militant Labor Forum, and the Resistance, on the left, and the John Birch Society, the Ku Klux Klan, and the Minutemen, on the right, are other examples. The Black Panther party, the Student Non-Violent Coordinating Committee (SNCC) under the leadership of Stokely Carmichael and then H. Rap Brown, and the new CORE under Floyd McKissick are examples of similar formations in the black power movement.

Movements and movement parties are different from electoral parties and sects in that, as long as the movement is truly alive (it has a way of living on as myth after death, as in the case of the labor movement, for example), its apparatus consists almost entirely of activists who evolve rather quickly into functionaries of the militant type. The movement disdains the apparatchik, mistrusts the intellectual, and considers the politico positively immoral.

The result is a great waste of human energy—"you have to call a meeting to get a letter written." Whatever the movement is, it is not efficient. It can get things done, however. Efficiency is not necessarily related to effectiveness. Movements succeed when they are able to mobilize forces on a vast scale and channel them toward a narrow and specific end.

The militant is the archetypal functionary during the early, heroic phase of the movement. Everything is done in his style and reflects his spirit. But movements, like men, move into middle age; and at that point the apparatchik and the intellectual move in, and the politico moves in and takes over. In the normal course of events, the movement becomes deradicalized, efficient, and pragmatic: it becomes a sect.

The socialist movement today, or the wreckage of it, illustrates the aging process of movements. One tendency is for the movement to wither away in doctrinaire futility. As it fades, the old hero-militants somehow hang on and keep their miniscule party going. One thinks of Daniel DeLeon's Socialist Worker's party, a tiny remnant of the Marxist and anarcho-syndicalist Industrial Workers of the World. During and just after the First World War, the IWW threatened to engulf the labor movement and even overthrow capitalism in America—or so many people feared, including Attorney General Palmer.

Another tendency is for the movement to become a tame, reformist, lib-lab (liberal-labor) political sect, which is the path chosen by the Socialist Party of America under Norman Thomas. A third tendency is to forget both doctrine and mission and concentrate on building an apparatus of professional revolutionaries. This was the path taken in Russia by Lenin and later by Trotsky. As early as 1906 Lenin split the Russian Social-Democratic party (Marxist) by condemning it for its ideological and organizational disarray, which he blamed on its attachment to the forms of bourgeois parliamentary democracy. It had become nothing but a futile debating society, in his view, and so he pulled his followers, the Bolsheviks, out and organized the Third International.

Lenin's organizational dicta called for a totally new kind of party, one with the character of a paramilitary combat organization. All members were to be fully committed activists with quasi-military discipline. No more do-gooders, well-wishers, Sunday zealots, amateurs, dilettantes, schismatics. To be admitted to the party was to become part of an elite corps of professional revolutionaries under a single command. It was to join the secular version of a monastic order; the new member left everything behind him, all values and interests that might weaken his dedication or distract him from his duty as a Communist—he was twice-born and given a party name to symbolize his new identity (and to foil the police). He was chosen, trained, and commanded by the party, yet at the same time he was a responsible part of it, responsible for what it did and what it was. Through the device of "democratic centralism," which provided for upward delegation of authority, he was in duty bound to make his own view of correct doctrine known until the moment the Central Committee acted and made a decision for all. After that he was expected to embrace the general line and execute it fervently and faithfully.

The functionary spirit is carried to a high pitch in the Communist party, because of the thoroughgoing emphasis on functional rationality as a guide to conduct throughout the ranks. The serious use of the pseudo-scientific jargon of Marxism-Leninism shows this vividly. Ritualistic, cumbersome, and rhetorical as it is, it nonetheless provides a universal language of analysis and discourse.

The functionary style of thinking and acting, and even of feeling—it becomes a mode of relentless self-rationalization—is not supported by a significant functionalization of the organizational structure. The various functions are recognized and studied intensively, with the aim of developing technical expertise and applying it as widely as possible to party operations. But specialism as such is discouraged. In its constitutional logic, the Leninist party is a party of cadres (leaders, generalists). Every member is an expert, ideally, whether his activities of the moment happen to be of the apparatchik, the intellectual, or the politico variety. The only respectable functionary role is that of militant; but every Communist is a militant by definition, and so in theory it cannot be a specialty.

Theory, myth, and actuality always diverge, however, and the Communist party is no exception. The myth that the party is the vanguard of the revolution mobilized exceptional energies, and they made up for the loss in efficiency that followed from the principled refusal to be guided by the logic of functionalization. The myth thus governed duty assignments as well as the development of technological expertise. On the other hand, functionalization was in fact followed through: everyone was a militant, but after a time there were apparatchik-militants, intellectual-militants ("theoreticians"), and, of course, just plain rank-and-file militants. The militant style and demeanor became institutionalized as the functional equivalent of the uniform for men in the police or the military or other order-like organizations.

The archetypal movement man—one can hardly call him a functionary because the movement is such an organizationally shapeless association—is a militant. The Communist party presents itself as the vanguard of the revolutionary working class movement; ergo, a Communist must be a militant. But the actuality is different. The archetypal Communist functionary is a hybrid: an apparatchik-politico. The activities that absorb him most are mediating and fighting, coalition-building, playing the game of power—all activities that define the politico function. But in a Leninist party these things are illegitimate and must be carried out covertly. The best resource for pursuing power within the organization, under such circumstances, is to control and manipulate the apparatus. The top official of a Leninist party typically wears the modest style of general secretary. Behind the ritually flamboyant cloak of the militant and the colorless mask of the apparatchik is the daemonic face of the politico.

The Communist party, or any Marxist-Leninist party, is in its constitutional logic a paramilitary combat organization. The rank-and-file members are soldiers. The leaders are generals. The organization itself is purely and simply an instrument for the achievement of a collective purpose. Thus, on the extreme edge of the category of voluntary associations is an organizational form that brings the discussion back virtually full circle to the military. Like a military force, the Communist party does not act for itself but as the vanguard, the mailed fist of its constituency—"the people" or "the proletariat."

Like the modern technician-soldier, the ideal Communist party member is about as close to the pure functionary as it is possible to get. His passionless dutifulness in work is his highest virtue. The functionary in business or government is no more than a pale reflection of the soldier in this regard, just as the functionary in the more conventional voluntary association might be described as a halfway Communist. *Being a soldier and being a Communist require at least the outward trappings of total commitment.*

But it is precisely in this external similarity that one discovers the key to the inner difference between the two. The Communist must live the life of the cause through a conscious and unrelenting effort of will. He is accountable for his failings of discipline, to be sure, but only after the fact. He is mostly on his own in day-to-day conduct. The soldier, on the other hand, wears the uniform, lives in a barracks or officers' quarters, and is subjected to twenty-four-hour-a-day discipline, at least at some stages and during some crucial episodes of his career. Much of the time he is under direct and close surveillance by higher-ranking functionaries. This means that the soldier can live with a relatively relaxed moral commitment. He can be cynical about the cause and positively scurrilous—with a little discretion—about the shortcomings of his unit and of the military in general. The situation of the Communist is different. He has few external supports, relatively, and so he must rely on his own inner strength much of the time to keep the faith and maintain party discipline.

Evidently, both formal organizations, such as the military, and voluntary associations, such as the Communist party, develop a characteristic form of the model functionary, each with its own peculiar strengths and weaknesses. What happens when the features of both types are combined? There are several recent historical examples: the Soviet MVD, GPU, and KGB, the Nazi Gestapo, SS, and *Waffen* SS (armed for military combat), the British Commandos, the French Paratroops, and the American Special Forces. All are volunteer, highly selective elite corps, highly trained and indoctrinated with a stop-at-nothing operational ethic. The meld does seem to work. We may say, provisionally, that the closest thing to the pure functionary is a militarized man-of-the-cause.

Part Three

7

Power struggle in the prison

Only a few years ago the prison was a place of exile, a Devil's Island. The convict was isolated from society, to protect it and to punish him.

The guard was a "keeper," and keeping quite literally was the content and functional meaning of his work. He was supposed to do his job professionally, dispassionately, without conscious or personalized cruelty. The system itself was sufficiently harsh that the inmate who endured it for the period of his sentence was thought to have "paid his debt to society" and could be discharged with the presumption that his hands were clean. If he had "learned his lesson" at hard labor and in confinement, if he came out chastened, eager to prove himself redeemed, all well and good. If he came out broken, or if he came out bitter and mean and spoiling for another showdown—whether or not the experience was good for *him,* still society benefited from the example he provided that "crime does not pay." It was no business of the keeper's whether or not prison set a man straight. It was strictly up to the man.

Now things are different. The guard is not a keeper but a "correction officer"; his job is correcting, not keeping—or not primarily keeping. The modern prison is supposed to help as well. The correction officers are its functionaries.

The change in the guard's occupational title is in part an example of the old gambit of semantic upgrading (ward attendants in mental hospitals are now "psychiatric technicians"), but it also reflects a real change in the nature and goal of the prison and the work of its archetypal functionary. The new correction officer learns during his training and indoctrination to be "primarily custodial but treatment oriented." The new prison is not a Devil's Island but a "detention facility"; its ultimate purpose is to "rehabilitate the offender." At any rate, that is the theory. In fact, it still does a minimum of rehabilitating. Custody remains its real business. The trend is clear, however, and cannot be restrained for long: the custodial function is sure to be more and more eclipsed by the function of rehabilitation.

The correction officer is primarily a custodial functionary. As time goes on, what will happen to him? He may be replaced by a new breed of rehabilitationist functionaries, who will seize control of the administrative apparatus and drastically reorganize the operations of the prison. Or, though not so likely, the correction officers may change their occupational character and become themselves rehabilitationists. A third possibility, more likely in the short run, is that the custodial functionaries and the rehabilitationist functionaries will work out some sort of live-and-let-live arrangement, each group with its own sphere of jurisdiction.

Whatever the situation at a given moment, the fact that the modern prison is staffed by two distinctly different kinds of functionaries, each with a commitment to half of the prison's dual mission (custody *and* rehabilitation), and each with a credible claim to the right to control the apparatus of administration in order to realize their version of the mission, means that the two types are locked into a struggle for power. Custody and rehabilitation are not really compatible, myth notwithstanding, and the party that controls the apparatus effectively defines the mission. The form the struggle takes—tactics, weapons, counters of gain or loss—depends on the history and circumstances of the particular prison as an organization, but it also depends on the relatively universal differences in occupational character and functionary type between rehabilitationists (social workers, psychologists, psychiatrists) and correction officers.

In the pages to follow we can see how the conflict is structured and how it has been waged in an actual institution, and then analyze the logic of the correction officer's work situation in order better to understand his character as a functionary.

In the early 1960's I did a field study of staff relationships at "Faulkner's Point" (a pseudonym), a large, medium-security institution located near a major metropolitan center in the Northeast. I concentrated on the youth division because it was the more treatment-oriented of the two major branches. The inmates were from eighteen to twenty-one years of age, and were mostly petty offenders: the usual sentence ranged from three months to one year. Most were Negroes and Puerto Ricans who had spent their lives in the big-city slums and racial ghettos, and their offenses were what one would expect: theft, mugging, trespass, assault, and narcotics. I was reliably informed that nearly all of them used drugs in some form, perhaps close to half used heroin, and 15 to 20 per cent could be classified medically as addicts. (These figures were estimates made by prison personnel.)

I interviewed twenty-four correction officers, including several captains and two deputy wardens, and seven civilian staff members, most of whom were rehabilitationists, about their feelings toward their work and their relationships with colleagues. This provided the key data for an analysis of the (then latent) power struggle in the prison, and was quite suggestive for an analysis of the occupational character of the correction officer. In order to get a broader base of understanding, however, I interviewed the principal of the vocational school on the prison grounds, the warden, and the commissioner and several top officials in the downtown headquarters complex. Finally, I set up an experimental demonstration training project dubbed "Mock Tribunal" (MOCTRIB), in which uniformed officers and civilians played the role of members of the Inmate Infractions Board and the Classifications Board, which assigned inmates to living quarters and work details. This device was especially useful for bringing out attitudes people find hard to put into words.

Because the study was concerned with staff relationships I did not interview inmates, nor did I observe them except in a casual way. This means that I know nothing *at firsthand* about officer-inmate relationships at Faulkner's Point. I did make inferences from what officers and civilians had to say, however, and judging from this and from information in research reports about other prisons like Faulkner's Point, I believe it is safe to make certain assumptions, in particular that a pattern of summary punishment exists there, as it does universally in prisons, mental hospitals, and other types of "total institutions." [1]

The discussion below is organized by considering the officer and the civilian, the officer and his work, the officer in relation to the inmate, and a note on the correction officer as a functionary. Throughout, the struggle-for-power theme is basic. The correction officer must carry on a two-front struggle: against civilian rehabilitationists who would take his job (as he sees it), and against inmates who threaten to "get out of hand" and take his authority. The entire situation offers insights into the situation of a functionary who is at once typical and unusual.

OCCUPATIONAL IDENTITY AND INTERPERSONAL RELATIONS

Dress and demeanor

The kind of clothing one wears and the way he wears it is always a distinctive mark of social identity. This is more evident in situations in which one is expected to "dress," as in the downtown shopping district, than in places like the zoo or the park or at a sporting event where people assemble in an undifferentiated mass and have only the most fleeting and casual contact with each other. There the prevailing air of informality makes it positively "wrong" to have too sharp an identity; one is supposed to step—modestly—out of role.

The individual is most tightly "in role" when he must act according to a sharp identity thrust upon him by the situation he is in. He announces to others what they can expect of him by his style of dress and demeanor; and they do the same for him. This makes functional encounters and social interaction less awkward, less provocative of anxiety than might otherwise be the case. Situations of this sort, in which identities are defined with the greatest degree of precision, allowing for the least possible ambiguity, are found not in public places but in places that are private in a very special sense: they are *impersonally* private (unlike a personally private place such as one's own home). Erving Goffman calls them total institutions, and they include concentration camps, mental hospitals, military posts, convents and monasteries, ships at sea, and boarding schools as well as prisons.[2]

One of the first things one notices in the prison is that occupational and status identity is overwhelmingly important. In any encounter, the individual is almost literally tongue-tied until he knows the other's identity. This is because of the endemically totalitarian social atmosphere. No one has the right to privacy, only the privilege, in proportion and in kind corresponding to his identity. It is difficult to speak or act freely when you sense that what you say and do will be construed as either a calculated act or a self-revealing slip by your occupational *group* and not by yourself alone.

One consequence is that the individual makes the badge of his identity plainly visible and immediately recognizable, by dress and demeanor. Another is that he learns to think of himself and of others as "types," and to manage his interpersonal relations accordingly. Thus one is first of all an officer (in uniform), an inmate (in prison dress), or a civilian (in street clothes).

The uniform, which closely resembles the uniform of a big-city policeman, signifies intermediate to high status: the ordinary correction officer's uniform is rather plain, while the captain's is rather gaudy. Civilians wear either the standard business suit of the white-collar worker, the neat workman's dress of the supervisory or skilled blue-collar worker, or the whites of medical functionaries. The deputy wardens wear street clothes or the uniform, depending on their work assignment. The warden may wear the uniform, if he wishes, but except on rare, ceremonial occasions he wears a business suit. The inmate, like the ordinary correction officer, has no choice; but those with a high-status work assignment manage to appear in prison garb that is clean and neatly ironed, and fits.

The "money-education complex"

Practically every uniformed man will tell the inquiring outsider, "We get along fine" with the civilians, and mean it. This is as one would expect. Under normal circumstances the officers are a solidary, homogeneous occupational group with the prideful sense that they "own" the apparatus of administration. They are the core functionaries; the civilians are ancillary—their function is to service the prison. The officers can afford to be charitable because they are in a position of strength. Moreover, as a ruling class they have a vested interest in fostering the myth that "everyone gets along wonderfully well."

Surprisingly, the civilians' first response is basically the same. They have a stake in the harmony myth, too. Nobody wants trouble. There are grievances, but not enough to justify "war." With a little probing the reticence yields, however, and it becomes evident that the situation is at best one of peaceful coexistence between officers and civilians.

The civilians (excluding the manual workers) are college graduates, and a good many have advanced degrees. Moreover, their education is presumably functional. They see themselves as professional people, technically qualified through higher education for their work. The correction officer can make no such claim. All he must do to qualify is to finish high school and pass an examination. To be eligible for promotion he must pass another examination. This may call for some fairly strenuous efforts at self-improvement, through reading and taking vocational courses, but not of the sort that can be called higher education or professional training. Some officers, wardens and deputy wardens and a fair number of captains, have a bachelor's or even a master's degree. Very few entered the service with the degree in hand, however, and it is open to question whether a college degree for the correction officer is ornamental or genuinely functional.

The civilians are better educated than the officers and do a higher type of work, as they see it. Yet on the average the officers, being career men, are better paid; the civilians tend to come and go. This is the rub, from the standpoint of the civilians.

From the officers' standpoint, the civilians' higher prestige and much greater autonomy in work and in their movements around the prison complex are a source of envy and irritation. The officer sees the civilian, usually a man who earns no more than he does, and often less, enjoying the privileges that the officer achieves only with advancement to high rank.

The officer "can't understand" why the civilian is not better paid if his skills are really "so wonderful," and the civilian "can't understand" how a man so "obviously inferior" as an occupational type, in terms of education, skill, and autonomy, can earn as much as *he* does or even more. Education is a caste mark in our society, regardless of its functional meaning, and so is autonomy in work. The officer ranks lower than the civilian professional in both, yet his pay is roughly the same. These incongruities of status are at the root of the problem of functional legitimacy that officers as well as civilians perceive as "the money-education complex."

The money-education complex causes friction but does not in itself produce conflict. It is a factor in preconditioning conflict and in structuring the relationship between the antagonists, however, because it provides a bedrock of meaning on which each's image of the other is erected.

CUSTODY VERSUS REHABILITATION

The point of departure of my study was the expectation that in a dual-mission organization such as the modern prison, in which custody and rehabilitation are equally legitimate but not harmonious goals, the functionaries would establish "counterpart relationships" on roughly equal levels in each of two structures of command and control, or else there would be an open struggle for power—control of the administrative apparatus—between the two. As it turned out, I found neither open conflict nor the functionally rational accommodation of partially conflicting interests.

The situation of the rehabilitation staff

Of the three civilian staffs, the schoolteachers experienced the least friction with the custodians, and the rehabilitation specialists (social workers and psychologists) the most. The amount of friction between the medical staff and the custodians appeared to be low to intermediate.

It is important to note that the school and the hospital are actually enclaves within the larger institution and are functionally symbiotic in relation to it. They service the prison. In the logic of their operation they are ancillary: they exist for the prison; not it for them. They do not presume to *be* the prison, nor to run it. Each has a physical plant of its own, and each is administratively responsible not to the warden but to a higher outside authority. Moreover, the nature of their operations is such that they are predictable and can be routinized, which removes another source of irritation in their relationship with the custodians.

Perhaps the decisive advantage of the school and the hospital, compared with rehabilitation, is that their function is highly specific and precisely located and limited institutionally. The correction officers see schoolteachers and nurses and doctors as doing something understandable and necessary, something which has a "home" in the organization. They pose very little threat in terms of jobs, power, or functional jurisdiction. There is operational friction, but it is of the chronic, picayune, low-keyed sort found in any organization. Status resentment there is, because of the money-education complex, but not a struggle for power.

Rehabilitation is another story. What is the prison for, to keep or to rehabilitate? To rehabilitate by means of keeping, or to keep in order to rehabilitate? What does rehabilitation mean? What does custody mean, operationally? Are security measures rehabilitative, counter-rehabilitative, or neither? These are the issues in a conflict that continues, although in the past few years it has been pushed underground. Certainly it has not been resolved.

There was a hot war at Faulkner's Point a few years ago, and now it is a cold war. What happened? What stopped the bloodshed between custody and rehabilitation?

Bureaucratization of communications

There are no counterpart relationships between functionaries in custody and functionaries in rehabilitation because they lack the freedom of action necessary to initiate them. All communications between the two groups are indirect, funneled through a liaison officer—who is of course a correction officer. The realities of power are vividly illustrated by a remark made by one of the social workers: "When I want to invade their territory, I go to Deputy Warden X for permission."

Some sense of why this draconic solution evolved, and why it was still acceptable to both sides years after it was first installed, is conveyed by the attitudes of correction officers and rehabilitation specialists. The rehabilitationists pointedly observed that there is little outright conflict with the correction officers now because there is little contact. "The situation was unbearable" before, however. There were "tremendous clashes." Now "there are no problems," or few. In the past, "the correction officer looked down on the civilians as fags, queers, do-gooders," and at the same time social workers and psychologists "felt guilty" to have to acknowledge that they saw the custodial people as "lousy" and "inferior." Now everything goes through channels—the important thing is to "find the right channel" and to "realize and accept the limitations of the system." It is difficult to make special arrangements, and important to adhere to standard procedures especially when it comes to anything involving inmate movements. Records is another "touchy area." Custody has charge of the records, and inmate clerks have access to them. This means that it is "awkward" to request information and "impossible" to keep sensitive information out of unauthorized hands. Still, peace is better than war.

The custodians, oddly enough, were rather more articulate about what had happened and why than were the rehabilitationists. "There were problems before, but they've been ironed out." Through weekly meetings the two groups are coming "closer to understanding each other." The civilians once felt that "custody doesn't know its job," but that is changing. The rehabilitationists now have a greater appreciation of the "responsibilities of the institution." They had to "learn their place" and realize that "the inmate has to be present at the census," and they had to realize also that "there is a personnel shortage . . . two or three jobs are done by one officer, and you can't split an officer." The civilians still have "an attitude of superiority" that causes "friction," and they are inclined to take a light and even contemptuous view of administrative necessities such as scheduling, and security matters such as the suppression of contraband, "but they are learning." One continuing problem is that they really have not seen "what we're trying to do" and yet they "belittle us." But "longevity" is reducing the dimensions of the problem— to such an extent, in fact, that "civilians are now trying to learn our job." (This particular custodian might well have added: "Just as we are trying to learn theirs.")

Bureaucratization of communications has separated the two

sets of functionaries and stopped the fighting. It worked because both sides were weary of the struggle and wanted an accommodation. It lasted because the individual chosen to perform the liaison function was an exceptionally able man who had the respect and confidence of both sides, but also because there continued to be a will for peace. Each party gained as well as lost by the terms of the accommodation bargain. It was a genuine compromise.

The accommodation bargain

On the face of it, the "accommodation" appears to be a total victory by custody. An important part of the bargain looks like the terms the victor imposes on the vanquished, but not all of it; and the meaning of those terms must be examined in the light of the fact that rehabilitation has the larger forces of change in society working for it.

What did custody gain? First, the concession by rehabilitation that "the interests of security are paramount"—which in effect recognizes the legitimacy of custody's continued "ownership" of the means of administration. Second, custody continues to have the right to regulate the movement of persons and things throughout the prison complex, particularly in those matters that involve contact with inmates. Third, custody may set up its own "counseling" programs and engage in its own "welfare" activities. Fourth, custody may, through a liaison officer, formalize and regulate all work-related contacts between rehabilitationists and correction officers.

What did rehabilitation gain? First, the right to participate in certain administrative actions: henceforth, rehabilitation was represented on the Infractions Board and the Classification Board. Second, custody recognized the legitimacy of the rehabilitationists' function by relinquishing intake and separation processing to rehabilitation, and by agreeing to cooperate by providing access to inmates and facilities for "therapy" and "treatment" programs, subject only to the overriding need to maintain security. Third, rehabilitation was conceded the right to define what "therapy" and "welfare activities" mean, operationally, and to have an absolute monopoly of expertise in the practice of "therapy" if not "welfare." Fourth, rehabilitation has the right to exercise ideological leadership within the prison by defining rehabilitation and having the opportunity to indoctrinate custodial staff with its nature and importance.

It is evident that custody managed to keep control of the apparatus of administration. The prison complex is like a state in miniature.* In form it is of the same species as a military dictatorship: the "government" and the "army" are made up of the same set of functionaries. Civilians still feel like outsiders, "nonpros," or at best like technical experts on temporary duty assignment. The career men are the uniformed officers.

Nonetheless, the civilian rehabilitationists have become part of the government, as they were not before. When they sit *by right* as members of the Infractions Board and the Classifications Board, they not only have a real voice in an important aspect of prison government, they get a window opened on the workings of the whole administrative establishment. Moreover, when the rehabilitationists have access to the inmates and to prison facilities for their treatment programs *by right,* the structure of the prison administration is changed. Before, the custodians claimed absolute jurisdiction. Now they must show cause, as it were, if rehabilitation accuses them of dilatory compliance or outright obstruction when a request is made through proper channels. Since any one of these requests may be turned down on grounds of security— which usually means administrative convenience—custody has the upper hand, administratively, in the short run. But in the long run rehabilitation likely has won structural legitimacy, that is, a

* The analogy is limited by the fact that all staff, officers as well as civilians, now live outside the prison and develop nonwork-related social affiliations the same as anyone else. Formerly there were staff residential quarters within the prison. It was undoubtedly much more of a "total institution" then, much more self-sufficient and state-like.

fundamental right to exist as a function of the prison government and within the prison government. It did not have this before.

In the long run, custody's right to hamper rehabilitation and frustrate its bid for power will depend on the strength of certain social forces. One of the most important of these is ideology. Unless the "ruling class" can keep faith in its doctrinal commitments, yet at the same time be sufficiently open to recognize new realities as they emerge, and accommodate itself to them, it cannot survive. It either commits suicide or is overthrown.

The structural concession implicit in the accommodation bargain clearly favors custody as the immediate winner. But the ideological concession seems to present the spoils of victory—at least in the long run—to rehabilitation.

Rehabilitation's gain was to become the official ideological mentor to custody. To be sure, there was a dual-mission formula: custody *and* rehabilitation. But the custodial part was all too obviously pale, negative, self-serving, and old-fashioned. The prestige of "science" and the weight of informed public opinion was all on the side of rehabilitation. *The accommodation bargain left the rehabilitationists still stucturally weak, in spite of their gains, but ideologically strong.* At the "Wednesday morning sessions," several rehabilitationists (usually including a psychiatrist, with the prestige of the M.D. degree to shore up the credibility of the rehabilitationist line) met with as many correction officers as could be spared from duty. Ostensibly the discussions were two-way, give-and-take. Actually the rehabilitationists lectured and the correction officers listened. In a less pointed way the same thing was true of the Infractions Board and the Classifications Board hearings. The "experts" were the rehabilitationists (although their advice was not always followed). Finally, the higher functionaries within custody itself were more than half won over to the treatment doctrine. What they read, wrote, and spoke in their occasional capacity as statesmen reflected either a conservative or a comparatively liberal version, in style and rhetoric, of the rehabilitationist point of view. Within the rank and file of correction officers, sentiment was less cautious, more polarized, with the reactionaries in the majority. It is surprising and significant, however, that a large and confident minority was doctrinally "radical" on occasion.

The correction officers were becoming "primarily custodial but treatment oriented"—surely an ideological victory for the rehabilitationists; but then *they* showed signs of becoming somewhat "custodially oriented"! One prominent theme in the remarks made by the rehabilitationists is that they must "go halfway and more than halfway" to meet the custodians. This means "understanding their problems . . . and understanding them." The implication is that the rehabilitationists have been "arrogant" and "organizationally naive" in the past and ought to change. As one psychologist put it: "We have to live by the principle, 'Render unto Caesar the things that are Caesar's.' " The naked fact of power—"they" have it and "we" don't—must be taken as given. Moreover, "Caesar" has a point. "We" have to change some of our thinking about what a prison is and what it means. "They spend eight hours a day with these kids . . . many are from the same background . . . they understand them very well."

Evidently the civilian rehabilitationists have a strong interest in making the accommodation bargain workable, for they fail to press the ideological concession as far as they could. Custody, in their view, is not merely a fact of life, to be put up with as an unalterable given in the situation. It has a reason for being. In a limited but important way, the correction officers know what they are doing—this is one theme. Another is that the custodians are totally "different" as an occupational group and "inferior." "They don't have the education, or maybe it's I.Q." "They lack verbal ability." "I would feel uncomfortable with them in any kind of informal situation." As the rehabilitationists see it, custody has a point, but the custodians are of questionable fitness.

THE CORRECTION OFFICER AND HIS WORK

"They think we're a bunch of idiots," said one correction officer ruefully, *"but that's what the job calls for!"* It is safe to say that most correction officers do not see themselves as doing "idiot work" most of the time, but some do. They are the minority of radicals who would do away with the whole system and have the officers take on the treatment function as their prime responsibility. Quite a few others would take a long step in that direction, but not one that would remove the uniform. These correction officers are the liberals. Most are conservatives, cheerfully cynical about the job, with no real desire for change.

Another minority, the "enlightened conservatives," takes pride in the workings of the system. In its view the work of the individual officer has no meaning in itself, but it is meaningful and can be satisfying if it is understood to be an essential part of a large collective enterprise. In a quasi-military organization, *somebody* has to "get these men in out of the rain," to recall a scrap of army humor. It may be idiot work as work, but considered as function it is necessary, responsible, and a source of pride if done with style.

The logic of the correction officer's situation has its key in what may be called the "rotation-examination-uniform" complex. It may provide some clue to the "security craziness" that afflicts the institution, and the idiocy—meaning mindlessness—of the correction officer's work.

The rotation-examination-uniform complex

The correction officer force is organized on a quasi-military pattern, reflecting its history as a body of "specialists on violence" who must be held rigidly accountable, individually and collectively, for what they do and fail to do. This pattern prescribes a peculiar organization and a corresponding set of attitudes toward the meaning of work and function.

The collective task is divided up, as in any body following bureaucratic principles of organization, into a number of complementary activities. Being quasi-military in spirit and structure, the prison is peculiar in that it not only fails to recognize individual expertise but positively forestalls its development. It fosters occupationally generic expertise instead: "how to be a good correction officer." Job-specific expertise ("how to run the clothes bin") and technical expertise ("how to apply psychology in the conduct of counseling sessions") are ignored, discouraged, or, at best, given little emphasis. Duty assignment by rotation and promotion by examination is how it is done; and the significance of the uniform is that it ties it together.

Periodic rotation of work assignment (post, duty, or tour of duty) is an ancient bureaucratic strategem for ensuring that power remains in the hands of one or a few top officials. It is functionally rational when the organizational mission demands swift and sure acceptance of orders from higher up, or when the heterogeneity of the components (social, geographical, or functional) hampers communication.

The classic three-year tour of duty of diplomatic and consular personnel is an example of how to cope with heterogeneity. Individuals on foreign duty assignment are encouraged to establish and maintain good relations with local people, not just officials, because they are supposed to have a "feel" for what is really going on and not remain insulated. But establishing and maintaining good relations means becoming rooted, however tentatively—"going native"—and in some measure losing one's objectivity. Routine, periodic rotation of duty assignment is an administrative device for reducing the likelihood that this will happen.

The need for swift and sure compliance with orders is best exemplified by the military. Unlike diplomatic and consular people, military men in overseas or even in domestic duty assignments need to relate to local people only minimally in order to do their job effectively. In fact, the organizational logic of military operations is such that fraternization is actively discouraged.

The danger of extended duty tours is not that the incumbent will go native but that he will begin to think "he owns the job": feudalization is the problem. The correction officers at Faulkner's Point recognized this in their criticism—mostly oblique, sometimes direct—of an officer on special-duty assignment who showed signs of "getting too big for his britches." The obvious solution was to put him back on the regular duty roster.

Promotion of officers at Faulkner's Point, as in virtually all bureaucracies, is based on a combination of seniority and merit. The trouble is these two attributes do not meld very satisfactorily. Assuming normal intelligence and effort, seniority virtually guarantees competence and rule-of-thumb know-how. But empirical expertise is not analytical intelligence, the ability to comprehend the whole and to understand and perhaps improve the structure of relationships among the functioning parts that constitute the whole. And so the need arises for a device that will select those most suitable for promotion, those who do have this higher ability, among otherwise equally well-qualified candidates. In a bureaucracy of the civil service type, such a device is a test, supplemented by a personal interview. The result is The List. Names of persons who pass the test and interview and who are thus deemed eligible are listed in order of "merit," as indicated by their scores. As vacancies occur, appointments are made from the top of the list.

The typical correction officer is a career man. He has job security, his acquired skill is not easily transferrable to another line of work, and after a few years automatic salary increments bring his income up to a level that prices him out of the general labor market. At the same time, promotions are slow. There are relatively few ranks in the prison custodial hierarchy, turnover is minimal, and general expansions of staff are infrequent. The result is long lists and few appointments. In any given year, most of those who pass the test are passed over for promotion. This is especially hard to take because proficiency in taking the test is not obviously related to doing well the work of a captain, a deputy warden, or a warden.

The theory of occupational testing is that those who get the low scores have less technical knowledge and less ability to learn than those who score high. But we have just seen that the management device of rotating duty assignments does not reward—and even covertly penalizes—strictly job-related expertise. The idea of a uniformed force demands virtuosity, not specialized excellence. The specialist is a threat. The preferred type is the generalist. This means that no body of technical knowledge is directly relevant to the correction officer's work.* The test for promotion is not rational in substance, which is why it is accepted only with great cynicism by those whose careers it affects. They know it is mostly ritual.

The test is not rational in substance but it is in function. It rewards rote memory rather than analytical intelligence, speed rather than care in problem-solving, prudence rather than creativity in innovation, knowledge of factual minutiae rather than understanding of significant facts in depth. But all of this is congruent with the constitutional logic of rotating duty assignments. They preserve and implement the commitment of the organization to solidarity above all else. Rotation neutralizes the compartmentalizing tendency produced by the division of labor, and the promotional examination does the same for hierarchy. The manifestly ritualistic character of The Test and The List and "promotion from the top" generates a sense of injustice among the merit-minded, but they are few in any case and become fewer as longevity weeds them out.

As an institution, the test means there is very little real technology of prison management to be learned, only a body of what must be called "occupational lore." The result is that the sense of difference among the ranks is minimized: a captain is a captain because he wears the insignia of office, "the brass." A mellow understanding of this makes for a sense of one-for-all-and-all-for-

* Criminology and penology are true applied disciplines, or technologies. But only the system designer or the two or three top management officials in the prison are in a position to make much use of them.

one, cutting across lines of rank and reinforcing a sense of being in the Service.

The highly visible symbol of the spirit and structure of the correction officer's work relationships is the uniform. A correction officer at Faulkner's Point looks very much like a big-city policeman. The attitude of most of the uniformed men is, "We like it that way." Others, a minority, are not so sure. They make self-demeaning jokes about "the monkey suit," or "explain" with heavy irony that it is a fringe benefit because it saves on clothing costs.

The warden almost never wears the uniform, although he is entitled to. The ordinary correction officer almost never appears at work except in uniform, because he has to. Captains and deputy wardens nearly always are in uniform, although in theory they are entitled to choose for themselves to wear it or not wear it. In practice, the deputy warden in charge of the youth division wears civilian clothes except on ceremonial occasions; this symbolizes a greater formal commitment in that division to treatment. The deputy warden in charge of the adult division, which is more custodially oriented, always appears in uniform. The assistant deputy warden in charge of personnel assignments—who is not on stage, so to speak, but does his work behind the scenes—ordinarily wears informal civilian garb. The officer in charge of liaison with civilians, a deputy warden in rank, is an interesting special case. He wears the uniform but seems uneasy about it. His coat is unbuttoned, his cap off, sometimes his tie is askew.

The ordinary correction officer is the first-line functionary of the prison, and his attitudes toward the wearing of the uniform most clearly reveal the logic of its constitution. The correction officer does not wear the uniform, or may choose not to wear the uniform, when he is off the regular duty roster and on special assignment. This may be any duty which requires him to be off the base or engaged in certain activities that are nonroutine.

Perhaps the clearest example is the Separation Cottage, an experimental unit which processes about thirty prisoners at a time and is designed to function as something of a halfway house, even though it is physically within the prison complex. The two "house fathers" are correction officers, but in theory they are not guards but helpers. They do not wear the uniform. Moreover, they see themselves as specialized experts in their work; the work itself comes first. "I break more rules than I keep," one remarked, pointing out that he violates the no-fraternization rule and keeps in touch with a good many of the inmate residents after they are released.

The few officers who do "counseling" are in an intermediate position. Unlike the "house fathers" of the Separation Cottage, who are almost totally isolated from their colleagues, those assigned to counseling are on the duty roster and subject to rotation; whether or not they stay in their semi-regular assignment or actually rotate through the duty posts with the rest depends on the discretion of the deputy warden in charge of their division. Because of this, they are unsure about whether the uniform should be worn or not. Some say, "They know who I am anyway, so why should I conceal it?" Others are inclined to think that the uniform is "like a red flag" to the inmates and should not be worn during actual counseling sessions.

The captains and deputy wardens who serve on the Infractions Board and the Classifications Board are similarly ambivalent. Does it help or hurt to be so visibly identified as "the cop"? In any case, is it "right"?

Wearing the uniform clearly creates stresses in the operation of the prison. And yet the custodial force clings to the practice (only the house fathers of the Separation Cottage do not wear uniforms regularly, and they seem to be virtual pariahs). It must be rooted deeply in the logic of prison organization, like job rotation and promotion by examination. As we have seen, rotation was an adequate coping response to the bureaucratic problem of compartmentalization induced by the division of labor. Promotion by examination was a response to the problem of segmentation by rank, or fractionation induced by hierarchy. Can we make the same sort of analysis in regard to the practice of wearing the uniform?

Prison guards have always worn uniforms because they are "specialists on violence," like soldiers and policemen. The uniform reminds the public that the wearer has the right to use force in the exercise of his duties. It also reminds the wearer that his right to use his professional expertise is highly circumscribed and highly visible. A man in uniform is constantly aware that he is "in role" while on duty and must be careful not to exceed his lawful prerogative; that if he slips out of role and acts improperly he may be observed, reported, and brought up on charges. At the very least, he may be chided, however mildly, and suffer the shame and guilt of having brought dishonor to the uniform. Thus the ability of the policeman or the correction officer to carry out his duties is enhanced by the awe and respect in which the uniform is held, but at the same time he feels less free to abuse his prerogatives.

This is to put the matter in very gross terms, however. The prison guard is no longer a keeper, a mere specialist on violence, but a correction officer who is primarily a custodian even though he is treatment oriented. The right to use force has become residual.

The key to the tenacity with which the staff as a whole clings to the uniform is the organization's emphasis on solidarity over functional rationality. This is the precondition for all other arrangements. Solutions to problems of hierarchy and the division of labor reflect this. Now we see that the uniform must be added to duty assignment by rotation and promotion by examination as part of a complex of administrative devices that persist because they implement a certain structural logic: the solidarity that is built into the very constitution of the prison.

To be specific, the uniform makes it possible to devise a solution to the problems of abstract rules, impersonality, and technical qualifications and tenure—all imperatives of bureaucracy—in a way that preserves the character-defining attribute of staff solidarity. Uniform wearers understand abstract rules as guidelines for the "higher-ups," not themselves. "The name of the game is 'kick it upstairs'—pass the buck." Impersonality in social relations at work is greatly simplified, as a problem, by the uniform. "You salute the uniform, not the man." * Technical qualifications and tenure are simply abolished, effectively, as a problem. Tenure becomes virtually absolute. It cannot be undone, so one learns to live with it. The uniform helps because it makes for a society of presumptive equals, in terms of technical qualifications and a mutual commitment to the good of the service. The psychological consequence is that the individual is inhibited from excelling.

The uniform is worn because it makes possible solutions to bureaucratic problems in a quasi-military organization committed to staff solidarity as a basic value. Putting the three terms together, we can now speak meaningfully of a rotation-examination-uniform complex which is characteristic of the social organization of prisons such as Faulkner's Point.

But why solidarity? It is necessary now to examine its causes and effects.

The obsession with security

Part of the routine orientation of the new inmate at a California Youth Authority institution is how to "go over the wire," to escape. The orientation officer shows him and his group the proper way to get over the top of the barbed-wire fence by using a leather jacket, a folded raincoat, or even just a couple of blankets as a shield against the barbs. The point is not to encourage escapes, of course, but quite the opposite. The demonstration dramatizes for the youthful offender that no great effort is made to prevent escapes, and so the act itself is not much of an exploit.

Faulkner's Point is very different, even though the type of in-

* The demeanor of the organization man without uniform is much more complicated. He must create and then wear a psychological uniform that is chameleon-like, changing with the light and the season.

mate is pretty much the same. The institutional obsession with "the count" is so great that even conservative officers are exasperated by it. At the end of every shift, a whistle is blown to signify that all inmates are present or accounted for. If the count is late, for whatever reason, no officer goes off duty until the discrepancy is corrected. Officers devote an enormous amount of time and energy to the mindless work of checking tallies, because an error in arithmetic can cause delay and irritation to scores of men who have learned to live by the clock.

The system of controlling movements is tight. Badges and passes are shown at checkpoints, remotely controlled barred gates are opened and shut, sidearms and keys and all sorts of contraband are checked in and out, lines of inmates waiting to be checked off of somebody's list are kept inside painted lanes in the corridor, schedules are obeyed with ritualistic rigor for fear an error will creep into the process of continuous surveillance.

"They're security crazy around here!" is a sentiment I heard expressed more than once by men in uniform, including some of high rank. A single inmate may go through a dozen checks a day. Why is there so much security craziness? What is at stake?

The official rationale is that the welfare and safety of the community must be protected, and so escapes must be held to the absolute minimum. But this is hardly credible in itself. The inmates are minor offenders serving short terms, which means they are not psychopathic killers, rapists, or even bank robbers. If a teen-age car-stripper escapes now and then, society will probably not suffer much; and there is a powerful deterrent to his even making the attempt, for he has little to gain—a few months, perhaps—and a lot to lose: escape is a felony.

Political considerations, obsolete facilities, an undermanned custodial apparatus (undermanned in terms of the job it has set for itself, which is substantively irrational), and just plain inertia, the weight of tradition, are the real factors behind the quest for security. What is illuminating, however, is that this seemingly irrational obsession with security becomes rational when considered in light of the uniformed force's strong commitment to solidarity.

A double and triple emphasis on security reinforces the sense of collective responsibility, and thus indirectly of solidarity, even when the measures are carried so far they provoke resentment in the individual guard. Having to wait until "the count is clear" before going off duty means sacrificing one's immediate personal interests—to safeguard the fundamental interests of the group. Solidarity is fostered by the experience of collective deprivation, even senseless deprivation, and the individual is reminded of his large responsibility every time he performs a tedious, routine act such as making a tally.

Summary punishment

Every solidary occupation has its "dark secrets"—events that must be covered up because of what they reveal about established but unacknowledged work practices. For example, the surgeon makes a mistake on the operating table and the patient dies or is maimed. The drill instructor pushes recruits in a Marine boot camp too hard on a field problem and some of the weaker ones drown. A manufacturer of pharmaceuticals inadvertently distributes a batch of dangerously toxic vaccine. Soldiers in combat shoot enemy troops trying to surrender, or kill prisoners when they are forced to retreat. A fighter-bomber pilot makes an error in identification and drops napalm on "friendlies." A policeman "works over" a suspect because he has not been sufficiently cooperative. A ward attendant in a mental hospital slaps a garrulous patient to shut him up. A correction officer who feels mocked and insulted "uses his hands" on an inmate to "teach him the proper respect" for authority.

Each of these examples could be documented as a particular instance. The more important question is whether it is part of a larger pattern. If there is a pattern, the next question is how and why it continues to exist.

Malfeasance or misfeasance that appears to be characteristic of the occupational group, not simply the act of an individual deviant, is a scandal. A scandal is a dark secret brought to light. It signifies collusion among insiders to conceal acts or a pattern of action from outsiders. The underlying attitude is that some occupational practices are really necessary even when hard to justify to noncolleagues who "wouldn't understand our problems." The risk of scandal and revelation adds an extra measure of discipline and cohesiveness to the occupational community. Every effort must be made to keep the dark secret dark, and the chances of being successful in doing this are in direct proportion to the level of occupational solidarity.

Summary punishment is one variety of the dark secret. It has the specific character of punishment, however, and so it is more risky than most patterns of illegal behavior covertly sanctioned by the occupational group. It is intentional, not accidental (although the perpetrator may miscalculate and go too far—unintended homicides do occur); it takes the form of a crime against a person, not just against things or against society; and its objective is to maintain the superiority of a functionary group over a subordinated client group. The attitude of the uniformed custodian in a total institution is that the inmates must be kept in line through terrorism. "They'll walk all over you if you let them."

The means of summary punishment vary, even though its general purpose is to foster respect for the uniform. Actual assault (shoving, slapping, punching, kicking, clubbing) is only the most dramatic of a number of forms it can take, from a show of coldness to a menacing gesture to outright psychological torture through bullying and humiliating the inmate, and finally to physical violence. The correction officer knows "it's your ass if you get caught," so he tries to rely on those milder forms that are within the letter of the law, even if they do controvert official policy.

Getting caught really means getting exposed, however, and so the fellowship of the uniform keeps up a united front of noncooperation with inquiring outsiders or higher officials as long as there is a chance of covering up an incident. Even the individual officer who feels it is wrong to use violence against an inmate—and most do not—is inclined to assume with the others that there are times when it cannot be avoided. The moralists close ranks with the more pragmatically inclined and stand together. "We" did it. It was a collective act. The guilt and responsibility must be shared, up to the point at which any further show of solidarity probably would not help the accused and would almost certainly weaken the all-important solidarity of the group. There does come a time when a man is really caught and must be thrown to the wolves.

THE OFFICER AND THE INMATE

Custodians and inmates universally are locked in a permanent struggle for power. The game they play has no beginning and no end. It is inherent in the logic of their situation that there can be no resolution, because they cannot combine to form a polity, nor can they disengage and form separate polities. The custodians are like a military force occupying a foreign country: they cannot hope to win the consent of the governed and so they cannot become a legitimate government, yet they must *be* the government; they cannot merge with the subject population, the "society of captives," yet they must have dealings with it. There is always the threat of violent rebellion. Under the circumstances, the best the two parties can hope for is a truce which will enable them to work out fair arrangements of convenience and necessity and thus ease the burden each must bear.

Power in the prison, as elsewhere, is primarily a function of numbers and organization. "God is on the side of the bigger battalions" only if they are at the same level of organization; a small well-organized force can prevail over a big, poorly organized one.

According to Robert Bierstedt,[3] power struggles are contests over prestige, influence, dominance, rights, and authority. If we focus on how correction officers and prison inmates actually carry on their eternal struggle over prestige, rights, and authority, leaving influence and dominance to be considered only indirectly, we may see how numbers and organization play a part in the chronic struggle for power in the prison, and learn more about the social character of the correction officer as a functionary type.

Prestige

Questions of inmate discipline and control are usually rationalized as questions of security by the correction officers. From the custodial standpoint, this has its advantages. Regulations for close surveillance, some of which seem quite trivial—such as forbidding all reading matter not checked out of the library as "contraband," or charging an inmate who stands out of line with being "out of bounds"—become sacred matters. The enforcer's prestige is correspondingly magnified. The inmate stands in awe of the man in uniform, who benefits from having his power enhanced and his work eased.

But there are disadvantages as well. Making sacred what are otherwise purely instrumental rules commits the prestige of the officer to their swift and sure enforcement—unless through an act of grace he waives the application of a rule in a particular instance. But if he waives too many he appears "weak." He must be constantly vigilant if he is not to lose face. Inmates are highly sensitive to this. Some, out of rebelliousness or simply a playful wish to commit mischief, exploit the artificially inflated significance of the rules and make a game of devising ways to break them. Officers with the talent and the taste for it accept the provocations as plays or moves in a game of wits and treat them as such, not without a certain sardonic pleasure. Others, less secure in their role, fall back on petty terrorism to crush them out.

Rights

Use and habit create stable expectations that take on the force of law. An inmate comes to have the substantive "right" to time off for good behavior, for example, although in legal form it is only a privilege; the authorities are not bound by law to honor it. It is one of a whole category of official privileges (library, commissary, mail, and so forth) which constantly threaten to become institutionalized as "rights." In addition, there are unofficial privileges: indulgences, dispensations, permissions—all those actions that fall within the officer's prerogative and involve waiving enforcement of a particular rule at a particular time.

The line between official and unofficial privileges becomes blurred with time, just as does the boundary between privileges and rights. Functionally, the privileges are stakes in a reward-and-punishment system of social control, and thus are counters in a game of power. Inmates feel unjustly treated when customary indulgences, or unofficial privileges, are periodically withdrawn under a let's-get-tough policy.

There is a cycle of "loosening up" and "cracking down." When things are quiet, officers find it in their interest to let occasional indulgences become established practice, and to add more and more indulgences to those already in force as part of the web of mutual expectations that constitute the relationship between them and the inmates. In effect, they buy peace and quiet—but only for a time, because the process is insidiously cumulative.

The officers get good will and cooperation, but only at the price of accepting more and more erosion of their power: the more unofficial privileges that become quasi-rights, the fewer options the officer has, the smaller his room for maneuver. Acts of grace in logic become, in custom, obligatory dues. Eventually, charges of administrative looseness, indiscipline, and even fraternization and collusion with inmates mount; suddenly, all unofficial privileges are withdrawn. The inmates see what has come to be rightfully theirs arbitrarily taken from them. They react with indignation and general restiveness, and this provokes a punitive withdrawal of some official privileges as well. The state of siege that ensues is the price paid for a period of peace bought through a liberal (although self-seeking) policy in administering privileges.

Authority

Authority endows its holder with the right to use sanctions in the lawful exercise of his function. Authority in the prison, like rights, is dual in nature. On the one hand, the correction officer is officially empowered to use force as an ultimate sanction, in self-defense or in order to quell a disturbance. On the other hand, he has certain unofficial powers of authority. He can grant or withhold privileges, some of which are extra-legal. He can make extra-legal demands. He can summarily punish a troublesome inmate by all means including physical chastisement, if he is discreet about it.

Authority is power exercised in accordance with law. But law exists in the form not only of formal statutes and regulations but of informal norms as well. The correction officer's official authority stems from the former; his unofficial authority from the latter. Moreover, informal norms in this case are of two sorts: the norms of the occupational group, and the norms of the prison community as a whole, *including the inmates.*

Unofficial authority is absolutely indispensable to the correction officer. With it he has the backing of his fellow officers and of the whole custodial establishment, and also, in a limited and of course variable way, the consent of the inmates. The struggle for power never ceases; but institutionalizing it introduces elements of form and structure that make life in the meantime more bearable.

The officers use their power to manipulate the system of rewards and punishments to gain acceptance of their right to command, their authority, from the inmates. A miniature social contract is established, analogous to the accommodation bargain. The commanded accept the commanders' right to apply sanctions against individuals caught in flagrant violation of at least some rules. In return the commanders agree to limit their exercise of authority according to the norms of the prison community. Both parties then know where they stand, and there is less turmoil, less mutual harassment than there would be otherwise. It is in this sense that the inmates play an important role in legitimating the (unofficial) authority of the correction officers.

Numbers and organization

The strictly tactical objectives of the power struggle are to build up and at the same time to use one's prestige, rights, and authority. As one party gains, the other party loses, so the contest has the logical structure of a "zero-sum game." The total of values at the beginning and at the end are the same. There is simply a redistribution from the loser to the winner, as in a game of poker.

Numbers and organization are primarily strategic rather than tactical, and so the zero-sum game logic does not apply. In the frame of any given contest—an episode in the continuing struggle for power—they are parameters (fixed values), not variables.

In the prison, each of the two parties does what it can over time to enhance its level of organization, and lower or weaken the organization of its opponent; neither has any control over numbers. Level of organization is not something you win from the other party, but rather something you try to develop in spite of the spoiling tactics of your opponent. Initially, inmates have the advantage of numbers, and custodial staff has the advantage of organization. Considering this, it is clear why correction officers have such a strong interest in maintaining a policy of close surveillance of inmates.

Inmates intuitively seek to build up their own organization as a counter to the tight organization of the custodians. First they try to establish a secure line of communications ("the vine") for transmitting and diffusing intelligence about the intentions and capabilities of "the enemy." This is the lowest level of inmate organization and is found universally, to some degree. Next inmates try to establish a system of procurement and distribution of goods and services. They become specialists in their underground roles: some are "merchants," some are "toughs." [4] Then a leadership structure emerges, a hierarchy of "con bosses." Some of the custodians are bought or intimidated into cooperating. In the extreme case, the men in uniform become virtual supernumeraries—at which point the inmates have really "taken over the joint."

Close surveillance is the custodians' chief spoiling tactic. Tight security sets up obstacles to inmate organization. Out-of-bounds restrictions limit social contacts and the flow of information through the grapevine. Added to this, the no-contraband restriction makes it hard to accumulate wealth, a prestige factor, and inhibits the flow of goods as currency, a factor in the system of sanctions any organization must have to survive. In this perspective it is evident the officers know what they are doing. Security policies that seem irrationally repressive to outsiders are in fact rational as a means to an end in the context of the inmate-staff struggle for power. If other things remain equal, relaxation of security rules undoubtedly leads to a higher level of inmate organization. This adds an increment of power to their ability to frustrate the ends of custody.

Just as the undeclared but real policy of the custodial force is to hold inmate organization down to the lowest possible level, through close surveillance and tight security, at the same time the custodians try to keep the level of their own organization high. The rotation-examination-uniform complex of work practices and institutions manifestly serves this purpose. Once an organization reaches a certain size, interpersonal solidarity and uniformity of action can no longer be sustained through personal contact alone. Rules and procedures must be formalized and their administration put on a rational, impersonal foundation. The custodians' solution to the problem of coordination is to simplify it by drastically minimizing heterogeneity and fostering solidarity. At the same time, they magnify the weight and scope of command authority at the expense of functional authority.

REFORM OR REVOLUTION?

The present order in the prison is not viable. History has caught up with it: it is locked into a technologically conservative mode in a society that is more and more technologically progressive. The inevitable adjustment must take one of two forms:

(1) Following the model of the modern military, the custodians from top to bottom will become technologists and technicians of rehabilitation but will retain their first identity, somewhat attenuated, as a quasi-military "order" of career men. Some civilians will be absorbed into the power structure, others will be retained as advisers, trainers, and highly specialized experts.

(2) Following the model of the modern mental hospital, the custodians will be dislodged from their "ownership" of the administrative apparatus by a civilian staff of technicians and technologists, and forced into the status of a mere guard force. Some custodians, suitably retreaded, will be kept in the power structure, and others will join the ranks of the civilian technicians. What is decisive is that the present quasi-military "order" of uniformed custodians will be reduced to a position of permanent subordination to civilian professionals

The first is a reformist type of accommodation, and the second is revolutionary.

The reformist solution

The consequence of an overriding emphasis on occupational group solidarity is technological conservatism. In a highly bureaucratized institution such as the prison, this means organizational conservatism too, because technological change makes organizational change necessary.

If the custodians realize that innovation cannot be stopped, they will accept reform and concentrate their energies on slowing the pace of change. They can do this in two ways. One is to isolate the particular sphere of operations affected, taking it out of the main stream of routine activities. Call it experimental, make it glamorous, but keep it dependent. The Separation Cottage is an example. The second way is to incorporate the new technique into main work routines but in adapted form. Make the innovation slowly, make it minimally disruptive, and the rate of overall change can be kept down. Shift the burden of accommodation to the new technique itself, even if this greatly reduces its effectiveness. A good example is the officer-conducted counseling program. It makes large organizational innovation unnecessary because it is small in scope. Moreover, it involves officers who are few in number and virtually without power, being subject to rotation. If they want to keep their assignment, they must find ways to integrate the program into established arrangements.

These are extremely small and cautious steps, and they are not enough to sustain a reformist commitment. Without continued pressure from "outside," the massive inertia of the custodial order, obsessed with security and the power struggle with the inmates, will weaken the chances of reform. This leaves the revolutionary solution as an equally plausible alternative.

The revolutionary solution

A clear-cut victory for the proponents of a "get-smart" over a "get-tough" policy for controlling crime might create pressure from outside for a revolutionary reorganization of the prison. What would this involve?

The rehabilitationists would seize control of the administrative apparatus from the custodians. The new officials would immediately downgrade security as a criterion of the prison's effectiveness and efficiency. In its place, priority would go to a "total push" treatment program for selected inmates. Next, one could expect that responsibility for all operations in the prison, including supervision of inmate work details, housekeeping, and so forth, would be taken out of the hands of custodians and given to civilian technicians and specialists. The uniformed force itself would be greatly reduced in size. The only functions left to it would be policing and guarding. Its role might be something like that of the military police in a training barracks.

To the extent that the total change in the power structure, the "circulation of elites," is genuine and thoroughgoing, the whole character of administration would change according to the occupational character of the new elite. Instead of interpreting administrative problems in terms of security, for example, as at present, the new regime would understand them as problems of securing maximum rehabilitation with the resources at hand.

The ultimate solution for the prison probably lies between these extremes—something more than foot-dragging mock reform and something less than revolution. Revolution is unlikely if only because known and tried techniques of rehabilitation have been unimpressive, to say the least. On the other hand, the prison as it exists today is beyond all doubt working against rehabilitation. Some kind of real reform must come, with or without a proven rehabilitative technology.

Real reform results when the incumbent elite is forced to coopt its challengers enough to weaken their drive for total victory. The "ins" must admit some of the key challengers to positions of real power, even though as a minority force in the beginning, and adopt enough of their program to bring about real change. The essence of the accommodation is that the Old agrees to meet the New halfway, and the New agrees, in return, to recognize the suzerainty of the Old. The result is a meld whose character is not clearly foreseen, or wished, by either: the Old loses its identity; the New loses its millennial militancy. On the other hand, each wins a share in the control of events and actions that will shape the future.

The evidence now is that the custodians will soon feel compelled to face up to the inevitable and save themselves by abolishing themselves—or almost. This means giving up the means by which tight group solidarity is maintained (the uniform, promotion by examination, work assignment by rotation) and settling for a looser, more technically modern form of occupational organization. Already many correction officers have become silent defectees, convinced at heart that "a machine designed by geniuses to be run by idiots," in the words of a novelist describing the old Navy, is not what the organization of a modern prison should be.

UNFINISHED BUSINESS: SOME CAVEATS AND QUESTIONS

The prison today is the scene of two very different kinds of power struggles. Rehabilitationists and custodians struggle for control of the administrative apparatus. Custodians and inmates, on the other hand, just struggle, endlessly, for the intangible "upper hand." The custodian is a professional at playing the game of power. It is his life. Competence in doing it constitutes most of his vocational expertise. The rehabilitationist is an amateur who will never learn it very well because it is alien to his main interests as a professional. The inmate is an amateur to begin with, but he very quickly becomes a "pro"; the correction officer and the civilian go off duty when the work day is over, while the inmate lives with and in the system twenty-four hours a day until he is released.

Viewed sympathetically, the correction officer is in the difficult position of having to fight a two-front war—and the tactics are different on each front. The fundamentals of the craft of custodianship are ancient, but the modern custodian finds that with inmates the rules of engagement are changing so rapidly that it is hard to be swift and sure, and confident, in applying the fundamentals. The rehabilitationists who threaten to overthrow him on the other front use ideology as a weapon and undermine his faith in the efficacy, even the morality, of the techniques of work he feels he must use. If they had a manifestly better faith and a better technique, his problem would be simpler. He might accept the wave of the future and follow the maxim, "If you can't lick 'em, join 'em," or he might resign himself to fighting a rearguard action. But the rehabilitationists have nothing better to offer. They seem terribly ignorant of the facts of prison life: that the inmates will take every inch they can get and keep up the pressure for more. The rehabilitationists just "don't understand our problems."

Viewed unsympathetically, the correction officer is an anachronism, terribly out of touch with the way scholars and scientists now understand human behavior in relation to social structure. He cannot realize that his problems are not "understood"— meaning understood his way—because he fundamentally misconstrues the nature of cause and effect as it operates in his situation. The prisoners do not make the prison; the prison makes the prisoners.

The man *under* the uniform often is an intelligent and decent individual, but the man *in* uniform tends to be the embodiment of everything that is stupid and mean and corrupt in the prison system. The inmate is assumed to be hard, vicious, and deceitful. He is treated that way, and so he acts that way. Of course he plays the game of power—what else is he to do when his humanity is denied and he is handled as a cipher by being checked off somebody's list twelve times a day? And it is "just routine," it is not even called punishment.

We have no theory that stands up about what should be done with the criminal. There is no rehabilitation technology that works. This is the unfinished business: we are pretty sure how and why prisons do not rehabilitate, but we are not at all sure what we might substitute for them that would do a better job. The caveat follows. The power struggle between custodians and rehabilitationists is not a morality play. It is not possible to speak of the "forces of reaction" frustrating "the forces of enlightenment" and bring much sense to the problem. The analysis above shows that the technological conservatism of correction officers and their use of summary punishment as a work technique, up to and including occasional acts of assault, are not manifestations of sadism or selfishness or laziness or arrogance but are rooted realistically in their experience.

As long as there are total institutions, as long as there are inmates and custodial functionaries, the functionaries will respond to the inmates' threat by unofficially institutionalizing summary punishment, informally stressing occupational group solidarity, and openly and officially demanding tight security rules. It is inherent in the logic of their situation.

If the rehabilitationists overthrew the custodians and took their place, without attacking the prison system at its roots, they would end up doing the same thing. This is demonstrated by the history of mental hospitals in this country and their organizational problems. Even so, there is an answer to the question of what should be done, not a very good one but better than none: do away with the system that exists. Almost any conceivable alternative would be better, no matter how flawed.

THE CORRECTION OFFICER AS FUNCTIONARY

Correction officers are a peculiar type of functionary because their occupational ethic, the kind of functional rationality they practice, is technologically conservative. In their situation, to be rational is to resist change. The prison's system of reward and punishment makes such an attitude inevitable. The prison builds a good record for itself by minimizing escapes and minimizing costs, not by maximizing rehabilitation. An industrial organization tries to keep costs down, too, but unlike the prison it can tap an impressive and proven body of technique for doing so. Moreover, unlike the prison it can do the same thing in making a good production record. The investment of capital and energy and the reorganization of social relationships at work is rational because the power of new technique is evident in increased production.

The social character of the correction officer is a realistic reflection of the conditions of his work. He must control the inmates, placate City Hall, and at the same time fight off civilian rehabilitationists who threaten to take over his job, or most of it. What can modernized technique do for him? His success, the efficiency and effectiveness of the organization he runs, is calculated in ways that make him the probable loser in prestige, power, and the autonomy of his occupational group if there is a move to devise rationally better methods of organization and operations. Under the circumstances, it is perfectly sensible for him to be less than enthusiastic about new treatment programs and to resist the growing power of the new civilian experts on rehabilitation.

The correction officer's strength is in his uniform, the vivid and omnipresent symbol of intense occupational solidarity and a high level of organization within the occupation. It is a reminder that group interests come first, and so it makes him continuously aware that there are group interests to be looked after.

The uniform is a militaristic device, and aside from its other meanings it serves to remind us that the correction officer is a type of militarized functionary. This raises certain questions. We noted in Chapter 3 that the modern military man is socially conservative but technologically innovative. In Chapter 7 we developed the implications of Philip Selznick's view of the Communist party as a paramilitary combat organization, and concluded that a militarized "man-of-the-cause" is in many ways the ideal functionary. He combines an unusually strong will and capacity for discipline with an uninhibited pragmatic bent to keep trying out new methods until he has found the one best way to realize his objective. He seeks group salvation through the application of ever newer and better techniques, organizational and operational.

The most important question presented by the case of the correction officer as functionary is that, if he is militarized and strongly disciplined, why does he resist innovation? The answer is not hard to find, and it offers a clue to the social character of the functionary in general.

First, the correction officer and the soldier are subjected to different kinds of discipline or, rather, a mix of kinds of discipline. *Peer* discipline has its source in the occupational group itself, the body of peers regardless of formal rank. *Official* discipline is bureaucratic: the individual is controlled and guided by duly constituted authority, extending up through the hierarchy of ranks within the occupational group and out beyond to the ultimate authority of the (ordinarily) civilian ministers in charge of the military establishment. Peer discipline is important for soldiers, but in all but exceptional cases official discipline carries the greater weight. The situation is the reverse in the case of the correction officer. City Hall (or State House, or the Sheriff's Office) is the ultimate source of outside civilian authority, but it is notoriously unstable, weak, and ineffectual most of the time (except for the federal system under the Bureau of Prisons). The result is that the higher-ranking functionaries within the custodial force become the creatures and captives of the body of peers that constitutes the occupational group.

Second, there is the matter of the cause, the mission, the reason for being of the institution and the occupational group. The soldier functions as a direct instrument of war only during infrequent episodes, but in a sense he is at war continuously. He trains, he practices, he acquires the lore of the professional military man which will sustain and guide him when he must face the moment of combat. "The cause" is abstract except when there is actual war, but it nonetheless exists. It enters into every important calculation, personal and organizational. The correction officer is at war continuously, too, but in a different sense. His battle is not abstract but concrete, with no beginning or end and not much rhyme or reason. He lacks a sense of cause, because there is no tangible objective and no way to calculate progress.

So the correction officer is a very special kind of functionary. Something is lacking. He has no cause, and he is disciplined more by peers than by officials. This explains his technological conservatism, which makes it hard for him to practice functional rationality. His situation is typical of the daily routine of a total institution.

Total institutions are not necessarily lacking in functional rationality, however. Some are, some are not, depending on circumstances. If there is a clear-cut goal or "cause"; if the functionaries who plan and oversee operations are not only permitted but encouraged to choose and apply means calculated to yield maximum effectiveness and efficiency in achieving the goal; if they are relatively unhindered by moral considerations, humanitarian sentiment, economics, or politics—in short, if they are instructed and enabled to give full and free play to rationality in adjusting means to ends, it does not matter much that the subfunctionaries of total institutions are inclined to be technologically conservative. The subfunctionary's ethos pervades the institution and dominates the higher functionaries only when goals are obscure or traditional and functional rationality is made all but impossible by a clutter of "don'ts" inhibiting the free employment of means.

The correction officer is a subfunctionary. In the United States today his type usually reaches up to structure the spirit and logic of the work carried on by the true functionary at the level above direct operations. It need not be this way, as we see in the next chapter. There we explore situations in which the tables are turned and the functionary is given virtually a free hand to stamp institutions and situations with the logic of his work procedure.

8

Extreme situations, total institutions, and the functionary

The experience of communist and fascist totalitarianism (Nazism under Hitler in Germany was a variant of fascism) just before World War II, and the war itself and its aftermath, produced several new ideas important in the analysis of modern society. One is that of the functionary as an occupational type—what this book is about. Other ideas that are especially germane to the problem of the functionary, and the trend toward universal bureaucratization and functionalization, concern total institutions and extreme situations.

The preceding chapter dealt mostly with the type of functionary to be found in one kind of total institution, the prison. The concept of the total institution was not developed in itself, however. Nor did we spell out its unique character as a sort of paradigm for the institutional shape of the modern social order, in which the functionary and functionary logic prevail.

The purpose of this final chapter is to show the direct logical connection between the situation of the functionary, stripped to essentials, and the structure of the total institution. The common denominator is that both seek to operate according to functional rationality, while treating substantive rationality as a remote factor in organizing any sort of action.

In commonsense language, both the functionary and the total institution—or the functionary *in* the total institution—want to worry only about means and forget about ends. They want to choose and employ means with the greatest possible efficiency and effectiveness, and this can be done only by installing bureaucratic discipline completely—untrammeled, immune from the inhibitions of "outside" law.

Our analysis must incorporate a third idea in order to make sense: the concept of extreme situations. Only in this way can we bring *people* back into our discussion and demonstrate how abstractions like functional rationality relate to the experience and life-interests of whole human beings.

The psychologist Bruno Bettelheim was one of the fortunate few inmates of the Nazi concentration camps who were released early in the war and managed to make their way to safety in Great Britain and the United States. He set down his observations and analysis of camp life as he knew it in a scholarly paper, "Individual and Mass Behavior in Extreme Situations," published in 1943.[1] It is primarily from this source that the term "extreme situations" entered social science literature.

Bettelheim discovered and named a phenomenon that since has been recognized as having tremendous significance for our moment in history. His conception of it was criticized from the beginning, however, as being too exclusively psychologistic and apocalyptic; it gained notoriety but not exactly what one could call wide acceptance. Sociologists and political scientists welcomed it as an important first approximation, but they found also that Bettelheim's exclusive focus on the lone individual in relation to a hostile environment was too simplistic to be credible. Where was the inmate social organization in the camp? The differentiation into groups and not just psychological types? The power structure? The political and organizational problems of the guard force, the SS? Bettelheim seemed to be saying that the inmate's only hope for survival was to be lucky enough to stay healthy, and to have enough strength of character to resist the self-altering pressure of the environment all by himself. Suspicion that this could not be accurate as a general picture of the camp experience was borne out by the accounts of other survivors published after the war (David Rousset, Eugen Kogon, and Margaret Buber, to mention a few).[2]

This chapter is about extreme situations, not concentration camps. As our understanding of the camp experience has broadened and deepened, so has our conception. The social scientist now sees extreme situations as related to what Erving Goffman calls total institutions—prisons and jails of all sorts, military barracks, mental hospitals, ships at sea, isolated mines and lumbering camps, convents and monasteries, boarding schools—any and all establishments in which there is more or less continuous coercive surveillance of "inmates" by "functionaries," with the consequence that the inmate is under pressure to alter his self.

The situation of all inmates, or quasi-inmates, is extreme in this sense. But we can generalize even further. There are recurrent situations in modern society that are not "inside the walls," or their functional equivalent, and yet are "extreme" in their fundamental character.

A SOCIOLOGICAL CONCEPTION OF EXTREME SITUATIONS

Situations are "extreme" to the extent that, bit by bit, the individual feels under pressure to accept a role and an identity that he considers intolerably degrading—a "fate worse than death." Concentration camp inmates wanted above all "to come out alive and *unchanged.*" The process they feared proceeds through stages. At each juncture the individual is asked to give up a little more of his autonomy, his dignity, his integrity. Eventually, he finds these cumulative small surrenders have carried him past the moral and psychological point of no return, and he has learned to accept a self altered and despised.

Goffman's "Moral Career of the Mental Patient" [3] describes how the new patient learns the patient role through devices best understood as "degradation ceremonies." Robert Jay Lifton's account of "thought reform" in Communist China [4] provides another example. The "trainee" discovers at a certain point that the magnitude of his surrender allows no turning back.

The functionary relates directly to the inmate in the total institution. Responding more to the logic of his situation than to any specific instructions, or to a planned pattern of conduct of the sort that has been called "brainwashing" (although the two cannot be separated), he grows accustomed to treating the inmate as a thing rather than as a human being.

In the most total of total institutions, such as the Nazi extermination factory at Auschwitz, which had the capacity to gas and burn fifteen thousand people a day, the inmate is nothing more than a horse or a block of wood: he is something to be used or destroyed, without moral scruple or inhibition. A man cannot meaningfully commit a crime against a horse or a dog; an SS doctor or hospital orderly or guard or inmate attendant could not meaningfully commit a crime against the miserable human cattle who were pushed out of the freight cars and onto the trucks that would take them directly to the gas chambers. They were simply "raw material" to be "processed."

Extreme situations in their classic form, such as those which developed in the concentration camps in their later stages, are the product of *de-legalization* of the functionary-inmate relationship, followed by *de-moralization*. First the inmate is denied the right to redress under law, which frees the functionary in the legal sense and permits him to be functionally rational in his dealings with the inmate. Then all humanitarian sentiment in the relationship is ruled out, which frees the functionary in the moral sense. The organization not only permits the functionary unlimited rationality in his choice of means but compels it; he not only can but he *must* treat the inmate as a horse or a block of wood.

The process as a whole may be called denormalization. All norms, unofficial as well as official, insofar as they stem from the value premise that the inmate is human and has rights, are taken out of the relationship. The result is something like Marx's "naked cash nexus" which defined the relationship between employer and employee in the period of early industrial capitalism. The nexus between functionary and inmate is one of naked functional rationality.

Modern mass society is governed more and more by the technologic of bureaucracy and mass communications. The result is that extreme situations are increasingly found outside of total institutions as well as within them. The rule of law is more and more attenuated, for one thing, as the rule of functional rationality renders it obsolete and forces it out. As modern society grows increasingly "massified," without structure, without communal bonds of cohesion, the old constraints break down; at the same time it grows more bureaucratized, which generates a new institutional logic and new constraints and imperatives. As the net of systematically rationalized and articulated social organization grows tighter and more pervasive, to fill the vacuum left by the decay of spontaneous ordering of social relationships; as the social type of the functionary is given ever more freedom to realize himself in his work, more and more people become his clients or else personnel he uses, and the situation of everyman comes to be essentially equivalent to the situation of the inmate in a total institution.

To many this will seem too apocalyptic—part of the charge brought against Bettelheim—to be plausible. But the question is, does it work? Does it yield insight? Is it consistent with the facts? As a test it will be useful to construct a number of types of extreme situations and see whether or not, and to what extent, they can be called extreme, and what the importance and the role of the functionary in each case is.

EMPIRICAL TYPES OF EXTREME SITUATIONS

The concentration camp

Concentration camps are established when conventional prison facilities are too small or in some other way unsuitable for the job. In the Soviet Union under Stalin, "detention and retraining centers" were established to isolate, house, and—in theory—transform "class enemies" (such as *kulaks*, peasants who resisted forcible collectivization of their farms) into "useful Soviet citizens." In Nazi Germany the camps were needed initially to house large numbers of political prisoners, then whole groups within the population (Gypsies, Jehovah's Witnesses, and especially Jews) who were considered "objectively criminalistic." Ordinary criminals and eventually Russian prisoners of war were added to the inmate population.

The common denominator in Germany was that such groups and individuals were considered unassimilable foreign elements within the pure "Aryan" body politic. Meanwhile, in the United States, all persons of Japanese ancestry, citizens or not, were forcibly removed from "sensitive" areas (along the Pacific seaboard) and sent to "relocation centers" for the duration of the war. They were thought to be "objectively" fifth columnists, potential spies and saboteurs, for the United States was at war with Japan.

These different concentration camp complexes varied greatly in the way the inmates were treated. The Nazi camp inmate faced more or less rapid starvation unless he was lucky enough to become a *Kapo*, or inmate functionary. The Japanese-American was merely sequestered and subjected to military authority, not starved.[5] One thing the two did have in common was that camp functionaries were comparatively free to operate outside the rule of law. Comparatively, not totally. It all depended on how totalitarian the sponsoring state apparatus was, and what the mission of the camps turned out to be.

To fall within the limits of our definition, the situation of the inmate was "extreme" to the extent that it was de-legalized, demoralized, and functionally rationalized. The American camps were not very extreme in this sense, even though the courts acquiesced in a public policy which flagrantly violated civil liberties guaranteed by the Constitution. At the other end of the continuum is the German case: an avowedly totalitarian state with the mission, as time went on, to let the camp inmates die through neglect and eventually to kill them off. But even in the German camps, surprisingly, there were rules against mistreating inmates, and they were sometimes even enforced. How is this anomaly to be understood?

If the SS guards in the Nazi camps were sporadically forbidden to mistreat inmates, it was not because of moral or humanitarian sentiment. Had this been a factor it surely would have been sensed by the inmates and reported in survivors' accounts. It is not. Instead, they testify that relatively small, personalized acts were more keenly resented than occasional mass atrocities: a considered slap in the face was more enraging than a random kick in the groin or two hours of push-ups in freezing mud for a whole barracks as punishment for the infraction of one individual. The personalized act signified a denial of the individual's fundamental humanity, *his* rights. The impersonal act was an act by the system directed at inmates as a group. It did not raise the question of individual rights, and so it was less frightening, less damaging to the individual's self-esteem. If an act is morally significant, it must question values which are generically human, universal in the person-to-person relationship. It seems clear that when the SS man was inhibited at all, it was not on grounds of moral principle.

If the grounds were legal, there should be evidence that inmates could effectively bring charges against the guards to complain of a violation of their civil rights. We are told that this did take place occasionally, and in at least one reported instance the abuses brought to light were halted. But the rarity of such reports indicates that such cases were most exceptional, and therefore there is no evidence that inmates generally had even rudimentary civil rights. There was no rule of law in the usual sense in the Nazi camps.

The fact that custodians were officially forbidden to mistreat inmates, at least at some times and in some places, is more plausibly explained as evidence of functional rationality than of legality. At issue was not the "rights" of the inmates but the welfare of the SS as an organization. It would have been contrary to its interests to permit its members to step out of their official role and pursue such purely private ends as sadistic gratification. The important thing was to forge the SS into an effective organizational instrument and keep it that way, which means it had to be guarded against corruption. It was functionally rational to look the other way when individual guards "irrationally" abused inmates, and even covertly to encourage a discreet and limited amount of such conduct as part of the toughening process for new recruits. But it would have been functionally irrational to permit them to forget that they were SS men, and under orders. The SS could not permit a continuous orgy of sadism and remain strong as an organization.

The mental hospital

A person found by a court of law to be "a danger to himself and others" by reason of mental illness is "committed" for "treatment" in a "hospital": this is the legal formula. Actually, he is deprived of his civil rights and locked up in a medium-security institution for as long as the judge sees fit, because society does not know what else to do with him.

The court takes its advice on commitment and release from doctors, who double in role as institutional custodians and functionaries as well. This means that the patient is an inmate who is judged by his jailers as to his fitness to be returned to society as a free man. Medical technology applied to the treatment of mentally ill persons is not very effective. So considerations of administrative convenience and necessity, more or less consciously disguised as purely medical considerations, constitute much of the real basis of the doctors' advice to the court. Goffman makes the point that the "medical model" [6] of operations is routinely subverted by the realities of institutional life.

The mental patient is subjected to incarceration in his own interest, in theory and to some extent in fact. (A considerable number request commitment voluntarily.) This mitigates the extremity of his situation, compared with the plight of his counterpart in the worst of the concentration camps. Still, he is enmeshed in a network of forces which profoundly threaten the self. The hospital is ordinarily isolated, and this gives the staff and management a comparatively free hand to determine the scope of moral and legal propriety to be observed in relations with inmates. They have the power and the will to make their definition of social reality prevail. As a result, the functionary-inmate relationship is de-legalized and de-moralized to a significant degree. It is administratively convenient, and it seems right because of the partly fictitious conception that the patient is incompetent and dangerous and that the staff is looking after his welfare.

Nor is the patient free from a realistic anxiety that he may be "destroyed" on functionally rational grounds. Lobotomy (surgical destruction of portions of the brain) was common practice a few years ago, and it produced extensive and permanent alterations in the self. Convulsive drugs and electric shock treatments are reportedly still used in some hospitals in the United States, although less frequently than in the past. Whether or not these techniques are supplanted by the powerful new tranquilizing drugs —it seems they may be—it is still true, as Goffman reminds us, that the implicit demand on the patient to give up certain values and attitudes and to accept new ones as a condition for release is in effect pressure to alter the self. Enforced socialization is a comparatively limited but nonetheless real form of destruction.

It seems fair to conclude that extreme situations are a characteristic feature of hospitalization for mental illness regardless of the treatment techniques used. The situation of the hospital inmate is ordinarily less extreme than that of his counterpart in the concentration camp, but the qualitative difference is not so large. What they have in common is more important than what separates them.

The ineffective state

A society which tolerates an ineffective set of institutions for securing justice and order and is divided, perhaps in open conflict, places whole categories of people in extreme situations. Quasi-official forces operate outside the law, either as vigilantes or as guerrillas. Vigilantes use extra-legal violence to incite terror and suppress minority populations. Guerrillas use insurrectionary violence to terrorize and eventually destroy "the oppressor." Ordinary people, nonactivists, find themselves inexorably drawn in. When they are not randomly chosen as targets by one side or the other, they are forcibly recruited, either as more or less secret collaborators or as open militants. One thinks of Vietnam, Algeria, Cyprus, Kenya, Angola, Mozambique, and the American rural South.

The reason there is no "war of national liberation" in the United States is that Negroes are overwhelmingly outnumbered. As the 1961 report of the U.S. Civil Rights Commission [7] shows, institutionalized vigilantism—the "white power structure"—has held the Negro to the status of second-class citizenship through a variety of legal and extra-legal means. An "uppity nigger," one who presumes to act like a white man, may expect to be fired from his job, evicted from his home, farm, or place of business, denied credit by the bank or the store, harassed by pool room toughs, intimidated by law enforcement officers, and, finally, beaten up and perhaps lynched by nightriders.

In the black-belt counties of the South, the black population nearly equals and sometimes surpasses the white. Not surprisingly, it is in these areas that the pattern of evading federal law is most fully developed. Local government functionaries, local notables, and local white-supremacist demagogues unite in a virtually explicit conspiracy to "keep the nigger in his place." This body of venerable institutions constitutes a shadow state which stands alongside and partially absorbs the visible legal state into its own apparatus. The effect is to deny Negroes redress at law, and so their situation is de-legalized. The body of white custom and sentiment alluded to by the phrase "our Southern way of life" inhibits the expression of humanitarian feelings in relations between blacks and whites. This means that the Negro's situation is de-moralized as well. The element of functional rationality comes in by way of the rationale used by both theorists and militant activists who make up the apparatus of the shadow state: "We have to prevent race mixing." This is virtually a genocidal declaration, under the circumstances. If the integrity of one's group is seen to be at stake, then surely there is a need to develop techniques and to implement them in the spirit of "anything goes." There is no developed "war of national liberation" in the United States, and so the casualties are all on the side of the oppressed minority. The whites have nothing to lose but their entrenched monopoly of power, not their lives.

This is not true in quasi-colonial countries caught up in civil strife. There the common man on both sides of the struggle is trapped in the crossfire of the militants, the establishmentarians no less than the revolutionists. Those who would prefer to be neutral find that role harder and harder to play as the situation polarizes. The guerrillas establish their own version of the shadow state and infiltrate the apparatus of the legal state. Their gruesome terrorist tactics become sharper and more dreadful as the vigilantes of the government in power react and carry on a full-scale "underground" struggle, matching atrocity with atrocity, through torture, while the war on the "surface" goes on. The situation of every man, woman, and child becomes extreme in such a beleaguered country. The game is total and everyone is a player, whether he wishes to be or not; the state is of no use to him.

The totalitarian state

Here we go to the other extreme, from the ineffective to the supereffective state. Its effectiveness is not for the individual, however, but for the collectivity; it is a party-state, a government run by a party that claims to speak for the whole national community. The individual does not get too little state attention, he gets too much, and of the wrong kind.

Totalitarianism—and one thinks immediately of Nazi Germany and Stalinist Russia as the prime examples—often is defined as the union of tyranny with technology. Tyranny, suspension of the rule of law, has occurred episodically since the beginning of civilization. But the technological base of totalitarianism, mass communications and all-pervasive bureaucracy, is as new as the twentieth century. Moreover, the new technology makes for a qualitative break. Totalitarianism is more than just old-fashioned tyranny by modern means; the new technology has created a new set of purposes. The social "good" that the activist state may seek is now so enormous that in time of crisis the temptation to set aside civil liberties—the institutions of juridical defense, as Gaetano Mosca called them—is so great that individuals are almost casually stripped of their immunities and guarantees and turned into a means to achieve a collective end.

Hannah Arendt [8] brilliantly demonstrates that the key institution of the totalitarian state is the secret police (in Nazi Germany the Gestapo and the SS, in the U.S.S.R. the MVD and GPU, more recently the KGB). The totalitarian secret police is freed from all moral and legal restraint in dealing with individuals who are labeled "objectively criminal" or "asocial." In the logic of the police bureaucracy, both are "surplus" and subject to "liquidation." A thoroughgoing functional rationality demands that nothing stand in the way of meeting the threat posed by the "criminals" and the waste incurred in maintaining the "socially useless." The secret police, like any other bureaucratic organization, needs these guidelines in order to act. Which things come first? Why? Is the proposed action worth what it will cost? By what standard? Will pursuing it interfere with some other end? Determining costs and setting priorities require clear criteria. This is as true of the totalitarian state and its apparatus as of any other organization in the modern world—because modern large-scale organizations are inevitably bureaucratic, totalitarian or not.

Administratively designating a certain category of persons as "criminal" or "asocial" immediately places everyone in it in an extreme situation. It strips away the immunities conferred by citizenship, and so the individual's situation is de-legalized. Functional rationality demands a speedy and efficient solution, unhampered by humanitarian sentiment (called "non-Aryan" or "bourgeois"), and so his situation is de-moralized as well.

When the categories "legitimately" subject to police terror are indefinitely broadened, as is the tendency of the totalitarian order, *everyone* is in an extreme situation. This is totalitarianism full-fledged: all moral and legal limitations on the state's freedom of action vis-à-vis the individual become revocable privileges, subject to being set aside at any moment. Hannah Arendt contends that a society so constituted has a built-in need for ever new categories of "surplus populations," to be destroyed in the interest of what is called the common good.

Genocide

Raul Hilberg appropriately speaks of the *destruction* of the European Jews. Terms like "killing" or "murder" do not convey the meaning of genocide because they have conventional moral and legal overtones, and the major significance of genocide is that conventional norms are altogether suspended. For the Germans—like Adolf Eichmann—who planned and carried out this largest of all "actions," there was no question of morality or legality. Only the end-in-view mattered: the cleansing of Europe, the elimination of vermin in human form. To the Nazi bureaucrats who conducted the operation, the meaning of the "final solution to the Jewish question" is best conveyed by their use of bureaucratic-technical terms like *Judenfrei* and *Judenrein* to describe areas "free" or "cleansed" of Jews. If we take what they said at face value, they thought of themselves as carrying out what was essentially a public health campaign, although a uniquely difficult and dangerous one. They were very much aware that those who developed and used the necessary techniques of extermination might deteriorate morally; and so they took extraordinary measures to foster the myth that a conspiracy to commit mass murder, as it has come to be judged by civilized society, was actually a noble and heroic task.

Paradoxical as it sounds, and painful, and regardless of the horror it evokes in the civilized conscience, the Nazi destruction of the European Jews was in the sociological sense an amoral and alegal act. An SS functionary might act humanely or inhumanely, correctly or incorrectly, toward a person in transport to the gas chambers, but in the context of that relationship he could not meaningfully commit an immoral or illegal act. An outsider—or an insider "out-of-role," for that matter—might judge an act to be immoral or criminal, but he would have to invoke norms of conduct that did not exist in that situation.

We have here, finally, the very essence of the extreme situation. The individual has neither a moral nor a legal claim on society. Society's functionaries are limited by no norms whatsoever, except the purely technical norm of functional rationality. The person who is the object of the functionary's interest is totally bereft. He has not even the right to be considered human, because the state has so decreed.

The totalitarian state abrogates the Hobbesian social contract. But instead of a return to the war of all against all, there is a newly created war of all against one.

Thermonuclear war

The soldier in combat is an example of one type of extreme situation: he is shot at only because he is categorically identifiable as "the enemy." The functionaries who oppose him know little if any immediate restraint, moral or legal, in their efforts to kill him. Ideally, they are governed entirely by considerations of functional rationality.

But this analysis needs some qualification: "All's fair in love and war" is true only of the moment of truth, of actual combat, and even then it is actually hedged with restrictions. The Geneva Convention outlaws the use of poison gas and soft-nosed bullets, requires the humane treatment of prisoners of war, and forbids the killing or wounding of noncombatants, medics, and civilians. Civilized nations have found it useful to make propaganda capital out of alleged enemy atrocities, but of course this makes no sense unless one can credibly distinguish between the atrocious and the nonatrocious. The only way to tell the difference is to refer to normative standards, and so functional rationality places certain limits upon conventional combat. Moreover, combat is only one of the many situations the soldier encounters in performing his military function; most of the time he is out of the enemy's reach.

Perhaps conventional warfare is thus not a good example of an extreme situation except for the actual clash of arms; and even then the play of functional rationality as a guide to conduct is limited by the Geneva Convention.*

Unconventional warfare is different. Guerrilla and counter-guerrilla operations are one type. It is often not logistically feasible to take prisoners, or to move prisoners already taken, so the tendency is to shoot them instead, unless there is a need for hostages or intelligence. Each side is inclined to treat the other—with some

---

* Soldiers in combat and in other closely related situations, such as taking and handling prisoners, often act illegally, of course. But the fact that certain conduct is *il*legal and not *a*legal is evidence of law and a sense of morality.

justification—as "traitors" and "war criminals" who have forfeited their rights under the Geneva Convention.

Another unconventional type is terror bombing, introduced by the Germans over London in World War II and rather quickly perfected by the British and the Americans. Hundreds, sometimes more than a thousand heavy bombers would strike a single city. The objective was to destroy the enemy's will to resist by bringing the war home to the civilian population. The traditional immunity of civilian noncombatants from direct attack by military force was ignored; the new technology and the strategy it dictated made it impossible to keep a firm operational distinction between military and civilian targets.

Thermonuclear war is an extension of terror bombing many times compounded. A thousand bombers in 1944 could expect in a single raid to drop a maximum of ten thousand tons of high explosives or fire bombs on the target and kill perhaps five thousand to ten thousand people. Now the standard operational ICBM (intercontinental ballistic missile) carries a warhead that is one hundred to two hundred times as destructive as a single one of those gigantic raids. The United States alone has about 1,800 deployed and capable of being fired in from three or four minutes to about half an hour.

The logistical cleanness and simplicity of the ICBM nuclear-warhead system greatly simplifies the moral problem as well. In fact, it virtually eliminates it. World War II terror bombing still involved an element of choice, for someone had to decide which cities to hit, in what order, and how hard. Thermonuclear war reduces all such nagging options to two: "if" and "when." The logic of the use of these weapons, assuming a more or less equally well-armed enemy, is that the first strike must be the hardest. The magnitude of destruction each side can inflict on the other, regardless of who fires first, is so enormous that all conceivable moral considerations seem picayune. Knowledge of what the bombs can do fosters a doomsday mentality.

Social relationships are altered by the introduction of thermonuclear weapons. Two sets of distinctions become blurred: between front- and rear-echelon troops, and between soldiers and civilians. Combatants now run no greater risk of getting killed than noncombatants. (In fact, those who make military decisions and actually direct the fire on "the front line," in hardened missile-launching sites or under thousands of feet of granite at Colorado Springs, are much less likely to be killed than the ordinary civilian.)

Virtually everyone is within reach of enemy weapons, and virtually everyone is a target. The effect of thermonuclear weapons and the tactics they demand is to transform the human condition itself into an extreme situation. The individual is an object of interest to functionaries not for what he does but for what he is: part of a social category tagged "the enemy." Moreover, he is "the enemy" in a new and dehumanized form. The functionaries' decision to kill him or not to kill him, and how, is an unmitigated expression of functional rationality. Against those who have the power and may find it necessary to annihilate him and his social type, he has no moral or legal claim. Given the full development of nuclear weapons and ICBM's, and their diffusion, every inhabitant of the globe will eventually find himself in this de-moralized, de-legalized extreme situation.

We have seen that extreme situations can be more fully explained by looking at norms and institutions than by considering only "the individual" in relation to "the environment." The simplest and clearest case is one in which the individual is an inmate of a total institution, or establishment, such as a concentration camp or mental hospital, and relates as an inmate to an institutional functionary. The inmate's situation is "extreme" to the extent that the functionary is legally and morally free from the need to respect the inmate's rights as a citizen and his dignity and worth as a human being. In conceptual shorthand, the inmate's situation is de-legalized and de-moralized. At the same time, the functionary is bound, by the logic of his situation, to be guided solely by considerations of functional rationality in his dealings with the inmate. He not only can but must treat the inmate as a thing and not as a person in order to do his duty.

Real life is more complicated than this abstract paradigm. Actually, there are varying degrees of extremity in the situation of the Negro in the American rural South, and in social structures of the colonial type in which the state is ineffective; in the plight of the ordinary citizen controlled by the secret police of a totalitarian state; in the plight of the individual member of a group undergoing the ultimate agony of genocide; and, finally, in the plight of everyone in the world as the clock ticks on toward the doomsday of nuclear holocaust.

There are two conclusions to be drawn. The first is substantive: what is real? The second is programmatic: what is to be done?

The substantive conclusion concerns the nature of modern society and is a central theme of this book. In our review of six empirical types of extreme situations, we found that total institutions occur in nontotalitarian social structures, and that extreme situations are not confined to total institutions. Does it follow that the ultimate source of extreme situations must be located in society itself, and not in the nature of aberrant groups and individuals or even "human nature"? If so, it makes little sense to continue trying to get factual knowledge about how institutional "breakdown" or epidemic neurosis is the cause of the mounting crisis of our times. The closer we look, the stronger is the evidence that the prime actors in the establishments and social enterprises that produce extreme situations are not criminals or madmen. Rather, they resemble the archetypal self-transcending hero (the dutiful functionary, the inspired fanatic) of our Western cultural heritage. It is not the failure of our institutions that is the cause of our deepest trouble but their very success.

The programmatic conclusion stems directly from this terrible paradox. Our civilization prides itself in the thoroughness with which it exploits scientific technique; its efficiency in organizing large numbers of people for cooperative enterprise; the breadth of vision in its conception of social welfare; and the intensity of its dedication to the ideal of duty in one's calling—work for the common good. Yet it was precisely these virtues which made possible the destruction of the European Jews, and which now threaten the extinction of civilization through thermonuclear war.

What can be done? There is no real answer. The problem does not trouble the social scientist very much, as a social scientist, because he lives in a world of questions, not answers. Quite properly, he proposes research that will help phrase the question better: broad comparative and historical studies and intensive studies of character and social structure, the kind Durkheim and Weber did a half-century ago. The result may be self-knowledge, insight, a grain of understanding of the "parceling-out of the soul" [9] that is the price exacted by advancing bureaucratization.

But the social scientist is a whole human being as well— unless as an individual he is some sort of monster—and so he craves answers as much as the next man. The answer I want is how and why the occupational psychosis called functional rationality threatens to become the ethos of the new age. I can only offer a hunch now: that the total institutions and extreme situations we have endured and continue to endure are bound up with the cult of technology (mistakenly called science) that we use as a curtain to hide the truth—that God is dead and nothing and nobody can save us, not even the scientist, most especially not the scientist.

What we can and should do is to scrape away the myths that cluster like barnacles around the base of our deified functionary— Comte's scientist-priest did not enter the stage of history on cue, and so we invented him—and find out for ourselves that he stands on clay and is made of clay.

Who knows? We might even find that the monster is capable of being put to some human use.

Afterword

This work is not a formal treatise, so there is no need for a chapter of "Conclusions." There are one or two things I would like to emphasize, however, in looking back over the whole book.

One is that I present the functionary, or images of the functionary, with a certain amount of ambivalence. Sometimes he is a likable, human-scale character, sometimes he is hateful; sometimes he is progressive and humane, intelligent and strong, and above all *right,* our hero, and then again he is a cunning, dirty little man, whoring after money and power; sometimes he is a lobotomized humanoid whose existence begins and ends with the job, and sometimes he is an "uptown hipster" who has learned how to step in and out of role with ease and even grace, with no apparent damage to his humanity and perhaps even some gain. Sometimes he is Adolf Eichmann and sometimes he is me.

These swings of imagery are so wide they raise doubt about the credibility of The Functionary as a sensitizing concept—but then the moment I write this the doubt is stifled by a flood of recollected encounters with functionaries, and with The Functionary in myself. Functionaries follow a universal logic—I follow it, too—in work because our work situations are at bottom the universal product of bureaucratization and functionalization.

The fact is that the functionary appears in one's experience in a great variety of disguises. At different moments he is "in role" in varying degrees, and this leaves room for a good deal of freedom in how the individual "comes on" or presents his unique personality in an encounter. Moreover, he often has occasion to shift from one functionary role to another ("change hats") in the course of his work, and this introduces another element of freedom in self-presentation. Again, the social meaning of the functionary's work varies enormously, even while the logic of doing it, functionary logic, functional rationality, remains essentially the same. Finally, the work itself is done in organizational contexts which never are completely bureaucratized and functionalized. The fact that some are much more so than others, taken with all the other variables, plausibly accounts for the ambivalence I have felt and probably everyone has felt in his encounters with functionaries.

A functionary who is nothing more than a functionary, whole-souled, is nothing less than a monstrosity, and extremes are always rare. Most people are human, and they take advantage of whatever looseness there is in the structure of their work relationships to be sociable. Functionaries are no exception. They want to affirm their humanity, and so they "socialize" informally with colleagues and even with clients, depending upon the pressure of work, their inclination of the moment, and the cues they get from the people they are with.

I say these things to answer myself as critic, and perhaps others, because my ambivalence toward my subject seems to need explaining. I do not wish to do more than that; in particular, I do not want to give the false impression that I have second thoughts about what some will see as an evocation of apocalypse masquerading as sociological discourse. I still think that bureaucracy and functionalization are handing the world over to more and more dehumanized functionaries, and that this makes both totalitarianism and thermonuclear war—either or both—more likely.

What can a man do? I think he must go on struggling for a better world. Even if the way is not clear—Marx is dead, God is dead—he must attack particular evils and try to catch a vision of a larger goal. As Camus writes in his retelling of *The Myth of Sisyphus,* to do so "makes of fate a human matter, which must be settled by men." Nothing happens "that cannot be surmounted by scorn." Even being herded into gas chambers by functionaries? Spending one's life and talent as a tiny cog in a big bureaucratic machine, writing ads for the back of breakfast cereal boxes? Perhaps. "Crushing truths perish from being acknowledged"—again, Camus. If a man can really and truly take the attitude that "his rock is his thing," he can gather strength and sanity and make his fate his own human project.

Appendix: Bureaucratization of the work environment

1. *Division of labor*

The governing patrimonial principle is that functions are specified, by assigning tasks and duties on an *ad hoc* basis; the procedure is to discover individual capabilities and "tailor the job" to fit them; the individual is thus able, in large measure, to *create his own role;* the enterprise is conceived as a tool, to be modified at will by the chief, who is a proprietor.

The governing bureaucratic principle is that functions are *specialized,* by rationally allocating tasks and duties in accordance with an overall plan; the procedure is to analyze the collective task into component "jobs" and to "tailor the man" to fit them; the individual is *assigned a role,* which he must accept and conform to; the individual (including the chief, a manager) is conceived to be a tool of the enterprise, to be modified or replaced as necessary.

2. *Allocation of authority*

Levels of activity emerge or shift in response to *changing constellations of personal roles;* authority is merely "lent" to specific individuals (conceived

Levels of activity are determined a priori in the form of a rationally systematic hierarchy; authority is *delegated* to graded ranks of officials; the power and responsibilities as "assistants") for the accomplishment of specific tasks; their power and responsibility, and communications between them, are *direct and personal;* administration, accordingly, is personal and colored by caprice and whim.

of the latter, and communications between them, are governed by the *chain of command* principle; that is, they are indirect and impersonal in character; administration in general is impersonal and systematic.

3. *Operations*

Operations are governed by *traditional or ad hoc procedures;* the ideal is to proceed *case-by-case,* taking into full account the unique circumstances surrounding each; in principle, means are "discovered"; facts are ascertained by *rule-of-thumb,* and decisions made according to "sound," *"time-honored"* principles; supervision is carried out by scrutinizing *results.*

Operations are governed by *abstract rules;* the ideal is that each case should be handled according to *standardized routine procedures;* in principle, means are *rationally formulated;* facts are ascertained and decisions made according to "scientific" criteria; supervision is carried out by scrutinizing *methods* in order to ascertain their *correctness* as rational means to an end.

4. *Interpersonal relations*

Interpersonal relations are personal in character, and are *taken for granted;* criteria for judging the actions of others are *moralistic* (as well as expedient); justice is *empirical* ("Kadi justice") in principle, and executed with full regard for unique circumstances.

Interpersonal relations are impersonal in character, and are conceived as *problematical;* criteria for judging the actions of others are objective; justice is *formally rational* in principle, and executed without regard for persons.

5. *Recruitment and promotion*

Ideally, personnel are recruited and promoted strictly on the basis of (subjective) *personal qualifications,* with no guarantee of tenure; the *rights of the employer* are the salient considera-

Ideally, personnel are recruited and promoted strictly on the basis of (objective) *technical qualifications,* with *tenure* implied; the *rights of the employee* are the salient consideration; in terms of motivation,

tion; in terms of motivation, *egoism* is presumed; nepotism is the rule, and *unlimited personal accountability* is expected. *altruism* is presumed; careerism is the rule, and accountability is *limited* to the *official* (or technical) sphere of competence assigned.

This conceptualization is derived in essence from the works of Max Weber, especially *The Theory of Social and Economic Organization,* trans. and ed. by A. M. Henderson and Talcott Parsons, Glencoe, Ill., Free Press, 1946; and the essay "Bureaucracy" in *From Max Weber: Essays in Sociology,* trans. and ed. by Hans H. Gerth and C. Wright Mills, New York, Oxford University Press, 1947. For restatements and commentaries I relied extensively on Reinhard Bendix, *Work and Authority in Industry,* New York, Wiley, 1956, and his *Max Weber: An Intellectual Portrait.* New York, Doubleday, 1960; and also on Peter M. Blau, *Bureaucracy in Modern Society,* New York, Random House, 1956, and Robert K. Merton, *et al.,* eds., *Reader in Bureaucracy,* Glencoe, Ill., Free Press, 1951. Reinhard Bendix read an early version and made valuable suggestions.

Notes

INTRODUCTION

1. Karel Capek, *R.U.R.*, London, Oxford University Press, 1923.
2. B. F. Skinner, *Walden II*, New York, Macmillan, 1948.
3. Sloan Wilson, *The Man in the Gray Flannel Suit*, New York, Simon and Schuster, 1955; Herman Wouk, *The Caine Mutiny*, New York, Doubleday, 1954; Alan Harrington, *Life in the Crystal Palace*, New York, Knopf, 1959; George Orwell, *1984*, New York, Harcourt Brace, 1954.
4. C. Wright Mills, *White Collar: The American Middle Classes*, New York, Oxford University Press, 1951; William H. Whyte, Jr., *The Organization Man*, New York, Simon and Schuster, 1956.
5. Raul Hilberg, *The Destruction of the European Jews*, Chicago, Quadrangle, 1961.
6. Hannah Arendt, *Eichmann in Jerusalem: A Report on the Banality of Evil*, New York, Viking, 1963.
7. Whyte defines the "social ethic" as "that contemporary body of thought which makes morally legitimate the pressures of society against the individual. Its major propositions are three: a belief in the group as the source of creativity; a belief in 'belongingness' as the ultimate need of the individual; and a belief in the application of science to achieve the belongingness." *The Organization Man*, p. 7.

8. Anthony Downs, *Inside Bureaucracy*, Boston, Little, Brown, 1967.
9. Reinhard Bendix, *Work and Authority in Industry: Ideologies of Management in the Course of Industrialization*, New York, Wiley, 1956.

CHAPTER 1. THE FUNCTIONARY

1. Seymour Martin Lipset, *Agrarian Socialism: A Study in Political Sociology*, Berkeley, University of California Press, 1950.
2. Robert Michels, *Political Parties*, Glencoe, Ill., Free Press, 1949 (first published 1915), trans. by Eden and Cedar Paul.
3. Two examples are Thurman Arnold, *The Folklore of Capitalism*, Princeton, Princeton University Press, 1937; and Adolf A. Berle and Gardiner C. Means, *The Modern Corporation and Private Property*, New York, Macmillan, 1936. A good review of the subject may be found in Daniel Bell, "The Breakup of Family Capitalism," in his book, *The End of Ideology*, Glencoe, Ill., Free Press, 1960, pp. 39–46.
4. Cf. A. C. Spectorsky, *The Exurbanites*, New York, Lippincott, 1955.
5. Cf. Joseph Bensman, "The Advertising Man and His Work," in *Dollars and Sense: Ideology, Ethics, and the Meaning of Work in Profit and Non-profit Organizations*, New York, Macmillan, 1967, pp. 9–70; and Martin Mayer, *Madison Avenue, U.S.A.*, New York, Harper, 1958.
6. Cf. David T. Bazelon, *The Paper Economy*, New York, Random House, 1963.
7. Stephen Potter, *Three-Upmanship*, New York, Holt, Rinehart, and Winston, 1962.
8. Thorstein Veblen, "The Instinct of Workmanship," in Max Lerner, ed., *The Portable Veblen*, New York, Viking, 1948, pp. 306–324.
9. Cf. Reinhard Bendix, *Max Weber: An Intellectual Portrait*, Garden City, Doubleday, 1960, pp. 455–456.

CHAPTER 2. WORK AND THE ORGANIZATION

1. This refers to five essential characteristics of bureaucracy adapted from Max Weber's classic essay: hierarchy, specialization, abstract rules, impersonality, and technical qualifications and tenure. See especially Hans H. Gerth and C. Wright Mills, eds., *From Max Weber: Essays in Sociology*, New York, Oxford University Press, 1946, pp. 196–198; and Max Weber, *The Theory of Social and Economic Organization*, New York, Oxford University Press, 1947, pp. 129–141. For

restatements and commentaries, see Reinhard Bendix, *Max Weber: An Intellectual Portrait,* Garden City, Doubleday, 1960, pp. 418–425; Peter M. Blau, *Bureaucracy in Modern Society,* New York, Random House, 1956, pp. 28–34; and several articles in Robert K. Merton, *et al.,* eds., *Reader in Bureaucracy,* Glencoe, Ill., Free Press, 1952.

2. The field has become quite large in recent years. The interested reader may wish to consult the journals *Human Organization* and *Administrative Science Quarterly,* and the following books: Amitai Etzioni, ed., *Complex Organizations: A Sociological Reader,* New York, Holt, Rinehart, and Winston, 1961; Sherman Krupp, *Patterns in Organization Analysis,* Philadelphia, Chilton, 1961; and James G. March, ed., *Handbook of Organizations,* Chicago, Rand, McNally, 1965.

3. Daniel Bell, "Work and Its Discontents," in *The End of Ideology,* New York, Collier Books, 1961, pp. 227–274.

4. Emile Durkheim, *The Division of Labor in Society,* New York, Macmillan, 1933 (first published 1893), trans. George Simpson, p. 43.

5. *Gemeinschaft* is an ideal-type concept which may be translated roughly as "communal society," in contrast to *Gesellschaft,* or "associational society." The distinction is most fully developed by the German sociologist Ferdinand Toennies. See Charles P. Loomis, "Gemeinschaft," in Julius Gould and William L. Kolb, eds., *Dictionary of the Social Sciences,* New York, Free Press, 1964, pp. 281–282. Durkheim used the terms "mechanical solidarity" and "organic solidarity" as analogous to *Gemeinschaft* and *Gesellschaft.*

6. Ruth Benedict, *Patterns of Culture,* Baltimore, Penguin Books, 1968 (first published 1934).

7. Elton Mayo, *The Human Problems of an Industrial Civilization,* New York, Viking, 1960 (first published 1933); Fritz J. Roethlisberger and William J. Dickson, *Management and the Worker,* Cambridge, Harvard University Press, 1939; W. Lloyd Warner and J. O. Low, *The Social System of the Modern Factory,* New Haven, Yale University Press, 1947; William Foote Whyte, *Human Relations in the Restaurant Industry,* New York, McGraw-Hill, 1948.

8. Reinhard Bendix and Lloyd Fisher, "The Perspectives of Elton Mayo," *Review of Economics and Statistics,* XXXI (1949), 312–319.

9. Julie P. Mayer, *Max Weber and German Politics,* London, Faber and Faber, 1943.

10. Joseph A. Schumpeter, *Capitalism, Socialism, and Democracy,* New York, Harper, 1942.

11. Mary Parker Follett, *Creative Experience,* New York, Longmans, Green, 1924.

12. Mayo, *The Human Problems of an Industrial Civilization.*

13. The Hawthorne studies of fatigue, worker morale, and productivity were carried out in the late twenties at the Hawthorne plant of the Western Electric Company. A major part of the findings and analysis is presented in Roethlisberger and Dickson, *Management and the Worker.*

14. Kurt Lewin, *Field Theory in Social Science: Selected Theoretical Papers,* New York, Harper, 1951. A critical assessment of small-group theory and research may be found in Lewis Coser, "The Functions of Small-Group Research," *Social Problems,* III (July 1955), 1–6.

15. Chester I. Barnard, *The Functions of the Executive,* Cambridge, Harvard University Press, 1938.

16. Herbert A. Simon, *Administrative Behavior: A Study of Decision-Making Processes in Administrative Organization,* New York, Macmillan, 1950.

17. Chris Argyris, *Personality and Organization,* New York, Harper, 1957.

18. Mayo, *Human Problems;* Warner and Low, *The Social System of the Modern Factory;* Elliott Jacques, *The Changing Culture of the Factory,* London, Tavistock, 1951; Charles R. Walker and Robert H. Guest, *The Man on the Assembly Line,* Cambridge, Harvard University Press, 1952; Whyte, *Human Relations in the Restaurant Industry.*

19. James D. Mooney and Alan C. Reiley, *Onward, Industry!,* New York, Harper, 1931; Adolf A. Berle, Jr., and Gardiner C. Means, *The Modern Corporation and Private Property,* New York, Macmillan, 1934; Peter F. Drucker, *The New Society: The Anatomy of the Industrial Order,* New York, Harper, 1950; Philip Selznick, *TVA and the Grass Roots: A Study in the Sociology of Formal Organization,* Berkeley, University of California Press, 1949; Alvin W. Gouldner, *Patterns of Industrial Bureaucracy,* Glencoe, Ill., Free Press, 1954; Wilbert E. Moore, *The Conduct of the Corporation,* New York, Random House, 1962.

20. Durkheim contends that the definitive characteristics of "social facts" are that they are exterior to the individual and constrain him in his actions. Emile Durkheim, *The Rules of Sociological Method,* London, New York, Free Press, 1964 (first published 1895), trans. Sarah A. Solovay and John H. Mueller, ed. by George E. C. Catlin, pp. 2–3.

21. Cf. Bendix, *Max Weber,* pp. 68–69.

22. "Imperative coordination" or "imperative control" is the rendering by A. M. Henderson and Talcott Parsons of Max Weber's concept of *Herrschaft,* which has no exact English equivalent. They write: "in a majority of instances . . . Weber is concerned with *legitime Herrschaft,* and in these cases 'authority' is both an accurate and far less awkward translation." (Weber, *Theory of Social and Economic Organiza-*

tion, p. 152n.) Reinhard Bendix thinks "legitimate domination" is more accurate than either "imperative coordination" or "authority." (Bendix, *op. cit.,* pp. 290–297.) I find Bendix's argument more persuasive in the context of ideology but not of technology—that is, the term "imperative coordination" seems to me to render the actual exercise of "legitimate domination" more precisely than does that term by itself, and so it is useful as a supplementary category.

23. Cf. William I. Thomas and Florian Znaniecki, "Three Types of Personality," in C. Wright Mills, ed., *Images of Man: The Classic Tradition in Sociological Thinking,* New York, Braziller, 1960, pp. 405–436.

24. See the works previously cited.

25. Cf. David T. Bazelon, *Power in America: The Politics of the New Class,* New York, New American Library, 1967; and Adolf A. Berle, Jr., *The Twentieth-Century Capitalist Revolution,* New York, Harcourt, Brace, 1954. Berle was one of the first to initiate the discussion of the "corporate conscience." He and others seem fascinated by the image Berle proposes of the new corporate archon as "something like a Norman duke," even though they disagree widely on the implications for policy of what they take to be the shaky legal foundations of modern corporate capitalism.

26. Mooney and Reiley, *Onward, Industry!*

27. *Ibid.,* p. 524.

28. Selznick, *TVA,* p. 9.

29. Robert Michels, *Political Parties,* Glencoe, Ill., Free Press, 1949 (first published 1915), trans. Eden and Cedar Paul.

30. House Document 15, 73rd Cong., 1st Sess. (1933). Cited in Selznick, *TVA,* p. 52.

31. Selznick, *TVA,* p. 12.

32. Philip Selznick, *The Organizational Weapon: A Study of Bolshevik Strategy and Tactics,* Glencoe, Ill., Free Press, 1960 (first published 1952).

33. Philip Selznick, *Leadership in Administration,* Evanston, Row, Peterson, 1957.

34. The psychoanalyst may or may not be interested in the therapeutic effect of his work; his one sure objective is to *know.* The psychotherapist seeks to know, and makes use of some version of psychoanalytic technique in his practice, but his objective is to *cure.* In short, the therapist is a technologist and the analyst is a scientist.

35. Alvin W. Gouldner, *Wildcat Strike: A Study of Worker-Management Relationships,* New York, Harper, 1965 (first published 1954).

36. Wilbert E. Moore, *Industrial Relations and the Social Order,* New York, Macmillan, 1951, rev. ed.

37. Frederick W. Taylor, *The Principles of Scientific Management*, New York, Harper, 1911.

CHAPTER 3. THE MILITARY

1. Harold D. Lasswell, *Politics: Who Gets What, When, How*, New York, McGraw-Hill, 1936, p. 100.

2. Cf. Alfred Vagts, *A History of Militarism, Civilian and Military*, New York, Norton, 1937.

3. Hagen points out that there is a "style of behavior . . . among men of Latin blood both throughout Latin America and along the Mediterranean wherever traditional culture and personalities prevail— the style of personality termed *machismo*. It has two aspects: incessant sexual adventure and an intense need to defend one's honor against any slight. The male is ready to regard his honor as put in question by the inflection of a voice or the turn of a word; he must defend it, not really against the attack of the other individual, but against his own uncertainty. Although uncertainty concerning one's manhood does not express itself in quite the same way in non-Latin traditional societies, it manifests itself in analogous ways. The duels and knightly sensitivity of the Middle Ages were probably reflections of the same species of authoritarian personality." Everett E. Hagen, *On the Theory of Social Change: How Economic Growth Begins*, Homewood, Ill., Dorsey, 1962, p. 147.

4. Sigfried Giedion, *Mechanization Takes Command*, New York, Oxford University Press, 1948.

5. Herman Kahn, *On Thermonuclear War*, Princeton, Princeton University Press, 1961, p. 145.

6. Cf. Morris Janowitz, *The Professional Soldier: A Social and Political Portrait*, Glencoe, Ill., Free Press, 1960.

7. See the Appendix, "Bureaucratization of the Work Environment."

8. Seymour Melman, *Our Depleted Society*, New York, Dell, 1965, p. 76.

9. Alfred T. Mahan, *The Influence of Seapower upon History*, New York, Sagamore Press, 1957.

10. Cf. Walter Millis, *Arms and Men: A Study in American Military History*, New York, Putnam, 1956.

11. Melman, *Our Depleted Society*, pp. 13–47.

CHAPTER 4. GOVERNMENT

1. Anthony Downs, *Inside Bureaucracy*, Boston, Little, Brown, 1967.
2. Cf. Joseph Bensman, *Dollars and Sense*, New York, Macmillan, 1967, esp. pp. 102–124 and 189–194.

CHAPTER 7. POWER STRUGGLE IN THE PRISON

1. Erving Goffman, "On the Characteristics of Total Institutions," in Donald R. Cressey, ed., *The Prison: Studies in Institutional Organization and Change*, New York, Holt, Rinehart, and Winston, 1961, pp. 1–107.
2. *Ibid.*, pp. 16–17.
3. Robert Bierstedt, "An Analysis of Social Power," in Lewis A. Coser and Bernard Rosenberg, eds., *Sociological Theory: A Book of Readings*, New York, Macmillan, 1964, pp. 143–156.
4. Gresham Sykes, *The Society of Captives*, Princeton, Princeton University Press, 1958.

CHAPTER 8. EXTREME SITUATIONS, TOTAL INSTITUTIONS, AND THE FUNCTIONARY

1. Bruno Bettelheim, "Individual and Mass Behavior in Extreme Situations," *Journal of Abnormal and Social Psychology*, XXXVIII (1943), 417–452.
2. David Rousset, *The Other Kingdom*, New York, Reynal and Hitchcock, 1947; Eugen Kogon, *The Theory and Practice of Hell*, New York, Farrar, Straus, 1950; Margaret Buber, *Under Two Dictators*, New York, Dodd, Mead, 1949, trans. by Edward Fitzgerald.
3. Erving Goffman, "The Moral Career of the Mental Patient," *Psychiatry*, XXII (1959), 123–142.
4. Robert Jay Lifton, *Thought Reform and the Psychology of Totalism: A Study of "Brainwashing" in China*, New York, Norton, 1963.
5. Cf. Alexander H. Leighton, *The Governing of Men: General Principles and Recommendations Based on Experience at a Japanese Relocation Camp*, Princeton, Princeton University Press, 1945.
6. Erving Goffman, "Medical Model and Mental Hospitalization: Some Notes on the Vicissitudes of the Tinkering Trades," in *Asylums:*

Essays on the Social Situation of Mental Patients and Other Inmates, New York, Doubleday, 1961, pp. 321–386.

7. United States Commission on Civil Rights, *Justice,* Report No. 5, 1961, Washington, D.C., U.S. Government Printing Office, 1961.

8. Hannah Arendt, *The Origins of Totalitarianism,* New York, World, 1951.

9. J. P. Mayer, *Max Weber and German Politics,* London, Faber and Faber, 1944.

Index

A Note on the Author

F. William Howton was born in Portland, Oregon, and studied at the University of Kentucky, the University of Arizona, and the University of California, Berkeley. Before teaching sociology he did research work for the Institute of Industrial Relations at Berkeley and for the System Development Corporation, and served as probation officer of Contra Costa County, California. Mr. Howton is now chairman of the Department of Sociology and Anthropology at the City College, New York. He is co-author of *Work, Self and Society* and co-editor of *Mass Society in Crisis*.